From Grimes
to Brideshead

From Grimes
to Brideshead

The Early Novels of Evelyn Waugh

Robert R. Garnett

Lewisburg
Bucknell University Press
London and Toronto: Associated University Presses

Associated University Presses
440 Forsgate Drive
Cranbury, NJ 08512

Associated University Presses
25 Sicilian Avenue
London WC1A 2QH, England

Associated University Presses
P.O. Box 488, Port Credit
Mississauga, Ontario
Canada L5G 4M2

PR
6045
A97
Z687
1990

Library of Congress Cataloging-in-Publication Data

Garnett, Robert Reginald.
    From Grimes to Brideshead : the early novels of Evelyn Waugh / Robert R. Garnett.
        p.   cm.
    Includes bibliographical references.
    ISBN 0-8387-5170-9 (alk. paper)
    1. Waugh, Evelyn, 1903–1966—Criticism and interpretation.
I. Title.
PR6045.A97Z687   1990
823′.912—dc20   89-42681
                                                                          CIP

PRINTED IN THE UNITED STATES OF AMERICA

Contents

Preface

When I first read Evelyn Waugh's early novels, I was struck by their happy disregard for conventional assumptions and attitudes, their irreverence for the usual pieties, their determination—as Waugh said of some undergraduate acquaintances—"to treat with the world on their own terms." The early novels were animated by irrationality, idiosyncrasy, impulsiveness, coincidence, madness; and, even more remarkable, despite a strong note of nostalgia they plainly sympathized with the irregularity and eccentricity of the fictional world they created. Here was an imagination that admired energetically disreputable characters and thrived on trouble, and here were unapologetic fantasies to fracture and subvert narrow perceptions, not least my own. Reading the early novels seemed to me an imaginatively liberating experience.

One of the first editions of Waugh I acquired was an old Dell Laurel paperback, with *Vile Bodies* and *Black Mischief* bound together inside a cover the color of dark orange marmalade; and in the odd way of associations, I came to associate that deep orange with the stimulating and zestfully imagined world of Waugh's early novels.

Later I began to read critics and found their Waugh a much dimmer figure: a snob, a misanthrope, or—worst of all—a relentless moralist.

Anyone reading Waugh's novels carefully, and reading his diaries and letters and others' reminiscences of him, cannot help but conclude that he was in fact a complex, many-colored figure; and he evokes complex, divergent reactions. His earliest critics were by and large reviewers who, though generally unsympathetic with his Catholicism and his political and social attitudes, could not deny the comic force of his early novels; Edmund Wilson is the best example. Toward the end of Waugh's life, however, and especially after his death in 1966, more formal academic criticism took Waugh in its grip; and most academic critics, seizing on his vein of moral earnestness, have been icily unsympathetic with his anarchic, comic impulses.

For example, a recent essay surveying criticism of Waugh's fiction observes:

> During the interim [the early 1960s], critics such as Bernard Bergonzi and Frank Kermode began to perceive that Waugh's social, religious, and

political opinions, so long regarded as damaging intrusions into his fiction, in fact constituted a powerful and productive "aristocratic myth," which gave lasting significance to his writing.[1]

Characteristic of recent criticism of Waugh is the strange assumption here that "lasting significance" in literature depends upon the "social, religious, and political opinions" it might express, as if literature had generally the same aims and functions as the more solemn articles on the op-ed pages of the *New York Times*. By this standard, of course, Waugh's early novels, not apparently weighted with opinions, seem in danger of insignificance—or, to quote the same essay, seem less "serious": "Many critics still praise Waugh's early comedies and disparage his later, serious novels, supposedly marred by declining ironic detachment and increasingly explicit dogmatism and pessimism." Critics still *mistakenly* praise the early comedies, one gathers—although the early novels are saved from complete insignificance by participating, embryonically at least, in Waugh's "consistent moral purpose": "Even in the early novels Waugh used satiric fantasy to expose the decay of society."

Almost invariably, contemporary criticism of Waugh (congratulated in the essay as "much more technically sophisticated in recent years") finds cause to regret the obtuseness of readers who enjoy the early novels as comedies rather than exposures of decay: ". . . Audience appreciation of Waugh's outrageous comedy hindered recognition of his satiric purpose, encouraged readers to resist any changes, and delayed awareness of the sincerity of his denunciation of declining civilization." The hallmarks of imaginative literature are thus "opinions" and "sincerity," and the implicit message to Waugh's reader is: *You may think these novels are funny, but in fact they're Deadly Serious; stop enjoying them, and wax indignant about declining civilization.* It may be a bad sign, however, when literary criticism begins to diverge so widely from the untutored reactions of most nonacademic readers, who quite naturally prefer the vivid comic gusto of the early novels to grave pronouncements about Western civilization.

I think Waugh should be serious reading, too; but not solemn reading, and not because of his philosophical views or doctrinal orthodoxy, let alone his opinions. It is the nature of literary criticism to want to sink its teeth into something "serious," but it is the inclination of comedy—including Waugh's early novels—to challenge accepted notions of what is serious. I think it is wrong—and unrewarding—to ignore or dismiss the unquiet, comically subversive Waugh; to applaud exclusively the novelist as social prophet, edifying moralist, and Augustinian theologian.

If the critical summary from which I have been quoting is an accurate representation of Waugh criticism—and I think it is, both in tone and in content—something has certainly gone wrong. Nothing could be further from the "lasting significance" of Waugh's early novels than his "social, religious, and political opinions" or the "sincerity" of his denunciations. Literature of permanent value springs from more fertile regions of the imagination than these. Waugh did not simply invent characters and stories to illustrate themes. His achievement was to create an autonomous fictional world that remains alive even though the era on which it was based now seems almost as remote as Chaucer's.

The world of the early novels is stamped with his own vivid and troubled imagination. He was vexed and stimulated by the various demons resident in a difficult temperament, an acute sensibility, and strong feeling; but chief among those demons, the comic demon reigned, fascinated by, instinctively drawn to, human crookedness and absurdity. He was—as he wrote of Cyril Connolly—"a man of high comic abilities in whom high spirits alternate with black despair."[2] His early novels preserve a distinctive voice and above all a distinctive vision, a trenchant and yet tolerant way of perceiving experience. I have thought it worth making the point, in the following pages, that the early novels are imaginatively rewarding not because of their "seriousness" in the mundane sense—their nuggets of admonition and advice touching on weighty issues in the "real" world—but because they can challenge and enlarge our narrow understanding of what is real, and serious.

This study follows Waugh's career up to 1945. A more natural stopping point for the early part of Waugh's life is 1939 (as in Martin Stannard's two-volume biography), when the Second World War changed his life dramatically and *Work Suspended* announced a sharp turn in his ambitions; but carrying the study forward to *Brideshead Revisited* makes the nature and consequence of those ambitions more apparent.

Several people were particularly helpful to me in the course of this study. Auberon Waugh, the late Christopher Sykes, and the late Christopher Hollis all very kindly granted me interviews (and hospitality) and made difficult-to-find materials available to me; Mark Amory allowed me access to his comprehensive files of Waugh's letters. Early work on this book was greatly assisted and encouraged by the late Irvin Ehrenpreis and by Leopold Damrosch, Jr. I am indebted to several libraries and their staffs: the English Faculty Library and the Bodleian at Oxford; the Humanities Research Center at the University of Texas at Austin; Mugar Memorial Library at

Boston University; the BBC Written Archives Centre; Alderman Library at the University of Virginia; and Musselman Library at Gettysburg College. Some of my research was done during a Fulbright fellowship at Oxford, and I received several travel grants for research from Gettysburg College.

Extracts from the writings of Evelyn Waugh are included by permission of the Estate of Evelyn Waugh and A. D. Peters and Company, London.

I am most of all indebted to my wife, who, though she could have married a doctor, never complained.

From Grimes
to Brideshead

1
Introduction: "I Hope There Will Be Trouble"

When he began writing *Decline and Fall*, Evelyn Waugh was twenty-four years old. His accomplishments were few, his prospects hazy. He had started other novels but had never managed to finish one, at least to his own satisfaction. He did not particularly want to be a novelist, in fact, and since leaving Oxford three years earlier had been dabbling instead in the arts and crafts, attempting first to become a painter; then a printer; then, while writing *Decline and Fall*, a cabinetmaker; he had also worked briefly as a probationary journalist. Most of the time, however, he had been muddling along as an usher in two obscure preparatory schools. Several months after an embarrassing dismissal from the second of these academies, he began to write *Decline and Fall*. After a few weeks he abandoned it. Somewhat later, however, having become engaged to marry, he felt obliged to finish the novel to demonstrate that he could support a wife. Up to this time he had been unable to support even himself.

The first publisher to whom he showed the manuscript of *Decline and Fall* expressed interest but would not agree to publish it without the deletion of various improprieties. Demurring, Waugh collected his manuscript and carried it down the street to a nearby publisher with whom he was familiar in the most literal sense, for the managing director of this firm, Chapman and Hall, was his father. Mr. Waugh was out of town on vacation, however; in his absence, his deputy offered to publish the manuscript, also insisting, however, on bowdlerizing changes. Eager to get the novel into print and disinclined to martyr himself in the cause of artistic freedom, Waugh consented to the alterations. To supplement the text he drew half a dozen stylized cartoon illustrations and executed a design for the dust wrapper, as well: he had acquired the habit of illustrating his own stories as a child, and his drawings had always been indulged at home.

Subtitled *An Illustrated Novelette*, *Decline and Fall* was a light, burlesque affair with no literary pretensions. As such, it was generally (though not universally) well reviewed, and sales were encouraging—better, probably, than Waugh had expected. But it created no stir in

English letters and hardly any stir even in his own family, for his father, in addition to his post at Chapman and Hall, was a respected man of letters and his older brother an established novelist. Waugh's mother wished her younger son had persisted with cabinetmaking.

Despite its modest ambition, potboiler motives, and inconspicuous debut, *Decline and Fall* was in at least one respect noteworthy, however. "I cannot forget the first sharp impact of Evelyn's first novel *Decline and Fall*," John Betjeman, an obscure young man himself in 1928, recalled years later. "It seemed to me then so rockingly funny, there could never be anything quite so funny again."[1] Spilling over with anarchic, comic exuberance, *Decline and Fall* disclosed Waugh's distinctive fictional genius; in its first few ebullient pages lay the promise of his future.

Sixteen years later he was well known and prosperous. He had published, in addition to six novels, a fragment of another novel, five travel books, two biographies, and a volume of short stories. He owned a large and handsome eighteenth-century manor house in Gloucestershire; he sat on the board of directors of his father's old firm, Chapman and Hall; he had commanded an entry in *Who's Who* for a decade. His ambition stretched even further. With the novel he began writing in 1944, in fact, he intended to vault beyond mere popular success by creating an enduring masterpiece, and when he finished writing it he was confident that he had succeeded. Looking back, he was now inclined to dismiss his earlier novels as mere apprenticework; *Brideshead Revisited* was his first mature work, the beginning of his career as a serious novelist.

Anyone who knew Waugh only as the improvident young man who wrote *Decline and Fall* would have had difficulty recognizing the eminent author of *Brideshead;* anyone who knew Waugh only by *Decline and Fall* would scarcely have recognized *Brideshead* as the work of the same person. The first novel had been a naughty, irreverent farce; *Brideshead* was a theological romance, soaked in nostalgia and pathos. *Decline and Fall* was ironic and understated; *Brideshead* was solemn, sentimental, opulent. *Decline and Fall* celebrated crookedness and disorder; *Brideshead* celebrated the high civilized style. *Decline and Fall* enjoyed the world, *Brideshead* shrank from it. This study aims to trace the course of Waugh's imagination between these two remarkably different stepsisters.

Reduced to simplest terms, the thorniest problem in Waugh criticism has been devising a critical formula that will make sense of both *Decline and Fall* and *Brideshead Revisited.*

It would be possible to account for the incongruity of the two novels by simply assuming that the anarchist of *Decline and Fall* at some point died and was reborn as someone quite different, an ultramontane Tory, leaving his earlier self behind. But such a radical imaginative discontinuity seems unlikely, and any attempt to deal with Waugh's career must somehow reconcile these two novels, somehow graph Waugh's career to produce a relatively plausible curve connecting these two antipodal points by way of the intermediate novels.

Various attempts to do this have been made.

One of the first critics to survey the full scope of Waugh's career, for example, James Carens, reads Waugh as primarily a satirist. "In fact, Waugh has always been a writer whose surface—apparently gay, sometimes bizarre, often even wildly uproarious—has masked a devastating satirical vision of the modern world."[2] As satire, however, both *Decline and Fall* and *Brideshead* are flawed, Carens judges. *Decline and Fall* lacks a moral center, a positive vision to oppose to the chaotic world it is presumably criticizing; it is wholly negative and morally confused. *Brideshead Revisited,* on the other hand, supplies a positive vision: "Differing from the earlier works, *Brideshead* springs not only from rejection but also from assent"; but the assent is too narrow: ". . . a Catholic framework which has been confused with a class-view. *Brideshead* makes no universal affirmation." In effect, Carens argues, while *Decline and Fall* rejects everything and commits itself to nothing, *Brideshead Revisited* embraces aristocratic values overenthusiastically, to the exclusion of larger principles. But at least *Brideshead* embraces something, which seems like progress; Carens, like most recent critics, detects an upward slope in Waugh's career.

The satiric reading, however, encounters problems. *Decline and Fall,* Carens notes with evident disapproval, takes shots at a bewildering assortment of satiric targets: "The principal objects of the satire in this novel are diverse, indeed, related to one another largely by the picaresque convention: Oxford, public schools, the smart set, the white-slave trade, modern architecture, prison reformers—these are all ridiculed." The very diversity of *Decline and Fall*'s targets, in fact, reveals the futility of reading the novel as a satire at all. Waugh had no strong feelings about the white-slave trade or prison reform, for example; the ridicule has a comic rather than satiric motive. Another critic has accurately observed: "To the satirist it is the *object* of his humour that matters, the point of view it serves; what matters to Waugh is the humour itself: it is vital only that the texture of life should be made to yield a comic response rather than a bitter or tragic one."[3] All of Waugh's novels contain satiric elements; few are pri-

marily satires. As for *Brideshead Revisited,* Carens admits that it is
"less a satire than a romance."

If by satiric standards both *Decline and Fall* and *Brideshead* lack an
adequate system of values—the former lacking values altogether, in
fact—to another critic, Jeffrey Heath, both novels are stern homilies
steeped in Augustinian moral theology.[4] Heath admits, at times,
dissonant motives in Waugh's fiction; for example, "The deep rift in
Waugh's psyche between the worldly and the other-worldly made
him unhappy, but it also generated the tensions which sustain his art
and give it its characteristic quirky complexity." Nonetheless, though
arguing that Waugh struggled to evade his vocation as a Christian
artist, Heath reads him as a militant rigorist, morally and theologi-
cally, from the beginning, and there is nothing either quirky or
complex about the novels as Heath explains them. He squeezes all of
them, even the early farces, into a consistent allegorical scheme:
"Waugh's early novels are surreal, fantasticated, and ostensibly
amoral, but on the figurative level they are parables about freedom,
servitude, and vocation. . . . In his four early satires the absence from
British history of faith and taste preoccupies Waugh."

There is some plausibility in imposing such a severe exegetical
scheme upon an overtly Catholic novel like *Brideshead,* but the
implausibility of *Decline and Fall* as a moralistic allegory is extreme.
For Heath, *Decline and Fall* is "an allusive history of the City of
Man"; the allusions are so skillfully concealed, however, that "unin-
itiated" readers, which is to say most, will fail to recognize them;
nevertheless they will operate "subliminally" to give even the uniniti-
ated reader a healthy dose of Augustinian theology, applied to West-
ern history from barbaric origins to the present. "Examples are
obvious enough when they are pointed out, but thanks to Waugh's
cheeky sleight of hand, they are seldom noticed," Heath explains to
account for the novel's so often being misread as comic.

For the initiate, the allegory-decryption and allusion-hunting re-
quired by Heath's method may constitute *Decline and Fall's* leading
charms, but most readers (I suspect) will rightly recoil from such an
exhausting and recondite exercise. To extract from the novel's anar-
chic zest a hidden theological allegory perversely ignores its most
powerful and plainly evident imaginative impulses. Heath himself
notes that the comic energy of *Decline and Fall* springs from "the
subversive and immature Waugh who rejoices in the anarchic self-
indulgence of Captain Grimes and his naughty world—and this is the
inventive and delightful early Waugh most readers know and relish";
but Heath himself, unsympathetic with *this* Waugh, advances instead,
as the more significant Waugh, a relentless and frankly rather trite

moralist whom few could like, let alone "relish." The uninitiated, unsuspecting readers are better in touch with *Decline and Fall,* for most such readers will recognize that the novel's strongest energies are expressed not in subliminal theological messages but in a comic gusto that ridicules just such moral sonority as Heath attributes to the novel.

One might impeach Heath's analysis of *Decline and Fall* on several counts: that it imposes an elaborate, weighty, and superfluous allegorical system on a farce; that it converts the novel from a burlesque accessible to anyone with even the slightest sense of humor into an esoteric document accessible to almost no one; that it ignores Waugh's perfectly explicit prefatory warning to the novel: "Please bear in mind throughout that IT IS MEANT TO BE FUNNY." But the root of the problem seems to be that an overdeveloped taste for moral sententiousness, an urge to locate grave universal pronouncements in all literature, has misled the critic into focusing on and exaggerating just one aspect of Waugh's fiction, and by no means the most interesting aspect. As the creator of a vivid comic fictional world, Waugh was remarkable, perhaps unique in his time; as a moralist, he was stern and occasionally provocative, but seldom distinguished.

Martin Stannard, in his biography of Waugh, is less extreme than Heath in his claims for the philosophical consistency of the early novels, and he is certainly aware of Waugh's temperamental complexity: "I see Waugh as a brilliant but awkward, isolated, and neurotic man, with many intimate friends and few lovers, almost frightened but with dauntless bravado, a scintillating manic depressive, not 'possessed' as Belloc suggested, but dispossessed, alienated."[5] Regarding Waugh above all, however, as a "serious artist" (at least after *Decline and Fall*), Stannard interests himself especially in Waugh's "developing aesthetic" and argues against tendentious readings of the novels: "A novel was to him neither a political tract nor an explanation of personal motivation."

For Stannard, nonetheless, Waugh's artistry was usually placed in the service of his philosophical, cultural, and moral opinions. Stannard is given to statements like: "But the most difficult aspect of all his pre-war novels is understanding their moral structure." In the case of *Decline and Fall,* for example, Stannard allows that "the consensus opinion" has always been that "*Decline and Fall* was clearly an entertainment rather than 'a book with purpose' "—but he then asks: "Is there more to it than this?" The answer, in short, is yes; *Decline and Fall* was heavily influenced by the young Waugh's reading of Bergson and Spengler: "Whether spelt out or not in the terms used in 'Paul's Meditations' [a passage deleted from the manuscript], the novel remains a metaphorical enquiry, albeit a light-hearted one, into the struggle for identity, of man as part of a 'chain of consequences so obscurely connected,' of time, space, continuity and 'position' in the chaos." The "albeit" qualifier suggests Stannard's tendency to suppress, or at least to subordinate, the comic impulses of the novel; they are not what interests him. (*Scoop* is later dealt with in almost identical terms: "it reflects, albeit humorously, the chaos Waugh saw around him in 1938 in a world rent (in his view) by humanist fallacies.") The comic thrust of *Vile Bodies,* too, is disparaged: "It is, of course, an amusing book but the humour no longer releases us into fantasy as in *Decline and Fall:* it teeters on the brink of hysteria." And any possibility that Waugh sympathized with the comic exuberance of the early novels is squelched in terms similar to Heath's: "So veiled had his irony been in *Vile Bodies* and *Black Mischief* that his outrage at a culturally degraded society had been mistaken for a celebration of anarchy." Again, as with Heath, the implication is that people have all along been misreading Waugh's early novels; that their *real* meaning, "veiled" and esoteric, is quite lofty; that moral "outrage," not comic energy, has created the novels; that a reader must suppress any frivolous pleasure in the comic, anarchic spectacle and instead nod gravely at a jeremiad against cultural degradation.

I think such arguments should be viewed with suspicion. What is askew in them is not their interest in Waugh the philosopher, moralist and cultural critic—but the assertion that these aspects of Waugh provide the major constituents of his fiction. It is true that the early novels would be quite different without the impress of his ideas and theories and religious beliefs; but without his mythmaking imagination, without his fascination with human crookedness and diversity, without his bubbling stewpot of unphilosophical, unmoral impulses and energies—without these, there would be no novels at all. The "high" Waugh, the novelist of elevated moral sentiments, would not have had a pulsebeat without the "low" Waugh whom recent critics seem so reluctant to acknowledge, the Waugh who happily kept company with the disreputable likes of Captain Grimes, Agatha Runcible and Basil Seal.

Carens, Heath and Stannard share the assumption that the motive impulses of Waugh's fiction are, or at least ought to be, thematic, whether the theme be philosophical, moral, ideological or whatever. Not every recent critic has agreed. Ian Littlewood instead reads Waugh's novels as evolving attempts to cope with the difficult and often painful experience of life: "They are . . . escapes and they are concerned with strategies of escape; they are about ways of avoiding reality and they offer in themselves an avoidance of it."[6] Discerning

five basic strategies of avoidance—detachment of tone, humor, ro-
manticism, nostalgia and religion—Littlewood finds that across the
years, the last strategy, Waugh's religious faith, gradually replaced the
first four as his response to the world. Though all the novels are
motivated by the compulsion of "escape," the strategies of escape
affect the novels variously; and while Littlewood sees Waugh's later
fiction moving toward a Christian (though not dogmatic) response,
he makes no improbable claims about the Catholic orthodoxy of the
early novels. His reading seems to me sensitive and sensible.

But I doubt that Littlewood's emphasis on escape, on avoidance of
reality and retreat from experience, adequately accounts for the comic
energy of Waugh's early novels. There can be no doubt that Waugh
often found the world unpleasant; as Littlewood says, "Waugh's
temperament is not sunny, nor are his books—even the funniest of
them. From *Decline and Fall* to *Unconditional Surrender* they are
shot through with an awareness of most of the things that tempt men
to despair: whatever lies between social boredom and the con-
centration camp, disappointment in love and the decline of a civiliza-
tion." But remembering himself and Harold Acton as Oxford
undergraduates, Waugh wrote: "What, I think, we had in common
was *gusto*, in the English use of the word; a zest for the variety and
absurdity of the life opening up to us."[7] That gusto, or zest, impelled
Waugh to seek out experience; it welcomed the world's diversity and
oddities and unpredictability; it was the major imaginative thrust
behind the early novels.

One of the few constants among the many vicissitudes of Waugh's
life was his affinity for trouble. When he was twenty-one, for ex-
ample, and had held his first job, a schoolmastering post, for less than
a week, he grew restless: "I think that things may become amusing
here after all because poor Mr Watson feels very strongly about
discipline and is stirring up a mutiny. . . . I hope there will be
trouble."[8] Thirty years later, fixed in his tastes and prejudices, his
gusto for life undoubtedly abated, he still welcomed the occasional
disruption. One friend recalled, for example, a boating mishap during
a visit to Jamaica in 1955: ". . . The raft slowly and surprisingly
disintegrated. . . . We swam for the shore, Evelyn doing a slow breast
stroke, blue eyes blazing and mood much improved, for he liked
things to go wrong."[9] Another, lifelong, friend observed: "I would
say of him that he had no liking for tranquillity. He liked life to be full
of disturbance."[10] His diaries invariably reveal him most interested in
his own life when it was least settled. During his rootless and dis-
turbed bachelor years in the 1930s, he longed to marry and retire to a

rural haven; but as soon as he finally accomplished this retreat he grew bored. "I have a natural zest for living; as long as something is happening I can enjoy myself," Waugh's elder brother Alec wrote of himself. "Eventlessness is the one thing I dread."[11] In this respect the brothers were twins. Waugh needed stimulus; and the best stimulus was the crowded, disorderly circus of human affairs, the more tumultuous the better.

Trouble was, after all, the most spectacular evidence of life. With the endless, ungovernable diversity of people, the quirks and aberrations of individual character, the impulsiveness and irrationality of human behavior, the prevalence of accident, coincidence, fortune, and misfortune—with all this, one could hardly expect things to go smoothly for long. Waugh was glad they didn't. He welcomed surprises and anomalies. "He loved waxworks and the monkey house at the Zoo, and when we were in Paris he used to rush to the Musée Grévin," an intimate friend recalled. "He was very fond of the Bramber Museum—I think it was Bramber—anyway, it had glass cases with stuffed animals in them—a guinea-pig pushing a kitten in a pram or a party of mice playing croquet. One could hardly bear to look, but he thought of the extreme oddity of the mind that had conceived this museum and it delighted him."[12] Spurning the neat herbaceous borders of English middle-class life, the young Waugh cultivated weeds, rank local specimens as well as more exotic varieties.

Trouble was the fuel of his early novels. Accident, conflict, violence, madness, and death regularly punctuate their action. *Decline and Fall* opens with the sounds of broken glass and an unprovoked assault on a blameless young divinity student, a fitting prelude to Waugh's career. Restless in England during the 1930s, he sought and found stimulus abroad: confusion in Abyssinia; madness in South America; returning to Abyssinia, a war. When in the autumn of 1939 England itself began to muddle into war, Waugh resented the inconvenience but enjoyed the disruption:

> This morning, depressed at the war news and the confusion of English services, I came down to breakfast and found the registration book for my car, for which I had applied, arrived by return of post. I reflected that there was really a great deal which went through smoothly in England, that we made a great fuss when anything went wrong and disregarded the vast machinery that was working successfully all the time, etc., etc. I then looked at the book and found that it referred to a totally different car. I further found that the number-plates of my car and its licence were different. Consequently most of the morning passed on the telephone between Steel's Garage and the Gloucester License Office.[13]

It was the only event of the day that he found worth recording in his diary, where it is retailed with obvious appreciation. Mix-ups like this stirred his imagination; in such wartime confusions, in fact, lay the origin of his sixth novel, *Put Out More Flags*.

Waugh's early novels create a world pullulating with diverse, tangential, reckless, and intersecting human energies. Few readers turn to Waugh's fiction for his ideas or philosophical views, for his moral or theological insights, for abstruse and ponderous systems of allusion. He was a popular novelist with a superb gift of comic irony, action, and characterization. His ability to populate and animate a fictional world, though not his fertility, was Dickensian. Love of trouble ran deep in Waugh's temperament, bubbling up in his early novels to lend them comic life, to liberate them from the narrow, the predictable, the merely conventional.

In a well-known observation, T. S. Eliot aphoristically remarked that Henry James "had a mind so fine that no idea could violate it." Though this statement does not apply to Waugh, a corollary might: whenever Waugh allowed ideas to invade his fiction, his fiction suffered.

By this I do not mean that Waugh's ideas were in themselves negligible or unworthy of expression, but rather that his genius was not for abstractions and systems; his distinctive literary gift was not the exposition of intellectual constructions. What Waugh did with almost unique ability was of greater value, however. He converted his most deeply felt—not rationalized—responses to experience into comic fables with mythic patterns and resonances. Waugh at his best was a writer not of ideas but of strong feeling—of nostalgia, longing for order, disappointment, resentment, despair—but the impulse that most animated the early novels was his fascination with the world of his experience, crooked and difficult as it was.

A comparison with one of Waugh's contemporaries illustrates this point. In Aldous Huxley's *Antic Hay* (1923), Gumbril Senior exhibits a large scale model of "London as it might have been if they'd allowed Wren to carry out his plans of rebuilding after the Great Fire." He goes on to explain its virtues:

> Wren offered them open spaces and broad streets; he offered them sunlight and air and cleanliness; he offered them beauty, order and grandeur. He offered to build for the imagination and the ambitious spirit of man, so that even the most bestial, vaguely and remotely, as they walked those streets, might feel that they were of the same race—or very nearly—as Michelangelo; that they too might feel themselves, in spirit at least, magnificent, strong and free. He offered them all these things; he drew a

plan for them, walking in peril among the smouldering ruins. But they preferred to re-erect the old intricate squalor; they preferred the mediaeval darkness and crookedness, and beastly irregular quaintness; they preferred holes and crannies and winding tunnels; they preferred foul smells, sunless, stagnant air, phthisis and rickets; they preferred ugliness and pettiness and dirt; they preferred the wretched human scale, the scale of the sickly body, not of the mind.[14]

I do not know if Huxley himself shared Gumbril Senior's enthusiasm for town planning, but it is in any event interesting to contrast the passage with Waugh's interest in the Mediterranean port cities he visited in the course of a 1929 cruise, when he was attracted to exactly the sort of slums Gumbril Senior deplored. Waugh delighted in the vigorous untidiness, "the wretched human scale," of crowded urban street life. His fascination with Mediterranean slums is a recurrent topic in his first travel book, *Labels*. First, for instance, he wandered about Naples:

> I walked for some time about the streets of the old town, where Baedeker commends the "diverse scenes of popular life." Small boys with long brown legs were bowling oranges about on the wet lava. The girls, at the orders of the priests, wore thick, dirty stockings. Bedding and washing hung from the windows as soon as the rain stopped; the uneven alleys rose in steps between high tenement houses; the smells were varied and intense but not wholly disagreeable. There were shrines at most of the street corners, honoured with artificial bouquets. Rudimentary trades were being pursued in dark workshops. The women gossiped and scolded at their doors and windows and innumerable balconies. (55)

In Port Said he investigated "Arab Town":

> I do not suppose that this part of Port Said is more interesting than any other Oriental town; indeed, probably much less so, but it was the first I visited and the only one where I stayed for any length of time. Their intensely human joviality and inquisitiveness, their animal-like capacity for curling up and sleeping in the dust, their unembarrassed religious observances, their courtesy to strangers, their uncontrolled fecundity, the dignity of their old men, make an interesting contrast with all the wrangling and resentment of northern slums, lightened by fitful outbursts of hysteria. (85–86)

Explaining his repeated visits to Arab Town in Port Said, Waugh wrote: ". . . it was not local colour or picturesque bits, or even interest in the habits of life of another race, which drew me there day after day, but the intoxicating sense of vitality and actuality" (85). As the cruise continued he became a connoisseur of the native quarters: in Malta, where to his great satisfaction he found what he thought must be "the most concentrated and intense slum in the world," the Manderaggio (131–32); in Athens, where he spent an unusually pleasurable evening of "Dickensian conviviality" among peasants in a bistro (153); in Algiers, where the Kasbar offered "that vivid street life that one sees in every old town which has a slum quarter inaccessible to traffic" (188).

Waugh's pleasure in the spontaneity and disorder of the slum quarters, as opposed to Gumbril Senior's preference for the broad, orderly avenues of Wren's plan for London, yields a glimpse into the chief imaginative source of the early novels. There is, in fact, a satiric sequence in *Black Mischief* reminiscent of Wren's plan, the Emperor Seth's plan to reorganize his capital city along more rational lines—a plan utterly defeated by the irregular vitality of Azania. Contradictory impulses—love of life's disorder and retreat from that disorder—clashed in Waugh's sensibility; but the primary source of his fiction was his gusto for "the variety and absurdity" of life.

Between *Decline and Fall* and *Brideshead Revisited*, Waugh's fiction was gradually undermined by his declining interest in the "vitality and actuality" that galvanized his early novels.

Most recent critics of Waugh look for progress in his career. Jeffrey Heath, for example, finds Waugh through the years moving toward an awareness of and resignation to his vocation as a Christian artist. Ian Littlewood sees him gradually shedding inadequate strategies of escape as he found that only religious faith could provide a fully satisfactory response to the contemporary world and his own discontents. Robert Murray Davis exhaustively traces his developing literary craftsmanship.[15] There is insight in all these areas of development, but I think it is also true that, whatever advances might have been made between *Decline and Fall* and *Brideshead Revisited*, Waugh's fiction had during the same period lost something of great value.

This viewpoint is not new. It was proposed early and most notoriously, perhaps, by Edmund Wilson, an admirer of Waugh's early novels who was bitterly disappointed and annoyed by *Brideshead Revisited*. But Wilson's attack on *Brideshead* was provoked partly if not entirely by his hostility to the novel's religious premises—Christianity being in Wilson's view no longer plausible, and a twentieth-century novel based on Christianity therefore being plainly out of touch, not to say obscurantist. So strongly did religious hostility prejudice Wilson's subsequent reading of Waugh that his criticism of later novels, for instance *The Loved One*, is merely absurd. Other critics, however, some more sympathetic to *Brideshead*'s religious premises, have also found the novel flawed by such defects as weak structure, snobbery, and sentimentality.

But beyond all these problems in *Brideshead Revisited*, there lurks a more fundamental malady. All are symptoms of Waugh's almost total imaginative withdrawal from the world of active experience, the world populated by every variety and extremity of character, the world as a novel in its own right. Littlewood's strategies-of-escape thesis nowhere makes better sense than in *Brideshead*, which reveals Waugh in headlong flight from contemporary life.

In fact, the impulse to retreat from life had been present in Waugh's fiction from the beginning. Many critics have noted that the disorder that fascinated him also repelled him and that he had a strong craving for order. "The artist's only service to the disintegrated society of today is to create little independent systems of order of his own," Waugh wrote in 1946; but this laudable public service was actually less a product of philanthropic motives than of his own strong appetite for order.[16] He valued traditional art and architecture, for example, especially domestic architecture, and he grew to love, in particular, the "high civilized style" of the past, especially the refined and carefully measured proportions of the neoclassical. He reverenced skilled craftsmanship, which imposed order on the amorphous and raw. From the social and moral flux of his own time he looked back wistfully to an ideal of Victorian class structure and Victorian standards of decorum and gentility. Christianity, for Waugh, was synonymous with the continuity and authority of Rome.

His ambivalent attitude toward disorder is illustrated by his two experiences in Abyssinia. During his first visit, in 1930, he was fascinated to observe an indigenous, technologically primitive culture invaded by an ill-assorted collection of European innovations and ideas, a pleasing confusion that inspired the robust anarchy of *Black Mischief*'s Azania. Yet even as he celebrated Abyssinia's cultural confusion, he despised it; and when Mussolini's Italy, which he imagined to be civilized and well disciplined, invaded Abyssinia in 1935, he applauded, choosing to regard the war as an exemplary assertion of traditional European order against semibarbaric disorganization and crudity. He was simultaneously the drunkard praising sobriety and the teetotaler thirsting for spirits.

These conflicting impulses appear in all the novels; the delight in disorderly energy that in turn energizes the early novels is invariably mitigated by wistful images of order. The novels are haunted by recurrent images of home, usually country houses; but what is essential to these homes is not their social status so much as their privacy and isolation, their domestic coziness, their routine and ritual placidity, their innocence. The rural sanctuaries of Waugh's early novels are not an idea but an impulse, a deep nostalgia for the kind of order afforded by a happy and stable childhood. They are not, as some would have it, a symptom of immaturity or arrested development; they manifest the universal appeal of the myth of edenic origins. If the early novels thrive on trouble, they also betray a longing to escape trouble, to retreat into a narrower, more secure circle of experience. The centrifugal energy of human activity, of life itself—the vital source of Waugh's fiction—wounded the wistful sensibility that sought the still center.

This opposition informs the structure of all the early novels, but not in equal proportions. In *Decline and Fall,* anarchy is almost unchecked; six years later, in *A Handful of Dust,* Waugh's tolerance for the crookedness of human nature had considerably diminished; in *Work Suspended,* five years later yet, he had lost almost all patience with the patent shortcomings of his own species. The trend of his early fiction, graphed across the years, shows him gradually retreating from the perturbations of contemporary life.

In part this retreat was simply a recoil from those features of the twentieth century that distinguish it so very sharply from earlier eras. Acutely sensitive to the advent of a new age, Waugh faced it with growing dread. His retreat soon became a withdrawal not from evil times alone, however, but from life itself. Misgiving turned into disgust, disgust into revulsion, revulsion into *accidia*. Sometimes accompanied by a vigorous rearguard belligerence, sometimes by mere apathy and dull resentment, his retreat began to exercise a deadly influence on his fiction. His interests and sympathies contracted; he became petrified in opinions; he turned away from the world's untidy hurly-burly to savor instead a cloying diet of private fancies and foibles. Like *Great Expectations*'s Miss Havisham, he closeted himself in a timeless, airless room, pulling the curtains shut on the activity of the street beyond.

Although this defiant sequestration may have afforded him a measure of private gratification, it cut him off from the stimulus that had kindled the early novels. The world around him in the 1930s and 1940s was in many ways chaotic, ugly, and degenerate, but it was the only world available to him, and to his fiction. There was no satisfactory substitute for life: when Waugh lost his zest for trouble, his real troubles began.

The following chapters argue that Waugh's early novels reveal him retreating, novel by novel, from the rough data of human experience. This retreat may have had some benefits for Waugh personally, but for his fiction it was a deadly hemorrhaging. Waugh's novels are not primarily interesting for their spiritual content, or moral theology, or satiric themes, or realistic presentation of life; their power resides in their creation of a living fictional world, a caricature that reveals elemental mythic patterns and tensions beneath the random, cluttered surface of life. It can be argued persuasively that Waugh's religious faith grew during the period I am discussing, and beyond; but it is not so certain that his fiction benefited very directly, if at all, and in any case the gains were more than offset by the losses. The novels beginning with *Brideshead Revisited* may have become more demonstratively full of moral uplift, but their comic uplift faltered; and in that comic uplift, fueled by his sympathetic fascination with crooked human energy, there was an even greater value.

2

Oxford and the Years of Ferment: "I Did Not Set Out to Be a Writer"

Three pieces of background—Waugh's undergraduate years, his early story "The Balance," and his biography of Dante Gabriel Rossetti—suggest some of the conflicting impulses behind his early novels.

Although he spent only two and a half years at Oxford, Waugh's undergraduate experience strongly stamped his imagination. He arrived from his public school, Lancing, a clever youth with artistic inclinations but circumscribed culture. Despite growing up in a literary family, his background was in most respects conventionally middle class. Once or twice in his novels he described, or caricatured, the sort of young man he had been in early 1922—as Paul Pennyfeather in *Decline and Fall,* for example, and later as Charles Ryder in *Brideshead Revisited:*

> My books were meagre and commonplace . . . and my earliest friends fitted well into this background; they were Collins, a Wykehamist, an embryo don, a man of solid reading and childlike humour, and a small circle of college intellectuals, who maintained a middle course of culture between the flamboyant "aesthetes" and the proletarian scholars who scrambled fiercely for facts in the lodging houses of the Iffley Road and Wellington Square. It was by this circle that I found myself adopted during my first term; they provided the kind of company I had enjoyed in the sixth form at school, for which the sixth form had prepared me. . . . (27–28)

But he was on the lookout for wider experience, and the opportunity came in his third term at Hertford, when an eccentric friend named Terence Greenidge introduced him to the Hypocrites Club, a rackety fraternity celebrated in the memoirs of many of Waugh's Oxford contemporaries, as well as in his own.

When Waugh joined the Hypocrites, it was becoming the center of an idiosyncratic, vaguely artistic, pleasure-loving undergraduate set, so extraordinarily congenial to him that he instantly forsook most of his more respectable connections. The Hypocrites Club became "the stamping-ground of half my Oxford life," he wrote; "the fount and origin of what I have called my boisterous bohemianism."[1] It provided the ideal outlet for his latent anarchic energies. In *Brideshead Revisited* he described the awakening of Charles Ryder in terms of a Yosemite geyser: ". . . the hot spring of anarchy rose from deep furnaces where was no solid earth, and burst into the sunlight—a rainbow in its cooling vapours—with a power the rocks could not repress" (44). In the fellowship of the Hypocrites Waugh found his own version of the enchanted Oxford he had imagined while reading *Sinister Street,* had anticipated ever since visiting the University with his father two years earlier, and had dreamed about still during his early, quiet months at Hertford. When he first walked up the stairway leading to the Hypocrites' seedy chambers in St. Aldate's ("up a tortuous staircase and long twisting passages to a room still filled with the atmosphere of beer, stale smoke and the nameless goings-on of the night before," the more studious A. L. Rowse recorded of his first, frightful, and only visit)[2]—Waugh had, like Alice falling into Wonderland, entered a wholly new world.

"Undergraduates recur," Warden Spooner of New College is said to have remarked, but Maurice Bowra, who saw many Oxford undergraduates come and go, distinctly recalled some of Waugh's contemporaries:

> The post-war generation had come to a close and was succeeded by something quite different. With the new arrivals of 1922 a dominant note was struck by a small and gifted party of Etonians, who set out unashamedly to be aesthetes and to revive some glories of the nineties. . . . They were splendidly courageous in defying their uncultivated contemporaries, who were first amused by them and then admired them.[3]

The undisputed leader of this vanguard was Harold Acton, a flamboyant and exuberant fellow Hypocrite who soon became one of Waugh's closest friends. Acton had spent much of his youth in his family's Florentine villa and commanded a cosmopolitan breadth of culture unique among his Oxford peers. Waugh's education was, by contrast, strictly insular. Christopher Hollis, another Hypocrite, later recorded a characteristic encounter:

> I remember well a dinner one evening at the Golden Cross, when Harold referred to Dickens with great contempt as "a writer whom my nurse used to make me read." He obviously knew little about him. Evelyn, who had been brought up by his excellent father, a man of letters, to tread well the central paths of English and especially Victorian literature, even if he

knew little of what he called "bloody abroad," knew and admired his Dickens well and took Harold severely to task.[4]

Acton thought Waugh a promising disciple: "At last you have escaped from the influence of that nice old maid who taught you illumination and whose drawings I have at the same time admired and deplored," he wrote in 1923, referring to Waugh's earlier artistic mentor, Francis Crease. "At last you are the modern you were always intended to be."[5] This congratulation proved deeply ironic, but though he never became the "modern" Acton hoped for, Waugh's encounter with Acton's style and enthusiasms opened up new prospects.

Many others also contributed to Waugh's "Kingdom of Cokayne" at Oxford, however. In *Brideshead Revisited,* Charles Ryder's undergraduate life is transformed by a single charming eccentric named Sebastian Flyte. Waugh's Oxford embraced a larger circle of friends and acquaintances with diverse backgrounds and multifarious charms and abilities, and Alec Waugh was surely correct in seeing Sebastian Flyte as the embodiment of a whole revelatory experience: ". . . though there was no Sebastian in Evelyn's life, there was, I think, an equivalent for Sebastian in the number of brilliant and elegant young men from a larger way of life who showed him in how narrow a world he had moved at Heathmount, Lancing and at Underhill."[6] Waugh was susceptible to dash, and at Oxford he came across young men who made an art of enjoying life stylishly, confidently, with aristocratic élan.

In *Put Out More Flags,* he wrote of his set at Oxford:

> In those days, the mid '20's at Oxford, when the last of the ex-service men had gone down and the first of the puritanical, politically minded had either not come up or, at any rate, had not made himself noticed, . . . a certain spiritual extravagance in the quest for pleasure had been the sole common bond between friends who in subsequent years had drifted apart. . . . (38)

Perhaps the finest example of this extravagance was the Railway Club—a group overlapping with if not identical to the Hypocrites—who periodically chartered a dining car on an outbound train for an evening of eating and drinking in congenial company. The bill of fare for at least one such occasion survives. The train left Oxford shortly after seven o'clock:

7.20 Bletchington: Hors d'oeuvres.
7.33 Fritwell and Somerton: Crême de Céléri.
7.45 Aynho: Filet de Sole, Poche Sauce Dieppoise.

7.51 King's Sutton: Roast Chicken and Sausage.
7.58 Banbury: Cauliflower, Brussels Sprouts, Potatoes. (Stop).
8.15 Woodford and Hinton: Cranberry Apple Tart and Cream. Mousse Framboise.
8.37 Rugby: Cheese and Biscuits. (Stop).
8.43 Lutterworth: Dessert, Coffee, etc.
9.0   Leicester, Central: L'Addition.[7]

Then the Railway Club changed trains and returned to Oxford, making toasts and speeches along the way.

Such deliberately extravagant exercises in the high eccentric style deeply impressed Waugh. Oxford opened his eyes to a different style of living: debonair, worldly, self-assured, scornful of the timid and conventional. He left the University without academic distinction but ambitious for experience, open to the world, eager to taste life in its great variety of intoxicating forms from beer to champagne—especially champagne.

In 1926 Waugh's first post-Oxford fiction was published, a story titled "The Balance."

Although he had written for several undergraduate periodicals, when he came down from Oxford in the summer of 1924 it was not clear to Waugh, or to anyone else, that his future lay in writing. Nonetheless, during his last months as an undergraduate he had been visited by inspiration for a novel "all about magic and madness."[8] "I began the *Temple at Thatch* last night and have written a dozen pages of the first chapter," he noted at its inception. "I think it is quite good."[9] He worked on *The Temple* intermittently during the summer, but "I find it in serious danger of becoming dull," he observed in early September, and the next day: "A suspicion settles on me that it will never be finished."[10] It evidently lay dormant through the autumn, but in December he was working on it again. "I am engrossed in the Discourses of Sir Joshua Reynolds—also in entirely rewriting my bad book," he wrote to his mentor Harold Acton before Christmas.[11] In January he carried the manuscript with him to Wales, where he had desperately taken a job as a preparatory school usher; in the evenings, supposedly monitoring the boys' studying, he continued working on *The Temple*, telling "any boy impertinent enough to enquire what he was up to," one pupil recalled, "that he was writing A History of the Eskimos."[12] But by the end of the day, he told Acton, he was "too sad and weary to write anything," and *The Temple* flagged.[13] He later recalled: "It concerned an undergraduate who inherited a property of which nothing was left except an eighteenth-century classical folly where he set up house and, I think, practised black magic"—a description that makes *The Temple* sound very much like his undergraduate writing.[14]

Acton's oblique censures condemned *The Temple* to the flames, but even before abandoning it Waugh had a new plan: "I want to write a story about Silenus—very English & sentimental—a Falstaff forever babbling o' green fields—but shall never have time," he wrote from Wales.[15] This book apparently never got underway, but a few months later he was struck by yet another idea: "I have quite suddenly received inspiration about my book. I am making the first chapter a cinema film and have been writing furiously ever since."[16] The "book" dwindled into a short story, but in that form, at least, he completed it at the end of August, after returning to London. "It is odd but, I think, quite good," he judged as he sent the manuscript off to a typist.[17] Eventually it was included in *Georgian Stories, 1926*, an annual collection of short stories his brother Alec happened to be editing for Chapman and Hall: there were advantages to having close connections in publishing.

The story was "The Balance: A Yarn of the Good Old Days of Broad Trousers and High Necked Jumpers," the subtitle facetiously alluding to contemporary Oxford fashion.[18] To call this his first mature fiction would be to apply too strong a word to it, for it is in many ways unripe, but in retrospect one can see in it distinctive marks of his later fiction.

The action of the story, abstracted from various complexities in the narration, is fairly simple. Adam Doure, a young art student just down from Oxford, has fallen in love with Imogen Quest, the debutante daughter of a wealthy aristocratic family. To forestall his courtship, Imogen's imperious mother rusticates her daughter. While Adam grieves, Imogen with a light heart and a copy of the *Tatler* entrains for a country seat named Thatch. Despairing and penniless, Adam sells his books to raise money, takes a train to Oxford, and there, planning to poison himself, tries to collect friends for a farewell party. After failing to muster anyone for the party, however, and instead spending a squalid, pleasureless evening in the company of a disagreeable acquaintance, Adam takes poison, only to vomit it back up. As the story ends, he is brooding over the meaning of this experience.

"The Balance" has a strong autobiographical flavor. The young hero, Adam Doure—middle-class, penurious, unworldly ("What's that?" he greets a plate of steak tartare), lovesick, weary of art school, dining out and nightclubbing beyond his means, and looking back to Oxford for friendship—strikingly resembles Waugh himself in 1924 and 1925, especially Waugh as he habitually portrayed himself in his diaries. Imogen Quest, the heroine, may be somewhat indebted, especially in her inattentiveness, to the young woman with whom Waugh was futilely in love at the time, Olivia Greene, but Imogen is far more glamorous, wealthy, and aristocratic. Imogen seems, in fact, an embodiment of the stylish and aristocratically spacious world Waugh had encountered at Oxford. Conjuring up a vision of his own middle-class home, Adam sees his plain sister Jane, "with her stupid pimply face and her dull jealousy of all Imogen said and did and wore": Imogen offers an escape from the narrow, conventional, plain world of Jane and home. Imogen's surname suggests her significance as an emblem of Waugh's intense, Gatsby-like ambitions, while Adam's despondency and suicidal broodings parallel Waugh's state of mind in the summer of 1925, as described in his diaries.

All this is conveyed in a series of narrative experiments, including not only the original idea of narrating the story in the form of a silent film, but also spare transcriptions of idle table chatter, a slow and dense stream-of-consciousness passage, contrapuntal choral commentary contributed by the audience of the silent film, and an interior debate in the form of a dialogue between Adam and his reflection in the water. It cannot honestly be claimed that all of these experiments were successful, but the confusion of techniques reveals Waugh receptive to innovation and willing to try whatever came to hand. Without knowing it, he was a novelist in search of a style, and while "The Balance" does not exactly find it, one or two of his trial-and-error attempts proved fruitful later. The convention of narrating a silent film, for example, while awkward, may have been a helpful lesson in the discipline of narrating with sharp visual images and dialogue succinct enough to fit into a subtitle. "The Balance" also reveals Waugh beginning to turn to fictional account his own generation of Oxonians and debutantes, staple characters in his early novels.

Despite the promise of several of its experiments, however, "The Balance" is an uneven accomplishment. The complexity of technique, by itself, makes for some uncomfortable reading, but behind this complexity lurks a larger problem originating in the story's autobiographical immediacy. The confusion of styles reflects Waugh's shifting perspectives on his own experience. In part he sought to treat his hero, as he often treated himself in his diaries, with ironic distance—in Adam's case by making him a two-dimensional and somewhat comic character on a cinema screen. But he also wanted to involve the reader in Adam's thinking and feeling. Thus the story is at times dramatic and farcical, at times tiresomely discursive and self-pitying:

REFLECTION: Is the balance of life and death so easily swayed?

ADAM: It is the balance of appetite and reason. The reason remains constant—the appetite varies.

REFLECTION: And is there no appetite for death?

ADAM: None which cannot be appeased by sleep or change or the mere passing of time.

REFLECTION: And in the other scale no reason?

ADAM: None. None.

REFLECTION: No honour to be observed to friends? No interpenetration, so that you cannot depart without bearing away with you something that is part of another?

ADAM: None.

Waugh did not repeat this particular experiment, but it suggests his occasional, dangerous temptation to become sentimentally self-absorbed. If the cinematic passages of "The Balance" foreshadow the early novels, the story's self-indulgent confessional tendencies look ahead to the first-person narration of *Work Suspended* and *Brideshead Revisited*.

"The Balance" gives a glimpse of Waugh at a difficult moment in his life. It is characteristic that, at the time of "The Balance," his diaries should mention his "perverse pleasure" in boring his pupils, his negotiations to buy a revolver, "the paradoxes of suicide and achievement," and his plans for a new book—all in a short entry for a single day.[19] "The Balance" reflects both his optimism and his suicidal depression, his alertness to the world around him and his tendency, under the pressure of unhappy experience, to retreat into himself. As such it is a prototype of much of his later fiction, both the best and the worst.

Except for one unmemorable short story, "A House of Gentlefolks," Waugh published no more fiction until *Decline and Fall*. He did undertake several other writing projects, however. One was a work he described in his diary in October 1926: "Some days ago I wrote to the publishers of the *Today and Tomorrow* series suggesting that I should write them a book on *Noah; or the Future of Intoxication*. To my surprise and pleasure they welcome the idea enthusiastically."[20] The publisher's enthusiasm disappeared when Waugh submitted his manuscript, however, and like *The Temple at Thatch*, *Noah* was apparently consigned to dustbin or flames; nothing of it survives, and given Waugh's characterization of it as "mannered and 'literary,'" its loss probably need not be regretted overmuch.

Earlier, in the autumn of 1925, laid up with a sprained ankle, he had immersed himself in study of the Pre-Raphaelites, and the following year he summarized his studies in "An Essay on the Pre-Raphaelite Brotherhood, 1847–1854," printed in small quantity by his close friend Alastair Graham. The "Essay" was partly an excursion into art criticism under the influence of postimpressionist, "significant form" theory, partly an exercise, under the influence of Lytton Strachey's *Eminent Victorians,* in satiric biography. Under neither heading is it very successful; the tone in particular—smug and condescending—is all wrong for Waugh:

> Now Ruskin today is universally, and, we think, justly regarded as out of date. He was a nice judge of a painting in just the same sense that his father had been a nice judge of sherry. . . . In *Modern Painters* Ruskin wrote: "Why we receive pleasure from some forms and colours and not from others is no more to be asked or answered than why we like sugar and dislike wormwood." Now these are, of course, exactly the questions with which modern aesthetics deal. The reason that he is out of date is not that he is démodé but decayed. He was for all his acuteness purely a superficial critic.[21]

As with "The Balance," he was searching for a style as he wrote this "Essay," and he was unfortunate in his selection of a model: there was little future for him in the Strachey vein.

Out of the "Essay" came something better, however, *Rossetti: His Life and Works,* written in the summer and fall of 1927 and published the following spring by Duckworth. Here Waugh immediately disowned the example of *Eminent Victorians'* mocking irony: "We have discovered a jollier way of honouring our dead," he wrote, alluding to Strachey's vogue. "The corpse has become the marionette. With bells on its fingers and wires on its toes it is jigged about to a 'period dance' of our own piping; and who is not amused? Unfortunately, there is singularly little fun to be got out of Rossetti" (12). *Rossetti* remains, however, though somewhat restlessly, under the influence of postimpressionist aesthetics. The autumn after leaving Oxford, intending to become a painter, Waugh had enrolled in art classes at Heatherley's Art School in London, but after several weeks dropped out. His career as a painter having been frustrated, perhaps he now entertained the notion of himself as an art critic like, say, Clive Bell.

Waugh the art critic was not to be, but the aesthetic discussion of *Rossetti* reveals, in retrospect at least, much about Waugh the novelist-to-be. It discloses, for example, the moralistic strain in Waugh: in his view Rossetti's failure as an artist—for Waugh's Rossetti was a painter whose great potential remained largely unrealized—was ultimately caused by weakness of character. Rossetti had avariciously and self-indulgently destroyed his own great talent, and Waugh concluded sternly:

> . . . there was fatally lacking in him that *essential rectitude* that underlies the serenity of all really great art. The sort of unhappiness that beset him was not the sort of unhappiness that does beset a great artist; all his brooding about magic and suicide are symptomatic not so much of genius as of mediocrity. There is a spiritual inadequacy, a sense of ill-organisation about all that he did. (226–27)

Combined with this severe note, on the other hand, is Waugh's romantic inclination, for, though he found Rossetti morally inadequate, he greatly admired several of Rossetti's paintings, especially *Beata Beatrix*. Inspired by Dante's *Vita Nuova*, *Beata Beatrix* is a mystical, sensuous painting; Waugh spent hours at the Tate Gallery studying it, absorbed in its details and lush color, awed by its otherworldly glow. *Beata Beatrix* by itself redeemed Rossetti: "It is, perhaps, the most purely spiritual and devotional work of European Art since the fall of the Byzantine Empire," Waugh gave as his "considered judgment," not simply an "ecstatic outburst" (130). In collision with his profound reverence for *Beata Beatrix*, his slender interest in academic aesthetic theory dissolved:

> Anyone who, confronted with its sublime and pervasive sanctity, can speak of it coldly in terms of saturation, and planes and plastic values . . . has constricted his artistic perceptions to an antlike narrowness. There are manifestations of the human spirit that transcend the materials in which they are discernible. (130–31)

Once again, a foreshadowing of *Brideshead Revisited*—the severe moral judgment on Rossetti together with this fervent religious response to the rich mystical suggestions of *Beata Beatrix*.

Several years earlier, in fact, during his initial Pre-Raphaelite enthusiasm, Waugh had conceived of the Pre-Raphaelites as good characters for a novel:

> The Pre-Raphaelites still absorb me. I think I can say without affectation that during this last week I have lived with them night and day. Early in the morning with Holman Hunt—the only Pre-Raphaelite—untiring, fearless, conscientious. Later in the day with Millais—never with *him* but with my biography of him—a modish Lytton Strachey biography. How he shines through Holman Hunt's loyal pictures of him. Later, when firelight and rum and loneliness have done their worst, with Rossetti, soaked in chloral and Philip Marston's "Why is he not some great exiled

king, that we might give our lives in trying to restore him to his kingdom?"[22]

Rossetti, despite its aesthetic concerns, is most memorable for its characterization of Rossetti and its sketches of his associates. Waugh's moral disapprobation competed with his admiration for Rossetti's bohemianism and personal extravagance. Besides Rossetti himself, his menagerie of friends and lovers—human counterparts to the exotic, scarcely domesticated animals that roamed about and devastated his garden—might well have populated a comic novel. The book's finest moments have nothing to do with art criticism, but with its diverse cast of characters and their relationships: Rossetti disrupting William Morris's quiet, healthy, industrious life at Kelmscott ("Here [Morris] returned from Iceland, 'all querulous feeling' killed in him, and the 'dear faces of wife and children and friends dearer than ever,' and here, in the autumn, came Rossetti, drug-soaked, crazy, haunted and driven by suspicion, a dark shadow across the sun-bathed water-meadows, the very embodiment of 'the confused and turbulent past.'"); Rossetti's marriage to the beautiful, consumptive Elizabeth Siddal ("The one exuberant, slangy, expansive, buoyant, widely educated and of some reputation, conscious of untried strength and unexplored potentialities, the other wan, and prim, already crushed by the difficulties of life, her strength failing daily, practically uneducated and entirely unknown, with only her fading beauty bearing the taint of underlying decay in its very height"); Rossetti's disgraceful liaisons with Fanny Cornforth ("this apparently soulless woman"— "there was no company into which she could be introduced without offence"). Waugh's instinct was to treat life in heightened farcical or dramatic terms, and with Rossetti and his circle he encountered very happy material. The biography's lasting value lies not in its aesthetic argument and outbreaks of censoriousness, but in its humor and expansive sympathies; in its foreshadowing, that is, of *Decline and Fall*.

3

Decline and Fall: "Grimes, You Wretch!"

In September 1927, staying with his parents at Underhill and still working on *Rossetti*, Waugh observed in his diary: "How I detest this house and how ill I feel in it. The whole place volleys and thunders with traffic. I can't sleep or work. I . . . have begun on a comic novel."[1] Sometime later he read the first ten thousand words to Anthony Powell, and at some point he read the early chapters to Dudley Carew as well:

> What he read to me that night, sitting in the chair where Arthur was wont to proclaim that beautiful Evelyn Hope was dead, were the first fifty or so pages of *Decline and Fall*. A happiness, a hilarity, sustained him that night, and I was back giving him my unstinted admiration as I did at Lancing. It was marvellously funny and he knew that it was. As was his habit in those old, innocent days, he roared with laughter at his own comic invention.[2]

According to Powell, the novel was originally called *Picaresque: or the Making of an Englishman*. But, Powell recalled, "Some months after the reading aloud of these chapters—probably a moment towards the end of the same year—I asked Waugh how the novel was progressing. He replied: 'I've burnt it.'"[3] He had not, in fact, but by November the manuscript seems to have been set aside and then ignored until after Christmas.

The later chapters advanced slowly. Early in the new year he wrote to Harold Acton: "The novel does not get on. I should so much value your opinion on whether I am to finish it."[4] Once again, as with *The Temple at Thatch*, he seems to have been ready to defer to Acton's critical judgment. In this case, however, Acton claims to have been enthusiastic about the manuscript. A draft of the novel was complete in April, but, worried about its length, Waugh wrote to Powell, who was working at Duckworth:

> I hope the novel will be finished in a week. I will send it to you as soon as it is typed & then want to revise it very thoroughly and enlarge it a bit. I

think at present it shows signs of being too short. How do these novelists make their books so long. I'm sure one could write any novel in the world on two post cards.[5]

In May he submitted the manuscript to Duckworth, where it was rejected on "the odd grounds of its indelicacy" (Waugh later wrote), with demands for alterations he declined to make.[6] Chapman and Hall soon accepted the novel but also stipulated some bowdlerizing changes. This time Waugh acceded, and *Decline and Fall* was published in September 1928, subtitled *An Illustrated Novelette*.

The facetious subtitle announced the novel's modest pretensions. As far as Waugh was concerned, it was a potboiler; weightier literary work might come later, but at the moment he needed money to get married. It also was something in the nature of an inside joke designed to amuse friends, for whom he inserted private allusions ranging from the Christian names of his two closest friends, Alastair and Olivia, to the surname of his detested Hertford tutor, Cruttwell. The names of two derisory minor characters so closely resembled those of two young men of Waugh's acquaintance that in the second printing new names were prudently substituted. The names of other friends and acquaintances had already been edited out in manuscript. The ideal reader was a recent Oxonian with Waugh's own aristocratic predilections and schoolmastering experience—someone like John Betjeman, for example. Perhaps swayed by the dedication to himself, even Harold Acton signified his approval; Waugh replied in acknowledgment: "I am glad to think it amused you a little. Anyway I enjoyed writing it which is more than I can say about Rossetti."[7] Fearing, however, that it might be damaging for a serious man of letters, or art critic, or whatever he might become, to have a comic novel in his canon, Waugh considered publishing it (Alec Waugh recalled) under a pen name.

Yet *Decline and Fall*'s comic accomplishment owed much to its lack of artistic ambition. Aside from urgent practical motives, Waugh's chief stimulus was playfulness, for in writing the novel he was burlesquing his own recent experience. He did not write it carelessly or in a spirit of holiday levity; he was serious about the novel, but he knew the novel itself was not a serious thing.

The challenge Waugh set himself was to exploit the comic potential of his material, "that the texture of life should be made to yield a comic response." Unlike life, which could be and in Waugh's case often was refractory and disheartening, language was something he could control and manipulate with confidence and élan; living was a skill he had not mastered, but writing was a game he could play well and one that yielded satisfying consolation when played successfully.

Much of the "meaning" of *Decline and Fall* lies simply in its deployment of language to achieve comic effect. In this first novel, Waugh achieved a concentration of comic style that he never really surpassed; *Decline and Fall* had no broad artistic ambitions or thematic motives to divert him from comic play or to persuade him to defer immediate effects for larger purposes. The page in hand was everything; the next page would take care of itself. His ambition was straightforward; as he insisted at the very beginning, "IT IS MEANT TO BE FUNNY."

Comic density and intensity were the goal; consistency was not a dominating concern. Waugh readily sacrificed consistency in tone, point of view, satire, or rhetoric if immediate comic impact could be gained by doing so. At one point, grandiloquent parody might serve the purpose, while in the next paragraph it might be severe understatement and, in the next paragraph yet, flagrant hyperbole; or he might at one point adopt the perspective of one of his characters, then a few sentences later suddenly step back from the same character with bland indifference. Behind all such variations, however, is a principle of understatement and precision, and *Decline and Fall*'s comic tone is based on a continual tension between the skillfully controlled language of the narration—selective, concise, lucid, exact, reticent (usually)—and the freewheeling, idiosyncratic energy of the novel's characters.

Playing with language meant, for Waugh, not primarily wit (he seldom played with words in the sense of puns or *double entendres*, for example) or elaboration, but sharpness and compression: packing the most significance into the fewest words. One of his gifts was finding the strikingly apt word or phrase; he preferred a single, well-aimed shot to a fusillade. But this effort of precise and accurate diction was part of a larger goal. Whether understating with clipped brevity or launching into mock grandiloquence, his object was to assert control over his material, and by extension over life, with skillfully deployed comic rhetoric. Near the beginning of *Decline and Fall*, for example, there occurs an often cited passage describing the annual Bollinger Club dinner:

> . . . from all over Europe old members had rallied for the occasion. For two days they had been pouring into Oxford: epileptic royalty from their villas of exile; uncouth peers from crumbling country seats; smooth young men of uncertain tastes from embassies and legations; illiterate lairds from wet granite hovels in the Highlands; ambitious young barristers and Conservative candidates torn from the London season and the indelicate advances of debutantes; all that was most sonorous of name and title was there for the beano. (13–14)

The passage is an adjectival extravagance, but scarcely an uncontrolled one: the rhetorical force of the description springs from the strong vocabulary and the carefully measured, rhythmically orotund sequence of balanced parallel phrases, alliterated almost like Old English prosody, building to the slangy anticlimax, "beano."[8] Though a long sentence, it has the effect of compression. Its comic force derives not simply from the jocular rhetorical deflation at the end, but even more from the mismatch between the promiscuous diversity of the Bollinger membership and the nicely calculated order and diction of their description.

Constantly crowded against this precise, controlled narrative voice is the spontaneous, quirky energy of the novel's characters. The narrator does not describe them; the characters describe themselves by their speech. We meet Lady Circumference, for example, talking to Paul Pennyfeather and Doctor Fagan about her son Lord Tangent:

> The boy's a dunderhead. If he wasn't he wouldn't be here. He wants beatin' and hittin' and knockin' about generally, and then he'll be no good. That grass is shockin' bad on the terrace, Doctor; you ought to sand it down and resow it, but you'll have to take that cedar down if you ever want it to grow properly at the side. I hate cuttin' down a tree—like losin' a tooth—but you have to choose, tree or grass; you can't keep 'em both. What d'you pay your head man? (81)

It is not psychological depth or complexity or even plausibility that Waugh was interested in extracting from the figure of Lady Circumference, but her "comic texture"—idiosyncratic character expressed in uninhibited, slangy speech. Though the vitality of the character is likely to attract a reader's sympathy (and Waugh's as well, I think), the narrative voice itself remains formally uncommitted and unappreciative.[9] Another passage, chosen more or less at random, will show some of the main features of *Decline and Fall*'s comic grammar:

> Ten men of revolting appearance were approaching from the drive. They were low of brow, crafty of eye and crooked of limb. They advanced huddled together with the loping tread of wolves, peering about them furtively as they came, as though in constant terror of ambush; they slavered at their mouths, which hung loosely over their receding chins, while each clutched under his ape-like arm a burden of curious and unaccountable shape. On seeing the Doctor they halted and edged back, those behind squinting and mouthing over their companions' shoulders.
>
> "Crikey!" said Philbrick. "Loonies! This is where I shoot."
>
> "I refuse to believe the evidence of my eyes," said the Doctor. "These creatures simply do not exist." (78)

Here the narrative voice initially seems to share the perspective of Doctor Fagan and Philbrick as they view with alarm the advancing musicians (as they turn out to be). Satire on the Welsh is a recurrent amusement in the early chapters of *Decline and Fall;* the particular tactic here is an extended metaphor crowding together vivid zoo and madhouse images in a series of rhythmic and balanced phrases and sentences. Scarcely a word fails to contribute to the joke, the smooth, urbane mastery of language by itself creating an ironic contrast to the Welsh provincials.

But with the switch from description to dialogue, the narrative voice at once recedes from the perspective of Doctor Fagan and Philbrick to a more remote vantage point, which surveys the musicians, Fagan, and Philbrick from roughly the same ironic distance. From this perspective, the latter are no longer privileged observers but comic objects themselves, with Philbrick's emphatic vernacular and dramatic, crudely violent impulse posed against the suave, ironic incredulity of Doctor Fagan. Their responses reveal their humors, and the juxtaposition of their clashing humors is the comic point. This single short passage thus contains several characteristic features of *Decline and Fall's* comic grammar: the concentration and marshalling of vivid language; the willingness, even eagerness, to shift point of view if the shift will augment the immediate comic effect; dialogue recorded without comment to display quirks of individual character and their comic confrontation.

Another passage shows some of the same methods. The subject is Margot Beste-Chetwynde's and Paul Pennyfeather's projected wedding:

> Society was less certain in its approval, and Lady Circumference, for one, sighed for the early nineties, when Edward Prince of Wales, at the head of *ton*, might have given authoritative condemnation to this ostentatious second marriage.
>
> "It's maddenin' Tangent having died just at this time," she said. "People may think that that's my reason for refusin'. I can't imagine that *anyone* will go."
>
> "I hear your nephew Alastair Trumpington is the best man," said Lady Vanbrugh.
>
> "You seem to be as well informed as my chiropodist," said Lady Circumference with unusual felicity, and all Lowndes Square shook at her departure. (176)

This passage is often cited for its shockingly casual disclosure of little Tangent's death, but its comic grammar is more complex. The first paragraph, with its mock deference to the notion of Society, Lady

Circumference's nostalgia for Victorian decorum, the French "ton," and the polysyllabic formality, momentarily establishes an elevated style of discourse and manners, in order to prepare for the sharp contrast of Lady Circumference's blunt style and savage insensitivity. Her rejoinder to Lady Vanbrugh's feline comment further compresses several comic elements: the countess gossiping with a chiropodist; the unusual and ambiguous authorial comment—"with unusual felicity"; the mock-heroic cliché "shook at her departure," applied absurdly to the aristocratically fashionable Lowndes Square. What ties all the techniques and jokes together is the play with language to achieve immediate and striking comic effect.[10]

Waugh was also playing with recent personal history.

The book Waugh had in mind when he began writing was a burlesque of his schoolmastering experience, especially his initiation into schoolmastering at Arnold House in North Wales. "The Balance," too, had sprung from his misery in Wales, but having escaped Wales, freed himself from schoolmastering, and reconciled himself to Olivia Greene's romantic indifference by the time he began writing *Decline and Fall*, he could look back on his griefs at Arnold House with greater emotional detachment and with a greater appreciation of their comic aspect. As Paul Pennyfeather, sitting comfortably in a London restaurant with his equally conventional Oxford friend Potts, reflects on his experience at Llanabba, it all seems a phantasmagoric aberration: "Llanabba Castle, with its sham castellations and pre-posterous inhabitants, had sunk into the oblivion that waits upon even the most lurid of nightmares" (145). In 1927, Waugh's own perspective on Arnold House was comparable, and *Decline and Fall* exaggerates the bad-dream metaphor into *Alice in Wonderland* dis-location, combining his departure from Oxford and his exile in Wales to create a myth of unheroic descent into a bizarre scholastic under-world, a purely comic Dotheboy's Hall. Beneath all the exaggerations and inventions of the novel, Paul's history follows a pattern similar to Waugh's: banishment from the agreeably sheltered life of an Oxford undergraduate, followed by a plunge into a strange and unsettling new world. Waugh's descent from Oxford to Arnold House provided the original comic impetus of *Decline and Fall*.

Although *Decline and Fall* parodies Waugh's experience, Paul Pen-nyfeather is not a close self-portrait of Waugh himself. A studious, mild-mannered undergraduate leading a blamelessly dull life, Paul is entirely unacquainted with Waugh's bohemian, pleasure-loving Ox-ford; he has certainly never visited the Hypocrites, and the circum-stances of his expulsion from the University scarcely resemble

Waugh's routinely unsuccessful departure. But Paul's middle-class background deliberately echoes Waugh's. Paul arrived at the University "after a creditable career at a small public school of ecclesiastical temper on the South Downs, where he had edited the magazine, been President of the Debating Society, and had, as his report said, 'exercised a wholesome influence for good' in the House of which he was head boy" (15–16)—very much like Waugh at Lancing. The difference between Paul and Waugh is that Paul seems hardly to have changed at Oxford; he seems, in fact, modeled on Waugh not as he departed from Oxford in 1924, but as he arrived from Lancing two and a half years earlier: spending his early months at Hertford quietly, reading and daydreaming, eating in hall, taking walks by himself in the country, making few friends; on Waugh as he might have remained but for the Hypocrites and Harold Acton. In ridiculing Paul's quiet sobriety, Waugh was mocking one possible version of himself. Not long before writing *Decline and Fall,* he had interviewed to become an Anglican clergyman; was there in Waugh the stuff of a placid suburban vicar?

Paul's relation to Waugh is thus ambiguous, partly autobiographical, partly antithetical. Although sometimes derisively conventional and dull-witted, polite to a fault, Paul is at other times a sympathetic figure—decent, ingenuous, abused, but uncomplaining. In this latter aspect he caricatures the unassuming, unlucky hero of Waugh's diaries, a semifictional character Waugh had been developing across the years for his own consolation and diversion. Paul Pennyfeather is such a diffident and unassertive hero that it is easy to overlook his importance to *Decline and Fall* and to Waugh's subsequent fiction. The buffeted, baffled, unworldly hero, of which Paul was the prototype, enabled Waugh to maintain an ironically detached perspective on his own experience and even on himself; self-caricature prevented self-absorption and self-pity. Paul Pennyfeather might take himself seriously, but Waugh can laugh at him; and in thus comically distancing himself from his protagonist, Waugh opened up to himself all the comic possibilities of his own experience, painful as it may have been at the time. The virtue of the reticent Pennyfeatheresque hero is amply demonstrated by his absence in *Work Suspended* and *Brideshead Revisited,* in which discursive first-person narration involved Waugh in unprecedented difficulties.

Waugh had a rough plot idea when he began writing—to follow Paul Pennyfeather's descent from Oxford to Llanabba—but *Decline and Fall* soon became improvisational, especially as the action began to move away from its autobiographical origins. Even in the novel's early chapters, when he was still drawing material from his school-mastering experience, Waugh seems to have let the plot develop as his daily inspiration directed, picking up and incorporating stray and unconnected bits of material as he wrote. The figure of Lady Circumference, for example, was closely modeled on Alastair Graham's mother, with whom Waugh was already well acquainted. But as he wrote some of the novel's early chapters he happened to be staying at her Warwickshire house, and the erratic hospitality he enjoyed there gave him immediate material and perhaps motive for sketching Lady Circumference's character. For example, as a friend of Alastair's who had often visited Barford before, Waugh was considered not so much a guest as a member of the household, and Mrs. Graham expected him to pull his own weight:

> This morning there was great trouble with a large truculent under-gardener who is under notice to go and will not allow his successor to use his cottage. Mrs. G.: "Here am I left without a *man* in the house"—looking hard at me—"if Hugh were alive he'd have *kicked* him out."[11]

This incident must have been fresh in Waugh's mind when he introduced this exchange into the novel:

> ". . . Greta, Mr Pennyfoot knows Alastair."
> "Does he? Well, that boy's doing no good for himself. Got fined twenty pounds the other day, his mother told me. Seemed proud of it. If my brother had been alive he'd have licked all that out of the young cub. It takes a man to bring up a man."
> "Yes," said Lord Circumference meekly. (83)

While this sort of extemporaneous borrowing helped to fill in the novel's first half, it became the governing method of the later chapters, when the novel wandered far beyond its original field of action.

By about the middle of *Decline and Fall* as it now stands, Waugh seems to have exhausted his schoolmastering experience, and from that point the novel grows remote from his personal history. As he resorted to other sources for material, his inventions became more exotic. His personal experience was limited in range, but he gathered scraps of material from here and there, piecing together current newspaper topics, gossip, sightseeing snapshots, and various of his own private interests. Margot Beste-Chetwynde's and Grimes's involvement in prostitution, for example, as well as Potts's sleuthing, was prompted by the well-publicized release in December 1927 of a League of Nations report on international white slave traffic. He set Margot's villa on Corfu because he had been impressed by the amenity of the island during a very brief stop there the year before, returning from a visit to Alastair Graham in Greece. Because its sources were eclectic, the second half of *Decline and Fall* grew more diffuse, topical, episodic, and peripatetic than the first half, and threatened to veer off into random satiric adventures.

Fortunately, however, by the time the autobiographical inspiration flagged, a new and accidental influence—Captain Grimes—had already begun to channel the novel's energies in a new direction. Grimes was modelled on one of Waugh's colleagues at Arnold House. "Young, the new usher, is monotonously pederastic and talks only of the beauty of sleeping boys," he noted in his diary a few weeks into his second term.[12] Young nonetheless proved a convenient drinking companion, and one evening as they drank together, he divulged some highlights of his personal history:

> . . . Young and I went out and made ourselves drunk and he confessed all his previous career. He was expelled from Wellington, sent down from Oxford, and forced to resign his commission in the army. He has left four schools precipitately, three in the middle of the term through his being taken in sodomy and one through his being drunk six nights in succession. And yet he goes on getting better and better jobs without difficulty.[13]

Waugh was greatly impressed by the narrative, "all very like Bruce and the spider." Several years later, with military rank and a wooden leg, Young became Grimes; and then, without, it seems, any clear intention on Waugh's part, Captain Grimes grew into the hero of *Decline and Fall*, the embodiment of the novel's sympathy with impulsiveness and anarchy.

On his first entrance Grimes appears an unlikely hero: "The door opened, and a very short man of about thirty came into the Common Room. He had made a great deal of noise in coming because he had an artificial leg. He had a short red moustache, and was slightly bald" (30). But when he discloses his history to Paul, his distinction emerges; he has a genius for falling "in the soup" and landing on his feet. Grimes is an emblem of spontaneity and irrepressibility; he is the weed poking up through the crack in the sidewalk. While his past more or less duplicates Young's, Grimes's powers of survival grow mythic. He cannot be extinguished. "I can stand most sorts of misfortune, old boy, but I can't stand repression," he remarks to Paul in prison, shortly before escaping (230). He glides undaunted through embarrassment and disaster. Mr. Prendergast, diffident and timid, a foil to Grimes's insouciant recklessness, is tormented by "Doubts," but as Grimes himself explains:

When you've been in the soup as often as I have, it gives you a sort of feeling that everything's for the best, really. You know, God's in His heaven; all's right with the world. I can't quite explain it, but I don't believe one can ever be unhappy for long provided one does just exactly what one wants to and when one wants to. The last chap who put me on my feet said I was "singularly in harmony with the primitive promptings of humanity". I've remembered that phrase because somehow it seemed to fit me. (45)

Grimes's revival in the second half of the novel, after apparently drowning, and his later escape from prison confirm his superhuman vitality. He becomes "one of the immortals," "a life force":

Sentenced to death in Flanders, he popped up in Wales; drowned in Wales, he emerged in South America; engulfed in the dark mystery of Egdon Mire, he would rise again somewhere at some time, shaking from his limbs the musty integuments of the tomb. (232)

After this panegyric, Grimes's reappearance would be anticlimactic; and his role in the novel, though not his spirit, here comes to an end.

If the figure of Paul Pennyfeather suggests the pre-Oxford Waugh, Paul's encounter with Grimes is analogous to Waugh's experience with the Hypocrites. Unexpectedly, the reprobate Grimes has a wholly salutary influence on Paul. Sober, studious, unadventurous, Paul has led a wastefully narrow life at Oxford:

For two years he had lived within his allowance, aided by two valuable scholarships. He smoked three ounces of tobacco a week—John Cotton, Medium—and drank a pint and a half of beer a day, the half at luncheon and the pint at dinner, a meal he invariably ate in Hall. He had four friends, three of whom had been at school with him. (16)

Paul's idea of nightlife is attending a meeting of the League of Nations Union to hear a paper on Polish plebiscites ("You talk as though all that were quite real to you," Waugh once remarked, incredulously, to a friend discussing central European politics).[14] After an evening of plebiscites, Paul retires to his rooms to read *The Forsyte Saga,* presumably Waugh's notion of respectable, dull reading, and smoke a pipe in solitude before bed. Imaginatively straitened by conventional ideas and personal inhibitions, Paul very much needs an infusion of Grimes's zest. "Paul had no particular objection to drunkenness—he had read rather a daring paper to the Thomas More Society on the subject—but he was consumedly shy of drunkards" (16). He is shy of life, in fact, academically cloistered and very unfamiliar with the exuberant variety and unpredictability of the world beyond Oxford, or even beyond his own small circle at Oxford, for he has never even heard of the aristocratic Bollinger Club, with its boisterous revelries.

After this bland closeted life at Oxford, Paul is astounded by Llanabba, whose inmates (except for Prendergast) are unreservedly eccentric. From a circle in which it is considered the height of daring to challenge a conventional opinion, even in an essay, Paul is dropped into a happy society of criminals and charlatans: Dr. Fagan with his absurd elegance, his fraudulent school, and his two horrible daughters; Philbrick the protean imposter; Grimes himself; and, super-added to the ordinary inhabitants, the Sports-day visitors, including the ill-matched pair of Lady Circumference, an earthy aristocrat in the Squire Western tradition, and Margot Beste-Chetwynde, the cosmopolitan adventuress, with her unexpected consort, the excitable Chokey. When all these characters assemble at the Sports, the conversation becomes a chaos of dissonant voices, representing in small scale the world of random and diverse human energies beyond Paul's straitened experience:

> "I had such a curious conversation just now," Lord Circumference was saying to Paul, "with your bandmaster over there. He asked me whether I should like to meet his sister; and when I said, 'Yes, I should be delighted to,' he said that it would cost a pound normally, but that he'd let me have special terms. What *can* he have meant, Mr Pennyfoot?"
>
> " 'Pon my soul," Colonel Sidebotham was saying to the Vicar, "I don't like the look of that nigger. I saw enough of Fuzzy-Wuzzy in the Soudan—devilish good enemy and devilish bad friend. I'm going across to talk to Mrs Clutterbuck. Between ourselves, I think Lady C. went a bit far. I didn't see the race myself, but there are limits. . . ."
>
> "Rain ain't doin' the turnip crop any good," Lady Circumference was saying.
>
> "No, indeed," said Mrs Beste-Chetwynde. "Are you in England for long?"
>
> "Why, I live in England, of course," said Lady Circumference.
>
> "My dear, how divine!" (94–95)

Even Prendergast gets drunk at the Sports and contributes with unwonted spirit, chatting volubly and shooting little Tangent in the foot. Though reticent and bemused, Paul is not unaffected. Llanabba's cheerful defiance of middle-class convention begins to erode the drab values he has brought with him from Onslow Square, school, and Oxford, and what begins as an awful ordeal turns into a liberating experience.

While Grimes best represents the spirit of Llanabba, another spirit beckons to Paul from Oxford: the ghost of his own past, embodied in the person of Arthur Potts, one of Paul's four friends. A monitory figure, Potts is what Paul was at Oxford, and what he might become. Potts, like Grimes, resembles one of Waugh's fellow ushers, in this case a certain Attwell whom Waugh knew briefly at Aston Clinton:

> He was educated at King's School, Worcester, and retains a slight accent, and at Christ Church, Oxford, where he seems to have led the dullest life imaginable. He is very keen on education and I have only just begun to cure him of talking to me seriously about it. . . . He took a second in English Literature and is not wholly uneducated, but he has a mean and ill-digested mind with a sort of part rationalism and part idealism.[15]

Even down to the keenness on education, this describes Potts almost perfectly. Potts, for example, writes to Paul at Llanabba:

> There is a most interesting article in the *Educational Review* on the new methods that are being tried at the Innesborough High School to induce co-ordination of the senses. They put small objects into the children's mouths and make them draw the shapes in red chalk. Have you tried this with your boys? (57)

The absurdity of such rarefied theory in the context of Llanabba reveals the great gap between Paul's arid Oxford education and the more fruitful lessons of Llanabba. While Potts combines rationalistic theories with a horrible complacency ("Are your colleagues enlightened?"), Paul has encountered actual life—irrational, intractable, disruptive, immensely vigorous.

Like good and bad angels in a morality play, Potts and Grimes compete for Paul's soul. The lines of battle emerge from Alastair Trumpington's offer to compensate Paul for his expulsion from Oxford. Recognizing the offer as "a test-case of the durability of my ideals," Paul deliberates conscientiously about whether to accept the money. The spirit of Grimes and Llanabba urges Paul to cast off his scruples. Even Prendergast counsels common sense: "My dear boy, it would be a sin to refuse" (55). On the other hand, the spirit of Potts whispers in Paul's ear, priggishly:

> If I refuse, I shall be sure of having done right. I shall look back upon my self-denial with exquisite self-approval. By refusing I can convince myself that, in spite of the unbelievable things that have been happening to me during the last ten days, I am still the same Paul Pennyfeather I have respected so long. (55)

The alternatives are clear—and Paul not surprisingly chooses Potts, explaining to Grimes: "I'm afraid you'll find my attitude rather difficult to understand. . . . It's largely a matter of upbringing" (55).

But the significance of the incident lies not in Paul's characteristic decision nor even, really, in Grimes's equally characteristic intervention—wiring Potts in Paul's name to send the twenty pounds—but in Paul's unexpected reaction when Grimes confesses that he has done so. Against all his upbringing and education, Paul is delighted: " 'Grimes, you wretch!' said Paul, but, in spite of himself, he felt a great wave of satisfaction surge up within him. 'We must have another drink on that' " (56). Potts, "something of a stinker," as Grimes astutely infers, writes in response: "I cannot pretend to understand your attitude in this matter" (56–57); but Paul has been liberated from the puritan self-righteousness of Potts and initiated into the more tolerant ethos of Llanabba:

> "To the durability of ideals," said Paul as he got his pint.
> "My word, what a mouthful!" said Grimes; "I can't say that. Cheer-ioh!" (56)

Free-spirited and impulsive, Grimes has defeated Potts—at least for the moment.

Paul's Llanabba has become the equivalent of Waugh's Oxford—not the insipid Oxford of Potts, but the sparkling Oxford of Harold Acton and the Hypocrites.

The Grimesian spirit governs *Decline and Fall,* but not without a murmur of dissent here and there, and particularly in the somewhat digressive chapter on the background of King's Thursday, which Waugh added in revision to help fill out the book.

This chapter focuses on Margot Beste-Chetwynde's Hampshire country house, the modernistic creation of one Otto Silenus, whose name recalls the book about Silenus ("a Falstaff forever babbling o' green fields") that Waugh had projected in 1925. The Silenus of *Decline and Fall,* however—mechanistic and indeed scarcely human—has little to do with Falstaff or green fields. A satiric allusion to the functionalist, factory-inspired "international style" creeping into England in the 1920s from Germany, Silenus combines the "significant form" aesthetics of Clive Bell and Roger Fry with the technocrat's passion for efficiency:

> The problem of architecture as I see it . . . is the problem of all art—the elimination of the human element from the consideration of form. The only perfect building must be the factory, because that is built to house machines, not men. I do not think it is possible for domestic architecure to be beautiful, but I am doing my best. All ill comes from man. . . . Man is never beautiful; he is never happy except when he becomes the channel for the distribution of mechanical forces. (142)

The unruly inefficiency of human energy saddens him:

> "I suppose there ought to be a staircase," he said gloomily. "Why can't the creatures stay in one place? Up and down, in and out, round and round! Why can't they sit still and work? Do dynamos require staircases? Do monkeys require houses?" (144)

And Silenus himself hums with turbo-electric energy, recharging as he lies sleepless at night, ". . . his brain turning and turning regularly all the night through, drawing in more and more power, storing it away like honey in its intricate cells and galleries, till the atmosphere about it became exhausted and vitiated and only the brain remained turning and turning in the darkness" (152). Rationalist and utilitarian, puritanically unornamented, the international style asserted values profoundly inimical to *Decline and Fall*'s celebration of spontaneity, diversity, and quirkiness—the Grimesian virtues. Gropius's leading academic champion, Nikolaus Pevsner, several years later summarized the ideological implications of the new architecture:

> The profound affinity of this modern enthusiasm for *planning* (architectural as well as political) with the style of Gropius's Fagus factory is evident. The forms of the building reveal the mind of an artist but also of a concentrated thinker. . . . The warm and direct feelings of the great men of the past have gone; but then the artist who is representative of this century of ours must needs be cold, as he stands for a century cold as steel and glass, a century the precision of which leaves less space for self-expression than did any period before.
>
> However, the great creative brain will find its own way even in times of overpowering collective energy, even with the medium of the new style of the twentieth century which, because it is a genuine style as opposed to a passing fashion, is totalitarian.[16]

A manifesto not greatly unlike Waugh's parody, but Pevsner wrote in earnest admiration, and the terms of his praise unmistakably suggest that there will be no place for someone like Grimes in the brave new world of the international style.

The new King's Thursday's chilly modernity contrasts sharply with the exaggerated backwardness of the old house, and it is in sketching the background of the original King's Thursday that Waugh's reservations about Grimesian anarchy emerge.

As part of his field researches for *Rossetti*, Waugh visited Kelmscott, William Morris's country house west of Oxford, shortly after he began writing *Decline and Fall*. A gabled Elizabethan manor house of

Cotswold stone, sitting snugly within a small enclosed garden, Kelmscott stands, still relatively isolated, among meadows flanking the upper Thames. Surprised by Kelmscott's compactness, Waugh wondered how it could have accommodated Morris's large household: "The rooms are very low and dark and the whole effect rather cramped and constricted. We could not conceive how so many people lived there."[17] The diminutive scale was a characteristic disappointment—"I had imagined it all so spacious"—for someone who preferred the grand scale of Brideshead. But during his study of Rossetti Waugh had developed a sympathetic appreciation of Morris's values and the little estate where Morris "found sacramentally embodied all that he held of high account of beauty and sweetness and dignity," as Waugh observed in *Rossetti*. "Here, in small compass, lay everything for which his art and his work was striving—peace, fellowship, love, childhood, beauty, simplicity, abundance" (183–84), Waugh wrote; then he quoted a character in Morris's utopian fantasy *News From Nowhere*, which concludes with a journey up the Thames to a house based on Kelmscott: "O me! O me! How I love the earth and the seasons and weather, and all things that deal with them, and all that grows out of them—as this has done" (184).

As Waugh thought about the sort of chic house suitable for Margot Beste-Chetwynde, Kelmscott seems to have come to mind as the exact antithesis to her turbulent modern spirit. Paul Pennyfeather first arrives at King's Thursday on a pleasant spring day:

> The temperate April sunlight fell through the budding chestnuts and revealed between their trunks green glimpses of parkland and the distant radiance of a lake. "English spring," thought Paul. "In the dreaming ancestral beauty of the English country." Surely, he thought, these great chestnuts in the morning sun stood for something enduring and serene in a world that had lost its reason and would so stand when the chaos and confusion were forgotten? And surely it was the spirit of William Morris that whispered to him in Margot Beste-Chetwynde's motor-car about seed-time and harvest, the superb succession of the seasons, the harmonious interdependence of rich and poor, of dignity, innocence and tradition? (148)

But such sentiments prove inept when the house itself bulks into view, for the venerable old King's Thursday, "enduring and serene," has been demolished and replaced by the creation of Otto Silenus.

The old King's Thursday was absurdly backward, but for all its absurdity it preserved certain William Morris values to which Waugh responded sympathetically:

The estate-carpenter, an office hereditary in the family of the original joiner who had panelled the halls and carved the great staircase, did such restorations as became necessary from time to time for the maintenance of the fabric, working with the same tools and with the traditional methods, so that in a few years his work became indistinguishable from that of his grandsires. (137–38)

Waugh's reading of Morris and his admiration for a well-cut dovetail here converged, products respectively of *Rossetti* and of his own recent carpentry lessons.

But such calm and stability do not prosper in the modern world as it is imagined in *Decline and Fall*. Governed by random, violent energy, that world resents the quiet enjoyment of life wherever such tranquillity might be lurking. When the slow-moving Pastmasters abandon King's Thursday, Margot Beste-Chetwynde quickly razes it, capriciously and perversely considering the rare old house common: "I can't think of anything more bourgeois and awful than timbered Tudor architecture" (140) ("I find that I am beginning to detest Elizabethan architecture owing to the vulgarities of Stratford-on-Avon," Waugh had written in his diary).[18] The image of Margot knocking down the old King's Thursday suggests Waugh's conflicting impulses: he was sympathetic with both the reckless impulsiveness of Margot and the quieter values enshrined in the old house, but in 1928 he was much more deeply enchanted with Margot.

A decade later, Waugh was mourning the demolition of many of London's old houses, but *Decline and Fall* is scarcely touched by such tender sentiments. The half-hearted attempt of Jack Spire, editor of the *London Hercules,* to save King's Thursday is derisive:

Mr Jack Spire was busily saving St Sepulchre's, Egg Street (where Dr Johnson is said once to have attended Matins), when Margot Beste-Chetwynde's decision to rebuild King's Thursday became public. He said, very seriously: "Well, we did what we could," and thought no more about it. (141)

Spire is a transparent allusion to J. C. Squire, who (Waugh thought) represented the folklore image of a merry-old, cricket-playing England that Waugh considered as spurious as modern timbered architecture. The Waugh of *Decline and Fall* scorned, or affected to scorn, sentimental wistfulness for preindustrial life, or at least for the quaint trappings of agrarian England. A year later he compiled a catalogue of what he considered antiquarian offenses:

. . . arts and crafts, and the preservation of rural England, and the preservation of ancient monuments, and the transplantation of Tudor cottages, and the collection of pewter and old oak, and the reformed public house, and the Ye Olde Inne and the Kynde Dragone and Ye Cheshire Cheese, Broadway, Stratford-on-Avon, folk dancing . . . (*Labels*, 55–56)

and so on at great length. Under the guise of historical preservation, entrepreneurs traded on nostalgic sentimentality to spawn middle-class tourist "attractions." Writing in 1929 in praise of the slums of Naples, he asserted: "In England, the craze for cottages and all that goes with them only began as soon as they had ceased to represent a significant part of English life. In Naples no such craze exists because the streets are still in perfect harmony with their inhabitants" (*Labels*, 56). The old King's Thursday harmonized with the indolent Pastmasters, who had never themselves arrived in the twentieth century, but the antiquarianism of people like Jack Spire or the Pastmasters' neighbors was self-indulgent, soft-boiled, dilettante:

"I thought we might go over to tea at the Pastmasters'," hostesses would say after luncheon on Sundays. "You really must see their house. Quite unspoilt, my dear. Professor Franks, who was here last week, said it was recognized as the finest piece of domestic Tudor in England." (138)

After calling on the Pastmasters, "they would drive away in their big motor-cars to their modernized manors" and sit "in their hot baths" (138). Perhaps this sort of weekend nostalgia was close enough to Waugh's own wistfulness to make him feel a little uncomfortable; perhaps Margot's wrecking ball was an oblique attack on his father's theatrical Victorian sentimentality. In any event, *Decline and Fall* does not go easy on nostalgia.

For all its confusion of grim factory style and splashy Art Deco— bottle-green glass floors and black glass pillars, malachite bath and kaleidoscopic drawing-room—Silenus's King's Thursday nonetheless represents the vital energy of the era. A "new-born monster to whose birth ageless and forgotten cultures had been in travail," it is an architectural image of 1920s England. In 1928 Waugh was twenty-four years old, his appetite for experience was keen, and the "new-born monster," despite its aesthetic horrors, represented the world as it lay before him. Despite his fond backward glance at the old King's Thursday of the Pastmasters, he confronted the contemporary world with high relish for its "vitality and actuality." *Decline and Fall*'s strongest sympathies are with the impulsive, anarchic energy of Grimes and Margot; and *their* impulse is to knock down old houses when the fancy strikes them.

From architecture *Decline and Fall* turns to other adventures: Margot's recruitment of prostitutes; Paul's trip to Marseilles; his arrest, trial, and conviction for abetting Margot's business; prisons; Paul's "death" at Dr. Fagan's bogus nursing home; his revival at Margot's villa at Corfu. Grimes turns up now and then in the later chapters, but Paul's continuing education is largely taken over by Margot. Wealthy, worldly, exquisitely elegant and fashionable, "the first breath of spring in the Champs-Élysées" (89), she is superficially very unlike the peg-legged, hand-to-mouth Grimes, but like Grimes she is spiritually anarchic, wholly amoral, beyond conventional standards of judgment. Although her restless energy leaves a wake of destruction, with Paul one of her victims, he easily forgives her; just as Grimes is one of the immortals, Margot too is a goddess. Neither can be confined by stone walls. Margot combines and burlesques two extremes, the criminal underworld and the high opulent style, spanning the novel's range of sympathies.

As Margot drives the action forward, Paul is pulled along behind. Though often baffling, his schooling in life continues, confirming and supplementing the lessons of Llanabba. Beyond the cramped circle of conventional respectability and neat academic theory to which he was previously limited, a multifarious and chaotic world flourishes. It can be ignored or condemned, but it refuses to be suppressed. The most spectacular collision between Grimes's and Potts's worlds is provoked by Sir Wilfrid Lucas-Dockery, the professorial prison warden whose enlightened reforms at Blackstone Prison, as irrelevant to actual prison conditions as Potts's educational ideas were to Llanabba, are dramatically refuted by the bloodthirsty visionary who decapitates Prendergast: a sad end for Prendergast, but a happy example of anarchy triumphant. Paul's passage through the underworld gives him the liberal education he was not getting at Oxford.

But Paul is not Grimes, nor was meant to be. At Llanabba, at King's Thursday, and in prison, he learns the limitations of his own background; but he can never quite escape it. His narrow, conventional self keeps surfacing. When Philbrick, for example, narrates one of his criminal fantasies, Paul responds indignantly: " 'But, good gracious,' said Paul, 'why have you told me this monstrous story? I shall certainly inform the police. I never heard of such a thing' " (70)—exactly what Potts would have said and done. Hopelessly naive about Margot Beste-Chetwynde's South American brothels, Paul travels to Marseilles, only to shrink from the crowded street life of the slums: "He turned and fled for the broad streets and the tram lines where, he knew at heart, was his spiritual home" (181). As he moves through the implausible events of the novel's latter half, he grows less censorious about the irregularities he encounters, but he can never really become a free spirit himself.

And in the end he returns to Oxford and to all appearances resumes the life he had led before his expulsion, reading divinity at Scone and bicycling to talks on Polish plebiscites, while a dull character named Stubbs replaces the dull Potts as his friend. After Paul's liberation from Potts at Llanabba, he seems to have fallen straight back into Potts's dreary milieu, a flagrant case of recidivism. But he actually belongs neither to Potts's nor to Grimes's world now, and instead stands aloof from both. Although his Oxford life is superficially unchanged, it has become a charade:

> On one occasion he and Stubbs and some other friends went to the prison to visit the criminals there and sing part-songs to them.
> "It opens the mind," said Stubbs, "to see all sides of life. How those unfortunate men appreciated our singing!" (247)

Paul doesn't answer; the gap between his varied experience of the world and Stubbs's complacent insularity is too wide to bridge. Though back in his old Oxford routine, Paul is no more at home at Oxford now than he had been at Llanabba. Outwardly occupied with his bland, studious routine and his circle of tedious acquaintances, Paul is nonetheless wiser and rather tougher now, aware of how much life pullulates beyond the smooth and tidy quadrangles of Scone. With this knowledge, there can be no genuine return to Potts.

Aware that Stubbs and Potts and their kind are *his* kind, however, and represent his future, he acts a deliberately chosen role, resigning himself to essay societies and cocoa, subduing his uneasy knowledge of his own futility, living at second hand in the passions of dusty theological controversies:

> There was a bishop in Bithynia, Paul learned, who had denied the Divinity of Christ, the immortality of the soul, the existence of good, the legality of marriage, and the validity of the sacrament of Extreme Unction! How right they had been to condemn him! (248)

Timid scholarly ferocity substitutes for any real engagement with life. The world boils with heterodox energy, with eccentrics and criminals, heretics and lunatics, with irrepressible weedlike vigor, but all that is outside and Paul has shut the door on it. Just beyond his rooms, in fact, the Bollinger Club is again partying noisily. Until the very last night of his first undergraduate career, Paul had never heard of the Bollinger, and if he had known of them he would have disapproved. Now, very much aware of them, he is neither sympathetic nor disapproving; but he does not want to get involved again, does not even want to be reminded of his earlier involvement with the Bollinger and all its consequences.

Peter Beste-Chetwynde, stumbling into his rooms, is a further reminder of the past, and Paul resents the intrusion. Peter is "dynamic" and Paul is "static"; Paul acknowledges this truth and disciplines himself to be content with his lot. When Peter leaves, Paul goes to bed—to sleep his life away, as it were, while others live theirs, awake.

Peter and Paul, in fact, both originate in Waugh himself. Peter is very drunk, but evidently more as a consequence of boredom than of celebration: "Oh, damn, what else is there to do?" he complains (252). Waugh too was sometimes a Bollinger in spirit, riotous and reckless; but he derived little solid comfort from his excesses, and, like Paul, he sometimes wanted to retreat, to close the door against the noisy outer world. Though bubbling throughout with comic effervescence, *Decline and Fall* ends on a subdued note of withdrawal.

The fruitless circularity of Paul Pennyfeather's experience, the uncertain mood of the ending, a series of playful religious and ecclesiastical allusions, and a knowledge of Waugh's later career—all these elements of the novel have, in some combination, led more than one critic to detect a deliberate and profound moral argument in *Decline and Fall*. Jerome Meckier, for example, finds the novel's meaning concealed in "symbolic shorthand"; in fact, "Symbols are always the key to Waugh's art." With this in mind, Paul's circular experience can be seen as a modern parody of the fruitful cycle of the seasons and the sacred cycle of the Christian calendar, models that expose the futility of the contemporary secular world. Paul, then, is "a parodic Christ"; Philbrick the butler is a "bogus Messiah" whose fantastic autobiographical inventions are a parody of the Transfiguration; Prendergast is a "parodic martyr"; and so on.[19]

This is one way to read *Decline and Fall*, of course—anyone who puts out money for the book owns his own copy—but it seems a particularly pedantic and humorless reading, and one that certainly would have astounded Waugh himself; the furthest thing from his mind was an allegorical parody of secular society or a history of the moral decline of Christian civilization. *Decline and Fall* is a mythic transformation of intensely private experience into broad comedy: an amorphous lump of his own life moulded into aesthetically satisfying shape. It had very little to do with his politico-religio-moral ideology, whatever it may have been at the time. The wistful and despairing tone of the ending suggests the novel's roots in Waugh's unsettled feelings, the comic possibilities of life competing with, and consoling him for, painful experience.

But the governing spirit of the novel is not at all ambiguous. *Decline and Fall* belongs to Grimes and Margot and their fellows, the characters who live most dangerously and most fully:

> Let us roll all our strength, and all
> Our sweetness, up into one ball;
> And tear our pleasures with rough strife
> Thorough the iron gates of life.

Decline and Fall is vernal and youthful, eager for experience, in love with the living and the actual. It is the novel of a young man on the outside, familiar with disappointment but unscarred, inclined to wistfulness but brimming with inventiveness and anarchic zest. Waugh's comic genius never flourished more happily.

4

Vile Bodies: "A Sharp Disturbance"

In the winter of 1929 Waugh and his wife of seven months left England for a Mediterranean cruise. Although the journey seems to have been taken partly or largely for her health—she had been seriously ill during the previous autumn—she immediately relapsed, and in Port Said, Egypt, she was taken off the ship on a stretcher and hospitalized. While she recuperated, Waugh had ample leisure to visit Arab Town, Port Said's native quarter, and to catch up on his correspondence. He wrote to his father: "Yes, I think I can promise a novel for the autumn and a very good one too," and a little later he wrote to his agent A. D. Peters: "I shall bring you two books at the end of May to serialise. A travel book and a fairly funny novel."[1] *Vile Bodies* was cooking.

Almost immediately after returning to England in the spring, he retired to the country to begin writing, explaining to Henry Yorke: "We found bills of over £200 waiting for us and each overdrawn at our banks so I must write a lot quickly."[2] Despite the concrete-sounding assurances to his father and to Peters, however, his thoughts about the novel seem in fact to have been fairly rudimentary as he began writing. "It was a totally unplanned book," he asserted later, perhaps with little exaggeration.[3] The leading principles of *Vile Bodies'* composition were simple: speed and improvisation.

The early chapters progressed according to this method. "Novel moving fast all characters seasick," Alec Waugh recalled Evelyn cabling soon after beginning.[4] Within a few days he sent an installment of ten thousand words to the typist and soon after dispatched a second installment. "I have written 25,000 words of a novel in ten days," he boasted to Henry Yorke.[5] About the same time, late June, he spent a weekend with his wife on the Hampshire coast, houseguests of a friend named John Heygate—an Oxford contemporary, a bachelor, an apparently unremarkable, inoffensive young man whom the Waughs had entertained at Canonbury Square before their cruise. As Waugh worked on his novel in Beckley, a village near Oxford, Heygate had continued to see much of Mrs. Waugh in London.

At the beginning of August she eloped with him.[6] Her defection seems to have come as a complete surprise to Waugh. He wrote to his parents, for example:

> I asked Alec to tell you the sad & to me radically shocking news that Evelyn has gone to live with a man called Heygate. I am accordingly filing a petition for divorce.
> I am afraid that this will be a blow to you but I assure you not nearly so severe a blow as it is to me.[7]

—adding in a postscript: "Evelyn's defection was preceded by no kind of quarrel or estrangement. So far as I knew we were both serenely happy." He was deeply grieved and humiliated. "I did not know it was possible to be so miserable & live," he wrote to Harold Acton soon after, "but I am told that this is a common experience."[8] Writing seven years later to Lady Mary Lygon, to console her on the death of her brother Hugh, he recalled his own desolation in 1929:

> I know from experience that being very unhappy is necessarily lonely & that friends can't help & that sympathy means very little. . . . The sort of dislocation you have had is a pain which cant be shared—but being unhappy is not *all* loss and I know you have the sort of nature that wont be spoilt.
> I only dare to say this because I was unhappy some years ago in rather the same way as you are now.[9]

In early September he filed a petition for divorce. In the meantime, amid these miseries and distractions, he resumed work on his novel.

His wife's desertion had interrupted the writing of *Vile Bodies* somewhere near its midpoint, and the later chapters betray the effects of, as Waugh later put it, "a sharp disturbance in my private life."[10] The first half of the novel is the book he intended to write, the second half the product of that disturbance, and he made no particular effort to harmonize the tone of the two halves. The first seven chapters—the last artifact of the very early, Grimesian Waugh—preserve his original concept; but when he returned to the manuscript several weeks later, he could not resuscitate that earlier spirit.

What he had originally meant to write was a topical, lightly romantic farce, using some new technical tricks he had picked up, but nothing very ambitious. Urged by bank overdrafts and working with congenial material, he struck off the early chapters with great speed. If, as he claimed at the time, he wrote the first twenty-five thousand words in ten days, he had already completed a third of the novel. He may well have been exaggerating, but he seems in truth to have written half the novel in scarcely a month. "I had the facility at the age of 25 to sit down at my table, set a few characters on the move, write 3000 words a day, and note with surprise what happened," he later wrote in reference to *Vile Bodies*.[11] He claimed at another time that his earlier novels were "six weeks work," including revisions.[12] This was not literally true of any of his novels, but had he sustained the early pace of *Vile Bodies* he might have come close.

As with *Decline and Fall*, he began writing with only a rough idea where the story was headed. The plot is extemporaneous and episodic, hardly a plot at all in any strict sense. The action required inventiveness, but he had this in good supply and did not worry overmuch about refinements. He was completely at home with his characters and their milieu: the Bright Young People, London society, a few comic caricatures. As with *Decline and Fall*, he leaned heavily on his own recent experience—his courtship of Evelyn Gardner, his partying, his success with *Decline and Fall* itself. The early chapters of *Vile Bodies* reflect his new confidence: whereas *Decline and Fall* opens with an ignominious banishment from Oxford, *Vile Bodies* opens with the hero's arrival in London from abroad, echoing Waugh's recent return from the Mediterranean but also suggesting his figurative arrival as a person of consequence, no longer the sad and obscure young man who had packed his bags for Wales four years earlier.

The narrative voice and comic grammar of *Vile Bodies* also offer suggestions of Waugh's improved circumstances and bolstered literary self-assurance. There is more diversity in the texture of the novel, with some passages reminiscent of *Decline and Fall*, but with others exhibiting a new tone and new ambitions. *Decline and Fall* had been largely a novel of idiosyncratic characters; *Vile Bodies* has similar characters—Colonel Blount and Lottie Crump, for example, with encores by Lady Circumference and Margot Beste-Chetwynde in minor roles—but to a larger extent *Vile Bodies* is a comedy of manners rather than of humors. The narrative voice is worldlier, venturing much further into refinements and nuances of social style. The narrative voice is also better informed, or at least not so reticent; whereas *Decline and Fall* had seldom or never probed the thoughts and motives of its characters, with the occasional exception of Paul Pennyfeather, *Vile Bodies* does so frequently, and not simply with the protagonist:

> To Father Rothschild no passage was worse than any other. He thought of the sufferings of the saints, the mutability of human nature, the Four Last

Things, and between whiles repeated snatches of the penitential psalms. (8)

"Square old Rampole," repeated Mr. Benfleet thoughtfully as Adam went downstairs. It was fortunate, he reflected, that none of the authors ever came across the senior partner . . . (29)

An innate dilatoriness of character rather than any doubt of the ultimate issue kept Edward from verbal proposal. He had decided to arrange everything before Christmas and that was enough. He had no doubt that a suitable occasion would soon be devised for him. (139)

And perhaps most noticeably from page to page, the narrative voice in *Vile Bodies* is more intrusive, more self-confident and more self-advertising than the narrative voice of *Decline and Fall*. There are frequent flourishes of rhetorical ostentation—staccato telephone conversations without attribution, the drugged reveries of Walter Outrage, the delirious reveries of Agatha Runcible, parodies of newspaper gossip paragraphs, the description of the Anchorage House reception and the catalog of parties in chapter 8, for example. The narrator often steps into the narrative with gratuitous comments and digressions that would have seemed out of place in *Decline and Fall*:

". . . Now just you wait while I look up these here *books*"—how he said it!—"in my list." (18)

"Do you know, I rather think I'm going to be sick again?"
"Oh, Miles!"
(Oh, Bright Young People!) (24)

It was too wet to walk, so he took a very crowded tube train to Dover Street and hurried across in the rain to Shepheard's Hotel (which, for the purposes of the narrative, may be assumed to stand at the corner of Hay Hill). (31)

. . . a thing known as a dressmaker's "dummy" (there had been one of these in Adam's home which they used to call "Jemima"—one day he stabbed "Jemima" with a chisel and scattered stuffing over the nursery floor and was punished. A more enlightened age would have seen a complex in this action and worried accordingly. . . .) (173)

There were six open churns behind Miss Runcible, four containing petrol and two water. She threw her cigarette over her shoulder, and by a

beneficent attention of Providence which was quite rare in her career it fell
into the water. Had it fallen into the petrol it would probably have been all
up with Miss Runcible. (183–84)

There are facetious explanatory footnotes at two points in the novel,
and in fact *Vile Bodies* occasionally veers close to mere facetiousness,
without ever quite falling over the edge. The flavor and tone of the
newspaper gossip paragraphs—bright, whimsical, casual, chatty—
seem to extend beyond specific parodies to influence the narrative
voice of *Vile Bodies* more comprehensively. Certainly *Vile Bodies,*
more than any other of Waugh's novels, sounds as if it might have
been written by one of the gossip writers who figure in the story.

As with *Decline and Fall,* the material of *Vile Bodies* draws exten-
sively from Waugh's recent experience. *Vile Bodies* never burlesques
the actual circumstances of Waugh's life as closely as the early chapters
of *Decline and Fall* had, but Adam Fenwick-Symes, a "brilliant young
novelist," revives an even earlier autobiographical figure, Adam
Doure of "The Balance." Four years older now, Adam otherwise
remains much the same character as the hero of the short story: a
professor's son and Oxford graduate, penurious, sentimental, and
lonely, in luckless pursuit of a fickle debutante. Waugh's self-portrait
in his diaries is the model for, or at least a strong influence on, both
Adams. *Vile Bodies* also borrows less importantly but even more
specifically from his undistinguished story "A House of Gentlefolks":
Doubting Hall, for example, resurrects the country house in the
story, while Adam's introduction to Doubting Hall echoes the story
closely, sometimes word for word. The borrowings tend to confirm
that Waugh was in a great hurry writing *Vile Bodies.*

The earliest chapters also borrowed their comic technique, as
Waugh later admitted, from Ronald Firbank. The previous year, after
finishing *Decline and Fall,* he had read all of Firbank's works and
distilled his critical observations in a short essay that throws light on
his own intentions in *Vile Bodies.*[13] He admired Firbank's craftsman-
ship, his delicate mosaic construction, his allusive dialogue, his
knowing worldliness, his naughtiness, his fine cavalier indifference to
plausibility. But Waugh's imagination thrived on robust characters
and action, notably lacking in Firbank's fiction, and after the opening
chapters of *Vile Bodies* Waugh left Firbank behind and, in his own
words, "struck out for myself."[14]

He did not in any event rest his hopes for success on *Vile Bodies'*
literary merits or sophisticated technique; the novel's immediate pop-
ular appeal, as Waugh well knew, was topicality. Deliberately and

shamelessly he made the novel a scrapbook of popular culture as defined by the popular press. He was not simply letting commercial calculation drag him down into the trivial and ephemeral, however, for he was honestly fascinated by the spectacle of contemporary life and very much interested in the 1920s as a distinctive historical epoch. English public school and University education, he wrote in *Labels* (in a passage incidentally summarizing his own formal education), produces the "sense of period":

> It consists of a vague knowledge of History, Literature, and Art, an amateurish interest in architecture and costume, of social, religious, and political institutions, of drama, of the biographies of the chief characters of each century, of a few memorable anecdotes and jokes, scraps of diaries and correspondence and family history. All these snacks and titbits of scholarship become fused together into a more or less homogeneous and consistent whole, so that the cultured Englishman has a sense of the past, in a continuous series of clear and pretty *tableaux vivants.* This Sense of the Past lies at the back of most intelligent conversation and of the more respectable and worse-paid *genre* of weekly journalism. It also colours our outlook on our own age. We wonder what will be the picture of ourselves in the minds of our descendants; we try to catch the flavour of the period; how will this absurd litle jumble of antagonising forces, of negro rhythm and psycho-analysis, of mechanical invention and decaying industry, of infinitely expanding means of communication and an infinitely receding substance of the communicable, of liberty and inertia, how will this ever cool down and crystallise out? (40)

This might well serve as a preface for *Vile Bodies.* Waugh was never more alive to the character of modern life, never relished the "flavour of the period" more than in its early chapters.

In particular, *Vile Bodies* reveals Waugh's immersion in London. Though suburban by background, he was urban in his tastes and ambitions, and London was the natural soil for his talents. "The sad thing is that 'Metroland' is my world that I have grown up in & I don't know any other except at second hand or at a great distance," he admitted later.[15] Until he found himself languishing in North Wales, however, he had never properly appreciated London. Returning from Arnold House in the summer of 1925, he embraced it joyfully:

> London was all. It was a town where I had spent little time—my holidays from school & vacations from Oxford had been mostly rural. But now London seemed alight & alive with fun & variety. More than this it

seemed a loveable place, dignified & beautiful, with its own inalienable character.[16]

Even if this recollection of thirty years later nostalgically exaggerates his earlier enthusiasm for London, there is no doubt that as a young man he seized avidly on London's pleasures and social opportunities. Waugh's London comprised mostly Mayfair, St. James, Belgravia, and their sister neighborhoods—the precincts of the wealthy and fashionable, where "The Balance"'s Imogen Quest and *Decline and Fall*'s Margot Beste-Chetwynde perfumed the air with romantic possibilities. Waugh himself was scarcely a member of fashionable London, but he was curious and admiring, much more than half in love with what he satirized.

Where contemporary culture and fashionable society intersected, Waugh found the Bright Young People, a recurrent topic in the popular newspapers of the 1920s. Observing the Bright Young People from the periphery, Waugh, though recognizing their aimlessness and futility, admired their reckless defiance of seriousness. Their distinctive argot, chic and childish, captured their contradictory qualities of worldliness and naiveté. Picking up this dialect from such of the smart young set as he knew, Waugh had begun to adapt it for fictional purposes as early as "The Balance." The young woman, for example, who in "The Balance" says: "But, my dear, you mustn't say anything against Basil because I simply adore him, and he's got the loveliest, vulgarest mother—you'd simply love her" (266) speaks the same dialect as the young woman in *Vile Bodies* who says: "The *most* bogus man. Miles discovered him, and since then he's been climbing and climbing and *climbing*, my dear, till he hardly knows us. He's rather sweet really, only too terribly common, poor darling" (23).

"Socially there was a general heightening of tempo," Alec Waugh recalled of the summer of 1929.[17] Nancy Mitford similarly recalled "the follies of the year" as exceptional, "perhaps the most extravagant of all those between the two wars."[18] *Vile Bodies* was written against a background of hyperbolically frivolous parties among the beau monde, chronicled in gossip writers' "paragraphs" and sometimes in the news columns of the popular dailies, and the novel's parties parody both the parties and the newspapers with little exaggeration. Almost all the action in the novel revolves about parties of one sort or another. With the whimsical jargon of the Bright Young People, with their stylish, festive, rather manic anarchy, and with the gossip columnists, Waugh had found the right material for his particular gifts, and the early chapters of *Vile Bodies* exploit and very much enjoy that material. After he had written several chapters, Waugh told Henry

Yorke that *Vile Bodies* was "rather like P. G. Wodehouse all about bright young people."[19] The comparison underscores the novel's origin as a light, romantic farce, a comedy of modern manners among the young smart set.

Then came his wife's defection. "The reader may, perhaps, notice the transition from gaiety to bitterness" in *Vile Bodies*, Waugh later remarked.[20] Chapter 8 seems to mark the transition; here the Ronald Firbank–P. G. Wodehouse tone gives way to a perceptibly darker, occasionally black mood.[21]

The chapter begins with the Bright Young People drifting through an unusually dismal evening, from a dirigible party to a squalid, illicit nightclub, and finally to the flat of a minor bore named Gilmour:

> Gilmour's place was a bed-sitting room in Ryder Street.
> So they sat on the bed in Gilmour's place and drank whisky while Gilmour was sick next door.
> And Ginger said, "There's nowhere like London really you know." (135)

All the gaiety of their first party in *Vile Bodies*, which had ended with Miss Runcible dressed in Hawaiian outfit at 10 Downing Street, has dissipated.

Meanwhile, as the Bright Young People mope at Gilmour's, the older generation are gathered at Anchorage House:

> . . . a great concourse of pious and honourable people (many of whom made the Anchorage House reception the one outing of the year), their women-folk well gowned in rich and durable stuffs, their men-folk ablaze with orders; people who had represented their country in foreign places and sent their sons to die for her in battle, people of decent and temperate life, uncultured, unaffected, unembarrassed, unassuming, unambitious people, of independent judgment and marked eccentricities, kind people who cared for animals and the deserving poor, brave and rather unreasonable people, that fine phalanx of the passing order . . . (136–37)

The reception at Anchorage House ("this last survivor of the noble town houses of London") is an image of Edwardian England: stable, orderly, decorous—but, in 1929, anachronistic, like the Tudor King's Thursday of *Decline and Fall*. Waugh's affectionate nostalgia for "Edwardian certainty" was not equal to his sympathy with the more vital energies of his own generation.

When in the second half of *Vile Bodies* the energies of the younger generation begin to flag, however, Waugh's sympathy with them descends into something like pity. Sitting sadly in Gilmour's mean cramped flat, the younger generation have inherited not the certitude and security of Anchorage House, Waugh implies, but its emblematic opposite, Doubting Hall. At the Anchorage House reception, Father Rothschild, S.J., delivers a short homily on this topic. Earlier in the novel Rothschild was a caricature of the intriguing Jesuit—ubiquitous, omniscient, meddlesome, purely comic; now he unexpectedly displays prophetic gifts. His subject is Waugh's favorite journalistic topic, the problems of youth, and on this topic Father Rothschild seems to preach with Waugh's authority:

> I don't think people ever *want* to lose their faith either in religion or anything else. I know very few young people, but it seems to me that they are all possessed with an almost fatal hunger for permanence. I think all these divorces show that. People aren't content just to muddle along nowadays. . . . (143)

Rothschild's citation of the divorce rate as evidence of the younger generation's quest for meaning, their refusal to "muddle along" in empty marriages, suggests that he is here giving voice to Waugh's own reflections in the weeks following the breakup of his marriage. By attributing the prevalence of divorce to the younger generation's honesty, Father Rothschild grants larger significance and rectitude to Waugh's refusal to "muddle along" with a wife "avowedly in love with someone else," even had she wished to muddle along with him.

Several other discussions about marriage, a subject not surprisingly on Waugh's mind, illustrate Father Rothschild's remarks. Ursula, the lovely young daughter of the Duke and Duchess of Stayle, rejects a long-expected marriage proposal from the dull young Edward Throbbing, considered by his elders "a nice, steady boy. . . . Quite one of the coming men in the party" (139–40). Though not at all a Bright Young Person, Lady Ursula is a perfect model of Father Rothschild's theories on the younger generation. She is not in love with Throbbing and wants nothing to do with him: "But, Mama, I don't want to marry him. I didn't know until it actually came to the point. I'd always meant to marry him, as you know. But, somehow, when he actually asked me . . . I just couldn't." The Duchess brushes off this quixotic delicacy: "It's a matter that only you can decide. After all, it's your life and your happiness at stake, not ours, isn't it, Ursula . . . but I *think* you'd better marry Edward" (147). Soon after, Adam overhears two working class mothers discussing *their* children: " 'It's a very good position,' I told him, 'and, of course, you can't expect *work* to be interesting, though no doubt after a time you get used to it just as your father's done . . .' " (150). More muddling along, in loveless marriages and spirit-breaking jobs. An impassable barrier of different values, we are given to understand, divides the parents and children of 1930.

We are given to understand this all too plainly, in fact. Temporarily obsessed with the generation gap and the difficulties of modern marriage, *Vile Bodies* was for several chapters made captive to Waugh's desire, perhaps compulsion, to place his private disaster in a larger context. No doubt he wished to deflect any suspicion (including his own) of personal inadequacy and to shift the blame for his cuckolding onto a basic maladjustment in the entire machinery of civilization, a "radical instability in our whole world-order," as Rothschild puts it (144). "I think they're connected, you know," he explains to Lord Metroland, who cannot see what the odd behavior of his stepson has to do with the world-order. "It's all very difficult," Rothschild concedes, however, and with this most readers will agree (145). Chapters 8 and 9 show Waugh stewing in his own miseries, consoling himself with the idea that they were precipitated by vast impersonal forces beyond his control, and inserting these plaintive ruminations into *Vile Bodies* without much regard for their dramatic relevance or interest. "The most boring subject I know," Mr. Outrage asserts of the younger generation, and certainly *Vile Bodies* wears the subject thin (142).

While interesting biographically, these middle chapters of the novel also reveal the less interesting moralizing that sometimes insinuated itself into Waugh's fiction: the vital mythmaking imagination eclipsed by mere opinions and preaching. But lectures on the younger generation soon faded from the novel, as he stumbled onto an experience that reawakened his imagination. Using his fiction for journalistic motives, making it a vehicle for his ideas, he lapsed into jejune and factitious invention. In a spectacle of surpassing uproar, he discovered far more potent images of his discontent.

The specific experience that rescued *Vile Bodies* from lachrymose self-absorption was an automobile race. In early August 1929, just after his wife's desertion, Waugh wrote to Harold Acton that he was "escaping to Ireland for a week of motor racing in the hope of finding an honourable grave."[22] Travelling to Belfast, he spent several days observing preparations for the Royal Automobile Club's Tourist Trophy Race, modestly described by *The Times* as "the greatest road race in history."[23] On the day of the race a half million spectators filled the grandstand and lined the sides of the course (favoring the most dangerous corners) to watch the autos speed around a long cross-country course thirty times. Waugh seems not to have cared especially who won; his interest was instead excited by the vast crowd, the routing of spectator traffic, the layout and amenities of the race course, the racers' gossip, the cult of the automobile, the obsessive and noisy pursuit of speed. Resuming *Vile Bodies* soon after, he immediately inserted a parody of the Belfast race, further evidence of the novel's extemporaneous inspiration.

The motor-racing subculture he encountered—a culture of coveralls, grease, carburetors, and noise; with its own language, rituals, and idols—was so alien to his own literary background and aesthetic sensibilities and St. James tastes that it strongly impressed him as a happily exotic, un-English phenomenon, rather in the same way he was impressed by Mediterranean slums several months earlier and Abyssinia a year later. In all three he was struck by the rude vigor that made middle-class English culture seem tame and bland.

But aside from its cultural, sociological interest, the motor race also seemed to Waugh an apt image of contemporary life.

Two passages from *Alice Through the Looking Glass* preface *Vile Bodies.* The first is this:

> "Well, in *our* country," said Alice, still panting a little, "you'd generally get to somewhere else—if you ran very fast for a long time, as we've been doing."
> "A slow sort of country!" said the Queen. "Now, *here*, you see, it takes all the running *you* can do, to keep in the same place. If you want to get somewhere else, you must run at least twice as fast as that!"

Vile Bodies' race cars formulated Alice's predicament in the terms of the 1920s. From the beginning, the pace in *Vile Bodies* is accelerated. Early editions carried a prefatory note:

> The action of the book is laid in the near future, when existing social tendencies have become more marked; I have postulated no mechanical or scientific advance, but in the interest of compactness and with no pretensions to prophecy, I have assumed a certain speeding up of legal procedure and daily journalism.

The Bright Young People are also speeded up, partying endlessly, hopping about restlessly from one amusement to the next. They are children of technological change and mass-produced machines; their toys are automobiles, telephones, phonographs, the cinema. Colonel Blount's keenness for the fruits of technology—vacuum cleaners, cinema films, the Rector's automobile—is a symptom of his balminess; but, after a manner, his quirk possesses the entire age. People move faster and faster, but to no useful end, like the racing cars at Belfast "running all jammed together like pigs being driven through a gate" (186), overturning at "Quarry Corner," hurtling off the road at ninety miles an hour, charging into hedges and crashing into one another (killing one driver), careering about, loudly, for four hundred miles at high speed, in circles, ending up just where they began. Like modern life, the racing cars vex the spirit with noise and frustration:

> The engine was running and the whole machine shook with fruitless exertion. Clouds of dark smoke came from it, and a shattering roar which reverberated from concrete floor and corrugated iron roof into every corner of the building so that speech and thought became insupportable and all the senses were numbed. (176)

When all that nervous energy is finally unloosed, it rockets out of control:

> Not so the *real* cars, that become masters of men; those vital creations of metal who exist solely for their own propulsion through space, for whom their drivers, clinging precariously at the steering wheel, are as important as his stenographer to a stock-broker. These are in perpetual flux; a vortex of combining and disintegrating units; like the confluence of traffic at some spot where many roads meet, streams of mechanism come together, mingle and separate again. (178)

The drivers have become the driven, slaves of their machines, not in control but only hanging on. When the restless Bright Young People and the demonically fast racing cars come together, the conjunction is inevitably disastrous. The heroine of the disaster is Agatha Runcible.

Agatha Runcible is *Vile Bodies'* freest spirit, the closest kin to Grimes and Margot Beste-Chetwynde; like Grimes in particular, Agatha often falls "in the soup." It is she who is singled out as a suspected smuggler and indelicately searched at Dover; who bolts from 10 Downing Street in Hawaiian costume and brings down the government; who is expelled from a restaurant for wearing pants. Her life defies the conventions and the odds, but unlike Grimes, the irrepressible survivor who always lands on his feet, Agatha is merely mortal, and when her characteristic carelessness is given simultaneous alcoholic and mechanical encouragement, she straightway destroys herself.

Drunkenly inspired to join the automobile race, Agatha soon veers off the course on a tangent, "turning left instead of right at Church Corner," speeds down a bye-road, "apparently out of control," and smashes into a village market cross (195). Like the demolition of the old King's Thursday by "all that was most destructive in modern machinery," Agatha's crash exhibits spiritual anarchy and mechanical technology in fatal combination. Carried to a nursing home, she has "the most awful dreams" of uncontrollable speed:

> I thought we were all driving round and round in a motor race and none of us could stop, and there was an enormous audience composed entirely of gossip writers and gate crashers and Archie Schwert and people like that, all shouting at us at once to go faster, and car after car kept crashing until I was left all alone driving and driving—and then I used to crash and wake up. (209)

When an impromptu Bright Young People party causes Agatha to relapse, the nightmare visions return even more frighteningly:

> There was rarely more than a quarter of a mile of the black road to be seen at one time. It unrolled like a length of cinema film. At the edges was confusion; a fog spinning past; "*Faster, faster,*" they shouted above the roar of the engine. The road rose suddenly and the white car soared up the sharp ascent without slackening of speed. At the summit of the hill there was a corner. Two cars had crept up, one on each side, and were closing in. "Faster," cried Miss Runcible, "Faster." (223–24)

It is an apocalyptic vision of the Bright Young People themselves, caught up in the compulsive and unravelling acceleration of modern life. The road race rescues *Vile Bodies* from Waugh's self-pity with an image characteristic of his best fiction: drawn from his active encounter with life, expressing his imaginative involvement with the world.

Critics have generally located the meaning of *Vile Bodies* in its satiric depiction of neurotic, dizzying, circular, futile action. For Alvin Kernan, "It is the arrangement of incidents and the overall pattern of events—plot—which ultimately establish the 'meaning' in Waugh's novels," and the pattern of events in *Vile Bodies* is expressed by the master image of the motor car race.[24] Stephen Jay Greenblatt follows Kernan in reading the novel as a study of the contemporary waste land: "With this technique of disconnected and seemingly irrelevant scenes, Waugh is attempting to portray a world that is chaotic and out of joint," and the novel's characters are only symbolically interesting: "Adam and Nina are significant only as representatives of the sickness of an entire generation, and their thwarted attempt to marry is meaningful and interesting only as a symbol of the frustrated search for values of all the Bright Young People."[25] And more recently, Jeffrey Heath follows much the same line, with the added insight that in *Vile Bodies* Waugh's "major target is aberrant religion. . . . through Adam's encounters Waugh examines the origins of England's spiritual bankruptcy." The basic problem in the novel is that "Adam never considers religion."[26]

All this loads a heavy weight of thematic purpose on *Vile Bodies,* some of which the novel will tolerate. But one should recall that P. G. Wodehouse and Ronald Firbank were the novel's early models; that two decades later Waugh described the composition of his earliest novels as purely extemporaneous; "When I began writing I worked straight on into the void, curious to see what would happen to my characters, with no preconceived plan for them, and few technical corrections."[27] Only when he was finishing up *Vile Bodies* did he sigh that "I am relying on a sort of cumulative futility for any effect it may have."[28] If a weighty thematic burden is dropped on it, *Vile Bodies* will crack. Waugh certainly proposed the disjointed and frenetic action of the novel as a metaphor of contemporary life, but the novel's images of chaos and futility spring more fundamentally from his own perplexed affairs and emotions. *Vile Bodies* is the complaint of a disheartened, baffled sensibility rather than a coherent cultural or religious argument.

The nontheological, nonideological imaginative origins of *Vile Bodies* are suggested by the image the novel itself opposes to the automobiles and partying of the Bright Young People—an image not of Periclean Athens or the City of God, but of the anachronistic, Wodehousian country house of Nina's dotty father, Colonel Blount, where Adam and Nina spend a short Christmas holiday, and where Adam enjoys his only interlude of peace and contentment.

Adam Symes is partly a cad, partly a sad young man abused by the world. In the novel's latter half, he bullies and cuckolds the rich but plebeian "Ginger" Littlejohn, for example, anticipating *Black Mischief*'s Basil Seal. Like Paul Pennyfeather, however, Adam is essentially a victim. His problems at the beginning of the novel are typically farcical, and even in the later chapters his mischances occur with comically predictable unpredictability. But though his courtship of Nina Blount is casual and disorganized, his determination to marry her distinguishes him from the apparently aimless Bright Young People. Father Rothschild asserts that the younger generation yearns for permanence, but among the novel's characters only Adam does anything concrete about it. Though he parties with the Bright Young People, he is not really one of them, and his response to the restless forces moving them is notably different from, say, Agatha Runcible's. Agatha might one day have slowed down enough to marry; but Adam wants to settle down now. More and more wistful for the stability of marriage, he is a lonely figure at the center of the novel's whirling energies.

The novel's second epigraph seems to refer to Adam's predicament:

"If I wasn't real," Alice said—half laughing through her tears, it all seemed so ridiculous—"I shouldn't be able to cry."

"I hope you don't suppose those are real tears?" Tweedledum interrupted in a tone of great contempt.

Adam's sensitivity is mocked and frustrated by the farce in which he is involved, as if Hamlet had somehow been miscast in Gilbert and Sullivan. He does not seem to share Father Rothschild's cosmic worries about the instability of the world-order, but he wearies of the flux and chaos of the world and seeks to order his own life by marrying. Nina is an attractive flapper, presumably, but like Imogen Quest of "The Balance" she represents a great deal more to Adam: not so much aristocratic freedom and elegance, in this case, as simple hearthside peace. In 1925, exiled in a distant and savage outpost, Waugh had longed for the glamor of London; in 1929, cast adrift by his wife, storm-tossed, he longed for a secure domestic haven.

We catch only a brief glimpse of it in *Vile Bodies,* however: Christmas at Doubting Hall. Just as Father Rothschild grows from a comic caricature into a prophet, Doubting Hall changes from the exaggeratedly backward country house of a mad old squire into a striking image of nostalgia. Early in the novel, Doubting Hall seems a Palladian version of the old King's Thursday; frozen in Edwardian prosperity, it has not changed since Nina was a child:

> There were several magazines in the library—mostly cheap weeklies devoted to the cinema. There was a stuffed owl and a case of early British remains, bone pins and bits of pottery and a skull, which had been dug up in the park many years ago and catalogued by Nina's governess. There was a cabinet containing the relics of Nina's various collecting fevers— some butterflies and a beetle or two, some fossils and some birds' eggs and a few postage stamps. There were some bookcases of superbly unreadable books, a gun, a butterfly net, an alpenstock in the corner. There were catalogues of agricultural machines and acetylene plants, lawn mowers, "sports requisites." There was a fire screen worked with a coat of arms. The chimney-piece was hung with the embroidered saddle-cloths of Colonel Blount's regiment of Lancers. There was an engraving of all the members of the Royal Yacht Squadron, with a little plan in the corner, marked to show who was who. There were many other things of equal interest besides . . . (73)

Colonel Blount loves the toys of technology, but Doubting Hall remains without telephone, automobile, or electricity (making it unclear how the Colonel will operate the vacuum cleaner he covets). Waugh's satire on places like Doubting Hall is never wholly distinct from his admiration; it was precisely because they were so comically out of touch that they were so attractive. Doubting Hall's value as an antidote to the frenetic urban pace of the Bright Young People is only briefly glimpsed in the early chapters, however, when Adam finds the peace of the old house wonderful therapy for a hangover: "When Nina and he were married, he thought, they would often come down there for the day after a really serious party" (74). At the end of the novel, however, Doubting Hall, calm and lonely, becomes much more profoundly therapeutic.

In the course of the novel, England has become physically uglier, a visible sign of its malaise. At the motor races, for example, industrial England looms squalidly through the rain:

> He looked out and saw a grey sky, some kind of factory and the canal from whose shallow waters rose little islands of scrap-iron and bottles; a derelict perambulator lay partially submerged under the opposite bank. (172)

Later, flying to the Continent on her honeymoon with Ginger Little-john, Nina surveys contemporary England:

> Nina looked down and saw inclined at an odd angle a horizon of strag-gling red suburb; arterial roads dotted with little cars; factories, some of them working, others empty and decaying; a disused canal; some distant hills sown with bungalows; wireless masts and overhead power cables; men and women were indiscernible except as tiny spots; they were marrying and shopping and making money and having children. The scene lurched and tilted again as the aeroplane struck a current of air.
> "I think I'm going to be sick," said Nina. (223)

From this prospect, and from Agatha Runcible's frenzied nightmares, the scene abruptly shifts to Doubting Hall, where "the park lay deep in snow, a clean expanse of white, shadowless and unspotted save for tiny broad arrows stamped by the hungry birds" (225).[29] Adam and Nina are pretending to be married. On Christmas eve Colonel Blount's film-showing at the Rectory is rather a failure, but this setback scarcely ripples the profound serenity of the season:

> Next morning Adam and Nina woke up under Ada's sprig of mistletoe to hear the bells ringing for Christmas across the snow. "Come all to church, good people; good people come to church." . . . Later they put some crumbs of their bread and butter on the windowsill and a robin redbreast came to eat them. The whole day was like that. (239)

It is a day of tradition and ritual at Doubting Hall: matins; an exchange of useless gifts; a glass of sherry in the servants' quarters;

carol singers in the evening ("*Oh, tidings of comfort and joy,*" they sang, "*comfort and joy . . .*"); and then a glass of punch for each ("each, according to his capacity, got a little more, but not much more, than was good for him") (243–44).

This tranquil idyll, unique in Waugh's early novels, balances the nightmare of the racing automobiles. Doubting Hall is a refuge from the noisy confusion of contemporary life, and from the disordered emotions of Waugh himself.

"I put off going abroad and came here to make a last effort at finishing my novel," Waugh wrote to Henry Yorke from North Devon late in the summer:

> It has been infinitely difficult and is certainly the last time I shall try to make a book about sophisticated people. It all seems to shrivel up & rot internally and I am relying on a sort of cumulative futility for any effect it may have. All the characters are gossip writers. As soon as I have enough pages covered to call it a book I shall join Bryan & Diana in Paris.[30]

Even were this explicit evidence lacking, Waugh's hurry to finish *Vile Bodies* quickly might be inferred from the ending he tacked on it. From Doubting Hall we are dropped onto "the biggest battlefield in the history of the world," where Adam is sitting on a tree stump surrounded by "unrelieved desolation; a great expanse of mud in which every visible object was burnt or broken" (247–48). Arbitrary and somewhat perfunctory, dictated by caprice and convenience, the epilogue wraps up an improvised novel with an impromptu conclusion.

But it is not an inappropriate conclusion. Like Paul Pennyfeather at the end of *Decline and Fall*, Adam is lonely and apparently resigned; and like Paul reading quietly and going to bed while the Bollinger Club revels outside his windows, Adam falls asleep in the front seat of the drunk Major's limousine while the Major and Chastity make love in the back seat. Life goes on, but without the hero. Chastity and the drunk Major, in fact, seem a desperate gasp of Grimesian irrepressibility in the face of adversity: the animating impulse of *Decline and Fall* survives, but in sadly atrophied form. Opening in high spirits, *Vile Bodies* ends in melancholy and begins the sequence of dark comedies between Waugh's two marriages.

Few would rank *Vile Bodies* among the best of Waugh's novels; Waugh himself ranked it low, citing its "many gross faults" (but it also had, of course, unhappy associations). Yet despite the unevenness of the second half, in which lugubrious discourse momentarily threatens to derail the action, Waugh's comic invention in *Vile Bodies* is almost always adept and often inspired. Emphasizing its pessimism obscures its achievement. A fantasy of ephemeral material, mixed mood, and erratic development, it is despite its problems a novel that only Waugh could have written; with it he confirmed his remarkable gifts.

5

Black Mischief: "Sunless, Forbidden Places"

At the beginning of 1930, the same week that *Vile Bodies* was published, Waugh's divorce decree was issued. Together these occasions marked a turn in his life. The novel became an immediate popular and commercial success. "Those Vile Bodies seem to be selling like Hot Cakes," he wrote exultantly to Peters shortly after publication.[1] For the first time, Waugh began earning a comfortable income.

His divorce, legally certifying him a bachelor once again, joined with his new literary renown to enhance his social life, as well. Though not single by choice, he seized without hesitation on his new opportunities. His diaries, resuming in May 1930 after a twenty-month break, record a succession of luncheons, teas, dinners, and cocktail parties, interrupted occasionally, when deadlines approached, by spells of concentrated work. More exalted social circles opened up to him, and diary entries often simply list names, sometimes quite prominent ones. After his discouraging years of schoolmastering and unemployment, and especially after the mortification of his wife's desertion, he glutted himself on the chocolates of success. If he was not to be a happily married man of letters, like his father, he would be a man about town, even a rake—like, say, Lord Rochester.

Neither his journalism nor his diaries, with the crowded social calendar, betray any hint of what he pondered in his more reflective moods, or, indeed, that he was ever troubled by reflective moods. During the early months of 1930 he was, however, meditating a decision of lasting consequence. Typically, the diaries' first hint of anything out of the ordinary is laconically sandwiched between luncheon and dinner in an otherwise routine entry: "To tea at Alexander Square with Olivia. I said would she please find a Jesuit to instruct me."[2] Olivia Greene, who (along with her mother) had converted to Catholicism five years earlier, sent him to Father Martin D'Arcy, S.J., whose "blue chin and fine, slippery mind" impressed Waugh at their first meeting, at which they "talked about verbal inspiration and Noah's Ark."[3] After briefly recording a few more sessions with Father D'Arcy, the diaries then ignore the matter for over a month, until in August Olivia Greene visited Waugh while he was staying in Wiltshire: "Olivia and I drove into Salisbury and bought some very good port from a slightly hostile wine merchant. That evening we got a little drunk and talked about religion."[4] Three days later he wrote to Father D'Arcy asking to be received into the Church. Olivia Greene had plainly been a decisive catalyst; he later asserted, in tribute, that "she bullied me into the Church."[5]

He took the final steps in this progress without ceremony and without visible emotion. When Penelope Betjeman later took instruction in 1948, Waugh wrote to her: "I am greatly impressed & edified by the depth of your studies. I just talked half a dozen times to Father D'Arcy about T. S. Eliot & Havelock Ellis, then popped into Farm Street on the way to dinner one evening & sat up with Driberg in the gallery of the Café de Paris to see a new negress singer."[6] Certainly there was little alteration in his workaday habits, at least as they are glimpsed in his diaries. "I am aghast now when I think how frivolously I approached (though it seemed grave enough at the time)," he told Edith Sitwell, "for every year since has been one of exploration into the mind & heart of the Church."[7]

Writing of his conversion for *The Daily Express* a few days after his reception, he had nothing to say about the mind and heart of the Church, however, speaking instead in very mundane terms: first, he wrote, he had discovered that Christianity was the alternative to Chaos and the "materialistic, mechanised State"; then he had determined that Christianity "exists in its most complete and vital form in the Roman Catholic Church."[8] He was strongly attracted by the Church as a visible institution representing order against instability, as a disciplined system of belief against moral and social disorganization. Though conceding that "there also remain the devotional needs of the individual member, for, however imposing the organisation of the Church, it would be worthless if it did not rest upon the faith of its members," he was reluctant to discuss his own faith in personal terms, making no reference to such things as God the Father, Son, or Spirit, the Incarnation or Resurrection, the seven sacraments or the four last things.

Yet the apparently cool rationalism of his conversion concealed an adamantine personal commitment, for he joined the Church against the opposition of his parents (his mother "very, very sad over news of Evelyn's secession to Rome," Arthur Waugh, who was also sad, noted in his diary[9]) and despite his belief that the Church would not allow him to remarry. Although he always took pains to discourage any suggestion of religious enthusiasm, preferring to attribute his beliefs solely to a rational, almost perversely logical, consideration of historical evidence, his conversion must have been owing to a convergence of feelings more compelling than any mere syllogism could have produced.

Less than two weeks after his reception into the Church, he left England for Abyssinia to attend the coronation of Ras Tafari as Emperor, an event casually recommended to him by his old friend Alastair Graham. He arrived in Addis Ababa in late October 1930. Expecting to find a pristine feudal culture, he was surprised to encounter instead a simple, leisurely tribal culture perplexed with an influx of Western innovations, a mongrel culture: "a tangle of modernism and barbarity, European, African, and American"; "a unique stage of the interpenetration of two cultures."[10] Haile Selassie's coronation intensified the contradictions and incongruities. "It is to *Alice in Wonderland* that my thoughts recur in seeking some historical parallel for life in Addis Ababa," he wrote; ". . . it is in *Alice* only that one finds the peculiar flavour of galvanised and translated reality, where animals carry watches in their waistcoat pockets, royalty paces the croquet lawn beside the chief executioner, and litigation ends in a flutter of playing cards."[11] By the time he departed Abyssinia he had accumulated the fictional material he needed. "I have the plot of a first rate novel," he wrote to his parents just after leaving Addis Ababa;[12] a few weeks later he informed a reporter in Uganda that he planned to write a "satirical novel on African monarchy."[13] He continued to wander, however—to Aden, Zanzibar, Kenya, and then toward the west coast, which he never reached, eventually emerging from the interior in Cape Town. After five months abroad he landed in England in March 1931, "looking very hearty, rosy & well; & bringing many delightful gifts, carved animals, & a canvas picture of the Abyssinian farmer's life," Arthur Waugh recorded of his son's descent on Underhill.[14]

After completing the travel book, *Remote People,* which he had been working on along the way, he began writing a novel based on his African experiences.

Several distinctly different motives informed *Black Mischief:* heightened literary craftsmanship; cultural ideology; the bitterness and humiliation of betrayal and abandonment; nostalgia; the stimulus of Africa, and especially of Addis Ababa during coronation week.

Black Mischief was, to begin, artistically ambitious. A new spirit of professionalism infuses the novel, Waugh's first to boast any sort of premeditated plot or deliberate structure. Its fabric is richer and more complex than that of the two earlier novels, weaving together broad farce, ideology, satire, comedy of manners, intrigue, adventure, the macabre; it is carefully stage managed, with characters making their entry one by one, converging near the novel's midpoint and accelerating through a rapidly developed crisis and suitably shocking catastrophe; the exotic setting is skillfully sketched with evocative detail. Gone is the improvisation (and something of the spontaneity) of *Decline and Fall* and *Vile Bodies,* with their haphazard digressions and stray intrusions. They were, by comparison, slapdash; *Black Mischief* is a piece of fictional cabinetmaking, with dovetails, beveled edges, and polished finish.

The novel's imaginative impetus, however, as distinct from its technical accomplishment, came from Haile Selassie's Abyssinia. Almost as soon as he arrived in Addis Ababa, Waugh seems to have recognized that he had stumbled onto fertile material, a scene of great "variety and absurdity."

> Every morning we awoke to a day of brilliant summer sunshine; every evening fell cool, limpid, charged with hidden vitality, fragrant with the thin smoke of the *tukal* fires, pulsing, like a live body, with the beat of the tom-toms that drummed incessantly somewhere out of sight among the eucalyptus-trees. In this rich African setting were jumbled together, for a few days, people of every race and temper, all involved in one way or another in that complex of hysteria and apathy, majesty and farce; a company shot through with every degree of animosity and suspicion.[15]

On his way back down to the coast he wrote to his parents: "I am not sorry to have left Addis," but: "All this trip is interesting me enormously. I think it is money well spent."[16] Waugh's cultural outlook, like his background, was narrowly English. Christopher Hollis remembered him declaiming loudly against "bloody abroad" at Oxford, no doubt taunting the cosmopolitan Harold Acton but also expressing a genuine strain of English insularity. His early career is a history of successive exposures to new cultures: Oxford, North Wales, Mayfair, now abroad. Almost every day in Africa he found English expectations surprised, English assumptions challenged. Mediterranean slums had been gratifyingly different, but Africa proved altogether novel.

The setting of *Black Mischief* is a pastiche of Africa (and Aden), but the novel's comic energy derived principally from Addis Ababa. Here, fresh from Europe, Waugh was startled to discover a native black culture, traditional and solid, dressed up in the latest Western fads and fashions—like the Emperor Seth, wearing "spotted silk pyjamas recently purchased in the Place Vendôme," yet haunted at night by "the inherited terror of the jungle" (52, 34). Ras Tafari's

coronation, attracting several hundred foreign visitors and jour-
nalists, seemed a good opportunity to impress the world with
Abyssinia's progressive outlook—an imposture, Waugh considered,
derisively exposed by the numerous absurdities and misadventures of
coronation week:

> If in the foregoing pages I have seemed to give undue emphasis to the
> irregularity of the proceedings, to their unpunctuality, and their occa-
> sional failure, it is because this was an essential part of their character and
> charm. In Addis Ababa everything was haphazard and incongruous; one
> learned always to expect the unusual and yet was always surprised.[17]

Indigenous Abyssinian culture struck Waugh as coarse. Abyssinians,
he felt, were arrogant and stupidly xenophobic; the women were
ugly, the men bullying. Religiously, artistically, socially, politically,
even gastronomically, Abyssinian culture offended him; it was raw
and uncouth, rather like the wild honey offered him at the monastery
of Debra Lebanos: ". . . two horns of honey, but not honey as it is
understood at Thame; this was the product of wild bees, scraped
straight from the trees; it was a greyish colour, full of bits of stick and
mud, bird dung, dead bees, and grubs."[18] (Characteristically, Waugh
dined instead that evening from a hamper of Fortnum and Mason
delicacies.) His tastes in honey and culture were fastidious, and the
relative crudeness of Abyssinia repelled him.

Yet Abyssinian culture, for all the shortcomings he detected and
deplored, possessed an undoubted and admirable vigor. Like Grimes,
native life continually slipped out from under the boot of authority.
Waugh sympathized with the Abyssinians' instinctive, inarticulate
resistance to imported modernization and progress. Their per-
tinacious backwardness, transferred to *Black Mischief*'s Azania, inoc-
ulated the novel with comic energy. Azania is incorrigible. *Decline
and Fall* had celebrated weeds poking up in the flower garden of
middle-class England; *Black Mischief*'s Azania is a lush jungle of
weeds, "things rank and gross in nature" possessing it entirely. The
few mail-order flowers from Europe are frail hothouse varieties su-
perbly ill-adapted to the Azanian soil.

A native family squatting under a wrecked lorry serves as a recur-
rent image of Azania's vitality. Despite intermittent harassments and
the general hurly-burly of Azanian politics—rebellion, moderniza-
tion, revolution—the family perseveres, unmoved and undaunted:

> A gang of convicts, chained neck to neck, were struggling to shift a rusty
> motor car which lay on its side blocking the road. It had come to grief
> there six months previously, having been driven recklessly into some

cattle by an Arab driver. He was now doing time in prison in default of damages. White ants had devoured the tyres; various pieces of mechanism had been removed from time to time to repair other engines. A Sakuyu family had set up house in the back, enclosing the space between the wheels with an intricate structure of rags, tin, mud and grass. (118)

The convicts damage the dwelling but fail to dislodge the family, the Emperor's triumphal progress to the train station is embarrassingly obstructed, and the tenacious family rebuilds: "In the derelict van outside the railway station, a patient black family repaired the ravages of invasion with a careful architecture of mud, twigs, rag and flattened petrol tins" (149). Several weeks later, the English animal rights advocate Dame Mildred Porch encounters the same family, still dug in: "Road to station blocked broken motor lorry," she records in her journal. "Natives living in it. Also two goats. Seemed well but cannot be healthy for them so near natives. Had to walk last quarter mile" (202). And at the end, after all the convulsions of Azanian affairs, after Seth's progressive policies, as well as Seth himself, have been swept away like dust in a gale, the family remains in place, having survived even the novelty of legal efforts to evict them:

> "We settled that case I told you about. You know, the one of the natives who built a house in a broken lorry in the middle of the road."
> "Oh, ah. Who won it?"
> "Oh we gave it to the chap in possession on both counts. . . . They'll have to make a new road round him now." (299)

Azania resists straight roads; it baffles rationalization and progress with irrepressible crookedness and spontaneity. The fiasco of Seth's railway departure for Debra Dowa, the native troops eating their government-issue boots, the never-finished road to the British legation—all assert Azania's cultural integrity, its unreflecting adherence to its traditional non-European character.

Amidst this flourishing native culture, the Emperor Seth raises the standard of modernism.

Conversion to Catholicism formalized Waugh's thinking about contemporary culture and energized him with ideas and opinions. Months of brooding, his new religious creed, and the journey through Africa had combined to widen his outlook, replacing *Vile Bodies'* parochial pity for the younger generation with anxiety about the future of European civilization, for which he now seemed to feel personally responsible. Several years earlier the rich comic potential of Abyssinia might have inspired a happy paean to anarchy like

Decline and Fall, but *Black Mischief*'s bacchic zest is qualified by didacticism. Though effervescent with farce, *Black Mischief* includes a dose of medicine, too.

While almost all critics have agreed that *Black Mischief* is strongly thematic, there is less agreement about the exact nature of the theme. Two principal ideas seem to inform the novel, however. The first was prompted by the cultural anomalies Waugh perceived in Addis Ababa, which had persuaded him that the elaborately ramified, delicately balanced edifice of European culture could not be quickly re-erected on the foundation of what he thought a rough and unmortared primitive society. Haile Selassie's Abyssinia demonstrated that the outer dress of European culture might be exported to Africa like a mail-order suit, but that the African donning the suit would remain essentially African; and that notwithstanding technology and ideology imported from Europe and America by the trainload, Abyssinia would remain essentially Abyssinia.

His actual interest in African modernization was slight, however. He was much more concerned with Africa's relevance to Europe, and here Abyssinia seemed to offer not only an example of cultural impenetrability, but also a warning of European decline. Europe was, in Waugh's bleak view, drying up, and Azanian fertility revealed by contrast European aridity. In November 1932, the month *Black Mischief* was published, he prophesied that if he lived long enough, "I am perfectly confident that . . . I shall see the beginning of a vast recession of the white races from all over the world—a withdrawal of the legions to defend what remains of European standards on European ground. I am less confident," he added pessimistically, "of how much will remain to be defended."[19] The legionary metaphor suggests the influence of Bellocian ideas about the Roman Empire.

Waugh's ideas, in fact, were not new—he had also read Spengler's *Decline of the West*—and perhaps the only excuse for introducing such ideas into the novel would be their memorable expression in character, action, or image. In this, *Black Mischief* is partly but not wholly successful.

The Emperor Seth is at the center of the novel's cultural statement; he embodies the concept of African modernization. Just as Basil Seal personifies (for Seth, at least) "all that glittering, intangible Western culture to which he aspired," Seth himself personifies the desire for that culture (142). His obsession is Progress, as the term is understood in the industrially advanced nations:

This is not a war of Seth against Seyid but of Progress against Barbarism. And Progress must prevail. I have seen the great tattoo of Aldershot, the

Paris Exhibition, the Oxford Union. I have read modern books—Shaw, Arlen, Priestley. What do the gossips in the bazaars know of all this? The whole might of Evolution rides behind me; at my stirrups run woman's suffrage, vaccination, and vivisection. I am the New Age. I am the Future.[20]

This jumbled catalog suggests not only the confusion of contemporary European culture, but also its inappropriateness for Africa. Imported novelties seldom work out quite as expected in Azania. Such is the case, for example, with Seth's ultimate weapon, the tank, and with the boots issued to the native troops. Such also is the case with the kindness-to-animals campaign of two Englishwomen in Azania, Dame Mildred Porch and Miss Sarah Tin, whose attempt to introduce the notion of compassion for animals is as futile as Seth's attempts to introduce other Western ideas. No one in Azania takes up the cause of humane treatment of animals; no one even understands the idea. Under the misimpression that Dame Sarah and Miss Tin are advocates of more advanced forms of cruelty, Viscount Boaz digresses from his official greeting "to recount with hideous detail what he had himself once done with a woodman's axe to a wild boar." Back in London, Lord Monomark is expounding on the vegetarian benefits of an onion and porridge diet, and Seth himself has confused notions about vitamins—but Azanians prefer raw red meat, preferably fresh-slaughtered and dripping.

Perhaps the strongest statement of this theme lies in Seth's self-destruction. He embodies not just the passion for modernization, but also its intoxicating effects on a stable traditional culture. Like Azania, he has only a shaky grasp on the European novelties he adopts; his enthusiasm is little more than a stew of fashionable ideas, indiscriminately modern, mostly trivial, wholly unassimilated. It has dangerous side effects, and Seth soon slides toward madness:

> It was as though Seth's imagination like a volcanic lake had in the moment of success become suddenly swollen by the irruption of unsuspected, subterranean streams until it darkened and seethed and overflowed its margins in a thousand turbulent cascades. The earnest and rather puzzled young man became suddenly capricious and volatile; ideas bubbled up within him, bearing to the surface a confused sediment of phrase and theory, scraps of learning half understood and fantastically translated. (189–90)

And as Seth, lurching from astronomy to ectogenesis to straw hats and gloves for the native peerage, loses his grip on sanity, Azania itself stumbles into anarchy. Seth's apparently benign reforms (like those of

Decline and Fall's prison warden, Sir Wilfrid Lucas-Dockery) unloose chaos, and Seth himself is the first victim. He represents the self-defeating attempt arbitrarily to impose Western culture on a non-Western nation.

Waugh also wanted, however, to illustrate the enervation of Western culture, quite apart from its implausibility in Azania. But while Seth's mania for progress is effective if not brilliant satire, the satire on European sterility, symbolized by the Emperor's birth control campaign, is heavyhanded. Birth control, like kindness to animals, is not easily appreciated in Azania, where, life being precarious, fecundity is prized. The Earl of Ngumo, for instance,

> . . . one of a family of forty-eight (most of whom he had been obliged to assassinate on his succession to the title), was the father of over sixty sons and uncounted daughters. This progeny was a favourite boast of his; in fact he maintained a concert party of seven minstrels for no other purpose than to sing at table about this topic when he entertained friends. (182–83)

Because Azanians value large families, the Emperor's birth control campaign encounters confusion and dissent. Waugh sympathized with their resistance. The banners carried in the Birth Control procession bear legends like *"WOMEN OF TOMORROW DEMAND AN EMPTY CRADLE"* and, paradoxically, *"THROUGH STERILITY TO CULTURE,"* but after street riots disperse the pageant, the symbolism of birth control appears starkly on one of the trampled banners: "Only one word was visible in the empty street. *STERILITY* pleaded in orange and green silk to an unseeing people" (246). In a talk composed for the BBC in 1932, Waugh made the point even more explicitly: "Physical sterility, whether artificial or organic, results from sterility of spirit."[21] Not just birth control, but the whole mixed assortment of progressive ideas percolating down to Azania implicitly falls under this condemnation.

With the Birth Control Pageant, however, *Black Mischief*'s ideas, as they become most obviously didactic, become labored and even shrill. In *Vile Bodies,* Father Rothschild's oracular wisdom directly expressed Waugh's personal views; but *Vile Bodies* had the excuse of being loosely organized, hastily written, disastrously interrupted, and only lightly revised. There was less excuse for such artless sermonizing in *Black Mischief.* Parts of the novel's satire on Africa and modern Europe are very funny; parts are merely jejune—unremarkable ideas imperfectly realized in character and action. Such satire as that on birth control, moreover, struck rather a false note: Waugh the would-be rake lamenting empty cradles.

Other motives strongly influence *Black Mischief*, not all of them artistic or edifying.

Despite Waugh's concerns about the decay of European culture, for example, *Black Mischief*, in the figure of Basil Seal, somewhat incongruously betrays Waugh's absorbing fascination with the aristocratic, man-of-the-world style.

Basil first appears in London where, from the exquisite little dinner parties of his mother Lady Cynthia to the bohemian languor and squalor of his friends the Trumpingtons, superannuated Bright Young People, we glimpse a superbly mannered and civilized—indeed over-civilized—society. Mayfair refinement and Azanian barbarity represent the novel's cultural antipodes, but the neat structural opposition provided by London happily coincided with Waugh's own inclinations. The London scenes reveal him pleased with his knowledge of high society and more than pleased to linger in describing it. Basil's day in London serves as a Baedeker's guide to Waugh's own London life, yielding in particular an insight into his love affair with the fashionable West End, the glamorous mistress he pursued for the next several years.

His absorption with this society can be seen, for example, in the lengthy description of Lady Cynthia's dinner party. She plans this affair to the last detail, and Waugh scarcely omits a single one. Lady Cynthia

despatched engraved cards of invitation a month in advance, supplied defections from a secondary list one week later, fidgeted with place cards and a leather board as soon as the acceptances began to arrive, borrowed her sister's chef and her daughter's footmen and on the morning of the party exhausted herself utterly by trotting all over her house in Lowndes Square arranging flowers. Then at half past five when she was satisfied that all was ready she would retire to bed and doze for two hours in her darkened room; her maid would call her with cachet Faivre and clear China tea; a touch of ammonia in the bath; a touch of rouge on the cheeks; lavender water behind the ears; half an hour before the glass, fiddling with her jewel case while her hair was being done; final conference with the butler; then a happy smile in the drawing room for all who were less than twenty minutes late. The menu always included lobster cream, saddle of mutton and brown-bread ice and there were silver gilt dishes ranged down the table holding a special kind of bon-bon supplied to Lady Seal for twenty years by a little French shop whose name she would sometimes coyly disclose. (96–97)

There is an undoubted suggestion that Lady Cynthia is tiresomely fussy in her arrangements, but the innuendo hardly seems worth such elaboration. It seems evident that Waugh was himself fascinated with the ritual of such aristocratic occasions. *Black Mischief* reveals him in the first flush of social success, relishing the fashionable world to which he had so recently gained access. In the figure of Basil Seal, at home (though not necessarily welcome) anywhere in aristocratic London, from the Trumpingtons' casual menage to Lady Cynthia's drearily respectable little gatherings, Waugh defined and celebrated his new social range.

Basil is very different from the heroes of Waugh's first two novels; he is in fact unique in the early novels. Paul Pennyfeather and Adam Symes were similar to the young Waugh himself in their middle-class background, their obscurity, and their relative poverty. Basil, on the other hand, is a flamboyant aristocrat, an adventurer, a cad: a product of Waugh's prosperity, but also of his injured pride. Basil was concretely inspired, Waugh later acknowledged, by two of his Oxford contemporaries: Peter Rodd and Basil Murray, who as undergraduates impressed him with their bold style. Though not fond of them, he confessed to admiration for their "insolence, a determination to treat with the world only on their own terms."[22] Basil, for all his defects, exhibits to an extremity the self-assurance of a born aristocrat. Whatever worldly success Waugh had achieved by 1932, or might yet achieve, he would always lack the intangible benefits that a gilded background (presumably) conferred. Though a rebel to the polite aristocratic society of his widowed mother, her fatuous friend Sir Joseph Mannering, and the sleepy old gentlemen of his club, Basil comes from wealth, privilege, Eton (no doubt), and Balliol, and conducts himself accordingly. Few really like Basil, but when he walks into a room, people take notice: "God, what I feel about that young man," says Lady Metroland (89); "My word he is a corker," remarks a girl at a cocktail party (91). To Waugh—the formerly obscure schoolmaster, the cuckolded and deserted husband—such commanding presence must have seemed very fine indeed. No one noticed *him*, even as a successful novelist, when he walked into a room.

One can speculate, in fact, that Waugh admired not only Basil's aristocratic presence, but even his arrogance and caddishness. A compulsive liar, a thief, and an adulterer, Basil takes advantage of anyone who lets him, and Waugh seems to have derived second-hand gratification from Basil's defiance of convention, his aggressive self-assertion, his exploitation of others. Even his boorish insensitivity must have seemed rather enviable.

Basil is not the only character suggesting Waugh's vicarious satisfaction in caddishness, moreover, for, though superficially quite different, the figure of Mr. Youkoumian rivals Basil in this quality. Omnipresent and irrepressible, Youkoumian is, like Grimes, a weed: a more noxious weed, actually, but so candid and affable as to disarm reproof. His instincts are directed entirely toward survival and profit; he is unacquainted with, or at least indifferent to, all delicacies of sensibility:

> Look, you give me hundred and fifty rupees I put Mme. Youkoumian with the mules. You don't understand what that will be like. They are the General's mules. Very savage stinking animals. All day they will stamp at her. No air in the truck. Orrible, unhealthy place. Very like she die or is kicked. She is good wife, work hard, very loving. (124)

Such genial villainy quickly wins over Basil Seal, and Waugh himself plainly felt some affection for Youkoumian. He is a survivor, not just scraping through but invariably profiting from the succession of upheavals and disasters in Azanian affairs.

Waugh was fictionally partial to this type, the bounder. But though Youkoumian recalls Grimes, they differ in ways that intimate changes in Waugh himself in the four years since *Decline and Fall*. While Grimes's special aptitude is for getting in and out of trouble, Youkoumian's flair is for swindle, an entrepreneurial faculty that thrives equally well in the disturbed climate of the Emperor Seth's Azania and the well-ordered Anglo-French protectorate that follows. Grimes is a free spirit, content to follow the impulse of the moment and let tomorrow sort itself out; Youkoumian is coarser and less childishly impulsive. Like Basil Seal, he exploits almost everyone who crosses his path, and sooner or later this includes most of the other characters. It is natural that Basil and Youkoumian should become partners and work well together. From 1928 to 1932, from Pennyfeather and Grimes to Basil Seal and Youkoumian, the tone of Waugh's fiction had changed.

The novel's sexual encounters reveal a similar alteration. In *Decline and Fall* sex was a jocular topic, as the worldly and lusty Margot Beste-Chetwynde initiated the virginal Paul Pennyfeather. In *Vile Bodies*, when the only slightly more experienced Adam seduces Nina Blount, sex is a romantic, comic, and fundamentally innocent adventure. Basil, however, is a rake, successful with women in a professional, rather contemptuous way. In *Black Mischief* lovemaking has lost its freshness and exhilaration. Basil's encounters with his London mistress, Angela Lyne, and his Azanian mistress, the ironically named Prudence, are loveless, and in the latter case squalid as well. For Basil, sex is no longer an act of initiation and discovery, let alone affection, but the perfunctory, almost boring diversion of a rake. "You don't do much for a girl," Angela Lyne remarks to him.

When *Black Mischief* was published, the bedroom scenes (among others) involved Waugh in an embarrassing contretemps with the English Catholic weekly the *Tablet*, which roundly condemned the novel as morally degenerate. No criticism seems ever to have upset Waugh more: for one thing, the *Tablet* was published under the aegis of the archbishop of Westminster; perhaps, too, the accusation seemed uncomfortably close to the mark. The *Tablet's* editor has been much abused by subsequent critics for narrow tastes and a censorious disposition, but his objections to *Black Mischief's* moral tendency ought not to be dismissed out of hand simply because of their puritanical spirit. Waugh indignantly asserted that the novel by no means condoned Basil's sexual transgressions; that, quite to the contrary, one scene in particular, a tryst with Prudence in Mr. Youkoumian's hotel, was portrayed with such sordid circumstantiality as to imply a salutary disapprobation of fornication. But this argument was slightly disingenuous. As Waugh claimed, the details of the assignation are repellent: "The atmosphere of the room was rank with tobacco smoke. Basil, in shirt sleeves, rose from the deck chair to greet her. He threw the butt of his Burma cheroot into the tin hip bath which stood unemptied at the side of the bed; it sizzled and went out and floated throughout the afternoon, slowly unfurling in the soapy water" (180). But the careful account of this rendezvous, as well as of Basil's cleaner-sheeted evening in London with the elegant Angela Lyne, suggests that Waugh's interest in such scenes was not actuated solely by moral indignation. His own social habits scarcely allowed him the luxury of reprobating the sexual indulgences of his characters, in any event, for the diaries disclose that after his divorce he enjoyed a number of different women. *Black Mischief* shows how far the unworldly romanticism and naiveté of a few years earlier, the wistfulness of the young man transfixed by *Beata Beatrix*, had been infected by worldly wisdom and even cynicism.

The result is an ambiguous tone in *Black Mischief*. Waugh was trying to juggle several different and sometimes conflicting roles: the prophet scourging European degeneracy, the connoisseur of high society, the man of the world. These ambitions, together with the novel's technical refinement and its delight in Abyssinia's cultural stewpot, make *Black Mischief* considerably more complex and perhaps more confused than *Decline and Fall* or *Vile Bodies*.

Other impulses animated the novel, as well.

In Abyssinia Waugh had been impressed by the placidly self-contained life of the British Legation several miles outside Addis Ababa, describing it in *Remote People:*

> The legation stands in a small park with the consulate next to it, and on either side of the drive a little garden city has sprung up of pretty thatched bungalows which accommodate the other officials. During the coronation a camp was pitched in the paddock for the staffs of the various visitors, and periodic bugling, reminiscent of an ocean liner, added a fresh incongruity to the bizarre life of the little community (41).

To Henry Yorke he wrote more frankly: "I have rarely seen anything so hysterical as the British legation all this last week—or so incompetent to cope with their duties."[23] *Black Mischief*'s British Legation originated in this isolated, inefficient (as Waugh thought) establishment, but as the fictional legation took on a life of its own, Waugh's satire mellowed.

At first sight, the Legation in Azania is a caricature of English muddle and bumble, a comic foil to the rough-and-tumble of Azania and the enthusiastic intriguing of the French legate. As the novel proceeds, however, the British Legation more and more becomes an enviable island of pastoral calm amid a sea of chaos, as if Doubting Hall had been uprooted from Buckinghamshire and replanted in Azania. The Legation is, as it turns out, less a caricature of the British in Abyssinia than a caricature of English country house life incongruously carried on in alien and hostile surroundings: a tribute to the English capacity for recreating England in unlikely places. Seven miles out of town on a nearly impassable road, the Legation looks as nearly English as possible:

> In its isolation, life in the compound was placid and domestic. Lady Courteney devoted herself to gardening. The bags came out from London laden with bulbs and cuttings and soon there sprang up round the Legation a luxuriant English garden; lilac and lavender, privet and box, grass walks and croquet lawn, rockeries and wildernesses, herbaceous borders, bowers of rambler roses, puddles of water lilies and an immature maze. (64–65)

Aside from Lady Courteney's exertions in the garden, life revolves about games and other amusements: bridge, tennis, bagatelle, dice, chess, croquet, a gymkhana, riding, "consequences," Pegity. When a few unexpected visitors, fleeing a revolution, arrive on the doorstep, Sir Samson, the legate, chafes at the interruption of his tranquil routine: "First there had been the Bishop, who arrived during tea with two breathless curates and an absurd story about another revolution and shooting in the streets. Well, why not? You couldn't expect the calm of *Barchester Towers* in a place like Azania" (253). But the provincial tranquillity of *Barchester Towers* is precisely the achievement of the British Legation, and it is in its absurd way an admirable achievement. With its bland indifference to the hurly-burly beyond its stockade, the Legation asserts its own quiet system of values: innocence, privacy, community, leisure—a finer statement of values, perhaps, than the novel's more loudly blazoned distress about European civilization.

The presiding genius of the Legation is the childlike Sir Samson, the envoy, but the more fateful and revealing figure is his daughter Prudence. A silly, inexperienced girl who has grown up amid the Legation's sequestered unworldliness, she is at the time of the novel an amorous teenager eager for wider experience. After a dalliance with one of the Legation staff, a character aptly named William Bland, Prudence is easily seduced by Basil Seal's raffish charms: " 'To think that I wanted to be in love so much,' she thought, 'that I even practised on William' " (177). For her, as for Paul Pennyfeather and Adam Symes, sex is still youthful and romantic. But not for Basil, and as Basil's mistress, Prudence alternates between two worlds; rooted in the Legation's prelapsarian innocence, she is lured by the siren call of Basil's worldliness.

Despite her compromising involvement with Basil, however, she seems to remain somehow unsullied in spirit; the Legation insulates her from adult experience. *"A woman in love . . ."* Prudence writes of herself after a tryst with Basil, but in fact she remains a child, and, as the title of her work-in-progress—*A Panorama of Life*—ironically suggests, she knows little of life. About to leave Azania, "a swift, gay figure under her red beret," she is poised to move beyond the Legation and her childhood, eager for new experience, still a girl:

> . . . already she seemed to be emerging into the new life which her mother had planned for her, and spoken of not long ago seated on Prudence's bed as she came to wish her good-night. Aunt Harriet's house in Belgrave Place; girls luncheons, dances and young men, week-ends in country houses, tennis and hunting; all the easy circumstances of English life which she had read about often but never experienced. She would resume the acquaintance of friends she had known at school, "and shan't I be able to show off to them? They'll all seem so young and innocent . . ." English cold and fog and rain, grey twilight among isolated, bare trees and dripping coverts; London streets when the shops were closing and the pavements crowded with people going to Tube stations with evening papers; empty streets, late at night after dances, revealing unsuspected

slopes, sluiced by men in almost medieval overalls . . . an English girl returning to claim her natural heritage . . . (276)

The Legation has preserved Prudence from adulthood—her parents themselves are still children, after all; she has even escaped Basil's corrupting influence, it seems, and faces life with a still childlike freshness and openness. Perhaps she represents an aspect of Waugh himself, seduced by aristocratic glamor and high society, eager to imagine himself a man of the world—the element of Waugh suggested by Basil Seal—willing enough to shed his inexperience and simplicity for smartness and worldliness; yet still drawn to the values of the Legation, with its Peter Pan reluctance to grow up and inherit the spiritual strains of adulthood, still half-wishing he could abandon Basil Seal and return to an earlier time.

But this was of course impossible, nor does Prudence herself, as it turns out, manage to escape Basil and return to England and her "new life." Sooner than he expects, Basil re-encounters her red beret, that emblem of bright promise. The cannibal stew of which Prudence is an ingredient and Basil a partaker completes his violation of her.

Innocence violated, not African barbarism or European civilization, is in fact *Black Mischief*'s darkest and most strongly felt theme. A similar pattern of violence occurs in *Decline and Fall* and *Vile Bodies*—King's Thursday is demolished, Paul Pennyfeather abused, the Christmas idyll at Doubting Hall disrupted, Adam Symes abused—but in *Black Mischief* the violation has become more savage. The Legation's innocence is shattered by chaos and brutality, evils of which the Legation had been splendidly ignorant. We last see Sir Samson and Lady Courteney keeping a sad vigil in Aden for their daughter: they "walked along on the cliff paths, waiting for news" (281). They have suddenly been thrust into a new and unpleasant adult world of anxiety and grief—things unknown in the edenic security of the Legation. But the world has proved inhospitable and indeed cruel to the values embodied by the Legation, to the "swift, gay" youth of Prudence. *Black Mischief* mourns the loss of innocence, and perhaps in this respect it springs from Waugh's regret for his own shattered romantic illusions—products of his childhood, victims of a wife's betrayal; and from regret for his subsequent decline into a less generous, less hopeful adult.

The climactic chapter of *Black Mischief*, beginning at the Legation with Sir Samson performing his leisurely morning toilet and grousing about an influx of refugees, progresses rapidly into terrible events in the jungle: Basil's discovery of Seth's murder, the murder of Seth's murderer, and finally the cannibal banquet itself—Basil's last, fatal rendezvous with Prudence. Waugh took pains to make this catastrophe as lurid as he could manage, and the chapter altogether was the most dramatically ambitious action he had yet attempted, not simply for its climactic disclosure but even more for its quick transition from the farce of a few pages earlier.

The editor of the *Tablet*, unimpressed by the artistry of all this, however, and already repelled by earlier scenes, recoiled from Prudence's grisly end, the very nadir of, as he put it, the novel's "foul invention."

Waugh responded:

> The story deals with the conflict of civilisation, with all its attendant and deplorable ills, and barbarism. The plan of my book throughout was to keep the darker aspects of barbarism continually and unobtrusively present, a black and mischievous background against which the civilized and semi-civilized characters performed their parts: I wished it to be like the continuous, remote throbbing of those hand drums, constantly audible, never visible, which every traveller in Africa will remember as one of his most haunting impressions. I introduced the cannibal theme in the first chapter and repeated it in another key in the incident of the soldiers eating their boots, thus hoping to prepare the reader for the sudden tragedy when barbarism at last emerges from the shadows and usurps the stage. It is not unlikely that I failed in this; that the transition was too rapid, the catastrophe too large.[24]

This gloss, often quoted as an authoritative statement of the novel's intentions, is in fact somewhat misleading, for Waugh had certainly designed the catastrophe to be as horrific as possible, hoping to shock just such people as the editor of the *Tablet*. Yet there is some truth to Waugh's assertion that, from the beginning, the jungle forms a "black and mischievous background" to the novel's action.

Characteristically, Waugh was fascinated by the savagery he professed to disapprove. Visiting Zanzibar in 1930, for example, he had been gratified to learn that voodoo thrived under the complacent British colonial regime: "Nowadays everything is kept hidden from the Europeans, and even those who have spent most of their lives in the country have only now and then discovered hints of the wide, infinitely ramified cult which still flourishes below the surface."[25] He inserted this sinister cult into Azania, too, just after that harbinger of progress, Basil Seal, arrives in Azania:

> And beyond the hills on the low Wanda coast where no liners called, and the jungle stretched unbroken to the sea, other more ancient rites and

another knowledge furtively encompassed; green, sunless paths; forbidden ways unguarded save for a wisp of grass plaited between two stumps, ways of death and initiation, the forbidden places of juju and the masked dancers; the drums of the Wanda throbbing in sunless, forbidden places. (150)

"Beyond the hills," the jungle waits, out of sight but never wholly out of mind: an uncharted region of fear in the deepest recesses of the imagination.

When Seth is overthrown and Azania lapses into anarchy, the narrative follows Basil Seal into the jungle, as if to probe the atavistic source of such chaos. Abandoned by his retainers, Basil ventures on alone, deeper and deeper into the interior in search of Seth. When he reaches his intended rendezvous, the atmosphere grows nightmarish. Seth is dead—murdered. In the night, a cry splits the silence—Lord Boaz, Seth's murderer, now murdered in turn by Major Joab, an adept at nocturnal assassinations. This revenge dispatched, Basil proceeds to Moshu, the capital city of the Wanda, for Seth's obsequies.

Preparations for the funeral feast are elaborate:

A pyre had been heaped up, of dry logs and straw, six foot high, in the market place. A large crowd was already assembled there and in another quarter a communal kitchen had been improvised where great cook pots rested over crackling sticks. Earthenware jars of fermented cocoa-nut sap stood ready to be broached when the proper moment arrived. (288)

The feast is inaugurated by dancing: "The wise men danced round the pyre, shaking their strings of charms and amulets, wagging their tufted rumps and uttering cries of ecstasy. They carried little knives and cut themselves as they capered round" (288–89). After sunset the dance accelerates: "Many of the tribesmen had joined the dance of the witches. With hands on each other's hips they made a chain round the pyre, shuffling their feet and heaving their shoulders, spasmodically throwing back their heads and baying like wild beasts" (290). After dinner, the dance continues, liberated by toddy and driven by increased frenzy:

Dancing was resumed, faster this time and more clearly oblivious of fatigue. In emulation of the witch doctors, the tribesmen began slashing themselves on chest and arms with their hunting knives; blood and sweat mingled in shining rivulets over their dark skins. Now and then one of them would pitch forward on to his face and lie panting or roll stiff in a nervous seizure. Women joined in the dance, making another chain, circling in the reverse way to the men. They were dazed with drink, stamping themselves into ecstasy. The two chains jostled and combined. They shuffled together interlocked. (291)

Finally, climactically:

Round and round circled the dancers, ochre and blood and sweat glistening in the firelight; the wise men's headgear swayed high above them, leopards' feet and snake skins, amulets and necklaces, lions' teeth and the shrivelled bodies of bats and toads, jigging and spinning. Tireless hands drumming out the rhythm; glistening backs heaving and shivering in the shadows. (292–93)

As the rhythm of the dance grows faster, as the dancers cast off all restraint, the dark, fierce energy of the jungle is unloosed: all the tattered clothing of civilization is torn off, and human nature exposed in its most terrifying, savage nakedness.

Next to this, all the toys and trifles of the novel's more civilized characters, from Lady Courteney's rock garden to Seth's modernization, appear as bubbles on the surface of frightening undersea depths of human superstition and ferocity.

Black Mischief is Waugh's version of *Heart of Darkness*, characterized by macabre irony instead of Conrad's sepulchral brooding. Yet Waugh, too, felt the "fascination of the abomination," abhorrence and attraction contending. For though he assured the archbishop of Westminster that *Black Mischief* dealt with "the conflict of civilization . . . and barbarism," as if they were two quite separate and incompatible categories, the novel actually suggests that the progress of civilization is like a series of expanding concentric circles, with savagery at the vital center; the more civilized a culture, the farther out and safer from that center, but the farther, also, from the primal source of energy. While modern culture in *Black Mischief* is anemic— birth control, Lord Monomark's onion and porridge diet, Gilbert and Sullivan ditties—savagery, like the cannibal dancers, is fire, blood, and sweat: a living, deadly passion.

Ultimately the wild frenzy of the cannibal feast, the horror of Prudence's death, and Basil's gruesome dinner all derived less from any considered thesis about human nature than from Waugh's own cookpot of emotions. Into the climax of *Black Mischief* he thrust all the gloom and resentment concealed behind his man-of-the-world façade and busy social life. Indeed, despite the obvious antimodernist satire of the novel and Waugh's assertion that the novel dealt with the antithesis of savagery and civilization, the imaginative currents in *Black Mischief* are ambiguous and even contradictory. He sympathized with the quiet communal domesticity of Sir Samson's Legation, with the riotous anarchy of Seth's Azania, with the murderous barbarity of the cannibals; he was both Basil the vicious and Prudence the victim, the predator and the prey. And it is tempting to speculate that the welter of diverse feelings exhibited by the novel reflects both Waugh's sense of injury and his determination to repay it, both his vulnerability and his revenge. *Black Mischief* reveals divergent impulses working themselves out in a complex fantasy, mingling nostalgic wistfulness, brutal violence, aristocratic glamor, and happy anarchy ("Its major flaw, perhaps, is that its exuberance is insufficiently controlled," one stern critic has complained).[26]

As a result of its sometimes uneasy mixture of ingredients, the flavor of *Black Mischief* fluctuates, and the moral tone hovers somewhere between the depravity detected by the *Tablet* and the rectitude professed by Waugh (and advanced by sympathetic commentators). But rather than suggesting Waugh's apostasy, as the editor of the *Tablet* would have it, *Black Mischief*—even the most dubiously virtuous passages—obliquely elucidates his conversion and loyalty to the Church, for Catholicism surely offered itself as an antidote to the chaos of feeling evident in the novel. In Addis Ababa in 1930, he had one day visited the local Catholic church: "Got up 7, went to Catholic church, island sanity in raving town."[27] The Church itself was an island of sanity to Waugh, a sanctuary less from the raving town than from his own disturbed emotions and impulses. "It seems to me," he wrote on the occasion of his conversion, "that in the present phase of European history the essential issue is no longer between Catholicism, on one side, and Protestantism, on the other, but between Christianity and Chaos."[28] Much of the chaos was within Waugh himself, however. The Church was civilized, stable, ritually and hierarchically ordered, transcendent, and dogmatically clear in its assertions: a refuge from the murky and disordered impulses evident in *Black Mischief*. Though not ostensibly a Catholic novel, *Black Mischief* indirectly suggests the deepest motives of Waugh's conversion.

The short final chapter of the novel is a deliberately anticlimactic epilogue, a decompression, shifting the scene from the whirling ecstasy of the cannibal banquet in Azania to the very indolent household of the Trumpingtons in London. As Basil returns home and Azania itself becomes dull, the nightmare recedes quickly.

Basil himself remains pure cad, apparently neither daunted nor chastened by his experience. Far from being deeply grieved by Prudence's death, he has added the cannibal banquet to his repertory of anecdotes: "I went to a party at a place called Moshu . . ." (296). For the first time, Waugh's hero has emerged from the maelstrom seemingly unaffected. Always glad to offend conventional sensibilities, Waugh insisted on the uninterrupted blackguardism of his cad hero.

Back in Azania, Seth has been succeeded by a well-ordered Anglo-French protectorate, a dreary paternalism inspired by Zanzibar, where, under benevolent and hygienic British administration, Waugh noted with disgust, everything is "legalised, controlled and licensed."[29] Like Zanzibar, Azania has become a place without problems, run by English civil servants dwelling in rows of identical bungalows. Gilbert and Sullivan tunes drift over the peaceful waterfront, just as, several years earlier, they had drifted down the stairway of the Onslow Square house of Paul Pennyfeather's bourgeois guardian. Regulated, sanitized, and policed, Azania has become to all appearances an English garden suburb. Seth's dream of Westernization has been ironically realized, with deadening completeness. The final pages betray nostalgia for the old Azania, barbaric and chaotic but very much alive, and contempt for the insipid new Azania, homogenized milk after the potent distillations of Mr. Youkoumian. Waugh the subversive still relished disorder, and the heroes of *Black Mischief* are the survivors: Youkoumian, outwardly conforming his shady enterprises to the new regime, avoiding "bust-ups" by faithfully observing closing time, for example, but radically incorrigible, foisting off army boots once again, this time on the protectorate; the native family camped under the lorry, confirmed in their squatting by the incomprehensible delicacy of British jurisprudence. Under the middle-class crust of the protectorate, Azanian life seems to go on much as before; and beyond the bungalows, in the sunless jungle, the cannibals no doubt persevere in their immemorial barbarities, "out of touch with modern thought," as Seth puts it (56). Azania has been only superficially civilized, and even that is a paltry suburban thing. By civilization, Waugh had written earlier, "I do not mean talking cinemas and tinned food, nor even surgery and hygienic houses, but the whole moral and artistic organisation of Europe."[30] Azania is no closer to this kind of "organisation" than before; the protectorate's Westernization is really just as sham as Seth's.

With Basil Seal unregenerate and Azania still flourishing ("Floreat Azania" concludes chapter 4 triumphantly), *Black Mischief* has more or less come full circle, a frequent pattern in the early novels. But though the pattern echoes *Decline and Fall*, the mood differs. The celebratory farce of the earlier novel, though only four years past, was looking very distant. The comic temper of Waugh's fiction was under strain. Even the confirmed anarchist Basil Seal sometimes feels old—

"I'm so tired I could die," he tells Prudence at one point—and at the end, after Basil's reunion with the Trumpingtons, Sonia remarks to Alastair: "D'you know, deep down in my heart I've got a tiny fear that Basil is going to turn serious on us too!" Perhaps this is just a reaffirmation of the Trumpingtons' own unrelenting frivolity—but perhaps it was an oblique comment on Waugh himself.

6

A Handful of Dust: "From Now Onwards the Map Is Valueless . . ."

"At 5:10 Evelyn returned, cheery, red-cheeked, with a car-full of luggage, & 5 stuffed crocodiles in a crate," Arthur Waugh recorded his son's arrival at Underhill on the first day of May 1933, home from several months of trekking through South American backwaters.[1] Almost immediately he retreated to the Grand Pump Room Hotel in Bath to soak himself in luxury. "Just back after a journey of the greatest misery," he wrote to Henry Yorke. "So I came to Bath which was absolutely right and live in a suite of rooms overlooking a colonnade with servants as it might be a club and a decanter of Crofts 1907 always on my sideboard and am getting rid of some of the horrors of life in the forest."[2] Typically, however, his next novel had its direct origins in "the horrors" of the bush, where he had conceived and written a short story on the theme of hopeless jungle imprisonment.

Almost a year later he journeyed to Fez, French Morocco, to expand the story into a novel. He found Fez very pleasant, "a city of astonishing beauty with running streams & fountains everywhere and enormous covered gateways in very narrow streets—no wheeled traffic, miles of bazaar, elaborate medieval fortifications, hills all round dotted with forts, olive trees, sand cliffs & spring grass, waterfalls," and at his pension, "good cooking & tolerable local wine."[3] *Work Suspended*, written several years later, opens with the first-person narrator, an author of detective novels, writing a book in Fez. Judging from the detective writer's routine, Waugh led a quiet, diligent life in Fez, staying at a modest hotel, dining at the British Consulate once a week, and visiting a brothel once a week. Judging from letters to his friends the Lygon sisters, he visited the brothel more frequently.

The book he began in Fez and finished a few months later in England was not only ambitious, but different in kind from his earlier novels. To Katherine Asquith, a lady for whose good opinion he was always anxious, Waugh wrote: "I peg away at the novel which seems to me faultless of its kind. Very difficult to write because for the first time I am trying to deal with normal people instead of eccentrics. Comic English character parts too easy when one gets to be thirty."[4] Perhaps his thirtieth birthday a few months earlier had persuaded him to shelve the broad farce of his first three novels. One of the titles he considered for the novel was *Fourth Decade*, referring to Tony Last's age but perhaps privately to his own as well. He was urged toward change by more than just his thirtieth birthday, however. Writing to Lady Mary Lygon he called *A Handful of Dust* his "good taste book"—only partly in jest. An ambition for respectability, both social and literary, as both a man of the world and a man of letters, seems to have suggested to him the propriety of a more serious, less anarchic vein of fiction. Irony was his staple, but he would make it thematic and structural, rather than merely comic. The texture of *A Handful of Dust* is often crisp and understated, dependent on innuendo and allusiveness, but also includes patches of elaborate writing unknown to the earlier novels (except in parody):

> 'Oh, he's not so bad, your Mr. Beaver,' Marjorie's look seemed to say, 'not by any means,' and he, seeing the two women together, who were both beautiful, though in a manner so different that, although it was apparent that they were sisters, they might have belonged each to a separate race, began to understand what had perplexed him all the week; why, contrary to all habit and principle, he had telegraphed to Brenda asking her to dine. (73–74)

Jamesian passages of this sort are scarcely frequent in *A Handful of Dust*, but that they occur at all suggests Waugh's emerging desire for a form and style more dignified than farce.

Also contributing to the "good taste" of *A Handful of Dust*, perhaps, were prudential considerations. Waugh was well known as a convert to Catholicism, and as such probably wanted to avoid scandal; especially, no doubt, he wanted to avoid such unseemly controversies as *Black Mischief* had provoked with the *Tablet*. Although he had rejected the *Tablet's* condemnation, he could scarcely have wished a recurrence of that annoying and embarrassing episode. *A Handful of Dust* was not intended as a specifically Catholic novel (nor did it, in the event, please the editor of the *Tablet*), but it could scarcely be construed as condoning adultery.

Further, Waugh was not in the right mood for farce. He had grown more militantly Catholic and more disaffected from modern England. Personal grievances and frustrations gnawed him. Despite his assertion that "comic English character parts" were becoming too easy, the case may have been the opposite. He had by no means renounced frivolity, but having come to regard his novels as serious artistic statements, he was not at the moment moved to produce a merely lighthearted entertainment. With *A Handful of Dust* he decided to go on the attack: to expose the savagery of contemporary life.

The structure of *A Handful of Dust* is based on a system of emblematic oppositions, representing savage modernity in conflict with traditional civilized values, moral chaos ranged against moral order. Waugh explained the novel to Henry Yorke: "The scheme was a Gothic man in the hands of savages—first Mrs Beaver etc. then the real ones—finally the silver foxes at Hetton."[5] Most critics discussing *A Handful of Dust* have taken Waugh more or less at his word. Jerome Meckier, for example, writes that "*A Handful of Dust* is best seen as a religio-philosophical satiric novel," with the specific theme being the modern world's futile attempt to substitute a secular "home" for its true spiritual home in New Jerusalem.[6] Another critic, Ann Pasternak Slater, observing that "Waugh's morality is comprehensive and unyielding," asserts that *A Handful of Dust* "is a novel whose meaning, and ultimately therefore its moral judgments, are the impetus to its form," although as to revealing the novel's exact meaning, Waugh "like most artists . . . is unwilling to give the whole game away, while pointing us in the right direction"—as if literature were a treasure hunt for the dubious prize of the author's "moral judgments."[7]

Yet the main force of *A Handful of Dust* does not derive from its moral nuggets or its religio-philosophical insights, and perhaps not even from its undoubtedly savage indignation. Although the novel's satire on modern England is trenchant, *A Handful of Dust* is not so much animated by pure satiric motives as it is haunted by unburied personal wraiths—disillusion, loneliness, despair—that, far from arranging themselves in tidy schematic formulation, wandered restless and discontented and formless through Waugh's imagination.

The genesis of the novel did not at first sight seem particularly well suited to ambitious expansion. Although "The Man Who Liked Dickens" is one of Waugh's few short stories of any merit, its lightness resembles that of most of his other stories.[8] The hero, a certain Paul Henty, is a bland, rather featureless young man, a passive victim. Not Henty himself but his grim predicament is the story's interest. As a hero, Henty notably lacks tragic weight:

> . . . an even-tempered, good-looking young man of fastidious tastes and enviable possessions, unintellectual, but appreciative of fine architecture

and the ballet, well travelled in the more accessible parts of the world, a collector though not a connoisseur, popular among hostesses, revered by his aunts.

His wife's adultery, the cause of his South American excursion, is treated with levity:

> "You are certain that you no longer love me?"
> "*Darling,* you *know* I *adore* you."
> "But are you certain you love this guardsman, Tony whatever-his-name-is, more?"
> "Oh yes, *ever* so much more. Quite a different thing altogether."
> "Very well, then. I do not propose to do anything about a divorce for a year. You shall have time to think it over. I am leaving next week for the Uraricuera."
> "Golly, where's that?"

Mrs. Henty's infidelity is no more than a convenient device for dispatching the hapless Henty to Brazil. But despite the ordinariness of the hero and the recurrently flippant tone of the story, the frightening notion of jungle captivity continued to interest Waugh. "After the short story was written and published," he recalled, "the idea kept working in my mind. I wanted to discover how the prisoner got there."[9] Henty was not really worthy of the finely imagined horror awaiting him in Brazil; a good revenge-play machination ("a 'conceit' in the Webster manner"[10]) had been wasted on a perfect cipher. *A Handful of Dust* originated not in moral earnestness, but in nightmare. Henty's grotesque, apparently lifetime confinement in the jungle, the satanic duplicity of his jailer, the superbly gratuitous torment of endless Dickens—these were potent images pulsing with mythic suggestion. But what exactly did they suggest? To find out, Waugh had to reinvent his hero.

In creating Tony Last, a man cuckolded and abandoned by a trusted wife, Waugh trenched closely on his own past. Older, settled in marriage, a father, Tony Last scarcely resembles the Evelyn Waugh of 1929. Tony is also much wealthier and better established, with a large country estate and an income of more than six thousand pounds a year, against Waugh's earlier hand-to-mouth journalism and two-bedroom flat in Canonbury Square. But though not specifically autobiographical, *A Handful of Dust* has its deepest emotional roots in Waugh's first marriage and its disastrous legacy. Tony Last's shipboard romance with Thérèse de Vitré offers a scarcely concealed parable of the lingering influence of Waugh's marriage. Young and unworldly, Thérèse is returning from a Parisian convent school to her home in Trinidad to marry one or another of the island's few bachelors of her own class; exactly which one hardly matters, for she feels no particular affection for any of them. Though ostensibly resigned to the limited field of candidates, she seems to find Tony an attractive potential alternative. But learning that Tony is already married, she abruptly drops him. This sad romantic interlude is marginally, if at all, relevant to the main action; but though a sentimental digression in the context of the novel, it was pertinent enough to Waugh personally, for it echoes in essentials his involvement with Teresa Jungman, whom at the time he wanted to marry.

The problem of Teresa Jungman, in fact, seems to have contributed not just to this particular episode but to the mood of the entire novel. Sometime in the autumn of 1933, hoping that his marriage would soon be ecclesiastically annulled, Waugh (as he informed Lady Mary Lygon in their private idiom) proposed marriage to Teresa Jungman: "Just heard yesterday that my divorce comes on today so was elated and popped question to Dutch girl and got raspberry. So that is that, eh. Stiff upper lip and dropped cock. Now I must go. How sad, how sad."[11] The bawdy flippancy made a brave show of what must have been a sharp discouragement, for his whole point in seeking a nullity decree had been to enable him to marry Teresa Jungman. His wife's betrayal seemed to gloom over his affairs, darkening not only his past but his prospects as well.

A Handful of Dust does not reproduce the circumstances of Waugh's marriage and its end—in fact, it steers well clear of close parallels; instead, it presents a fable that echoes the emotional rhythms of the experience. Tony Last's rather anachronistic sensibility, his naiveté, his trust in his wife, his bewilderment at her disloyalty—all glance at Waugh himself or, if not at Waugh precisely, at the self-caricature he had created in Adam Doure of "The Balance" and elaborated in Adam Symes of *Vile Bodies*. In 1934 he was not ready to deal with his marriage so directly as he had dealt with, say, his schoolmastering in *Decline and Fall*; but there can be little doubt that Tony Last's blood was drawn from Waugh's own veins.

But at the same time that *A Handful of Dust* probes Waugh's malaise, it also reflects the prosperous surface of his life as he wrote. His ambition to write a novel about "normal people instead of eccentrics" raised the interesting question of whom he thought "normal." As it happens, he meant the leisured upper classes, and *A Handful of Dust* is among other things a detailed study of contemporary West End and country-house culture. On the one hand, this is an asset, for Waugh had observed this culture carefully and studied its intonations and nuances lovingly and scrupulously; on the other hand, this exclusive focus on a narrow slice of aristocratic culture hinted at problems. The novel suggests that he had so thoroughly fashioned himself into a gentleman of the man-about-town variety, cutting himself off imaginatively from everyone else, that the world beyond the small circle in which he moved no longer held much interest for him.

The novel's action alternates between the West End and Hetton, Tony Last's large country house. Waugh's visits to country houses—a prominent part of his life in the early 1930s—made him very familiar with places like Hetton, where the squirearchical routine, the protocol of the weekend visit, and the ritual of the hunt meet are knowingly described. The London scenes reflect the other half of Waugh's life, his usual urban rounds—the St. James club, cocktail parties, luncheons at expensive restaurants, dinners with Mayfair hostesses, supper dances, and—in Tony's and Jock's visits to the Old Hundredth—his occasional dips into low life, especially his patronage of the notorious "43" Club, where a prostitute named Winnie (a name assigned to the daughter of one of *A Handful of Dust*'s tarts) received Waugh's particular attentions. The narrative moves about London with easy confidence, giving a partly sociological, partly satiric portrait of the man-about-town's world, from parvenus like Lady Cockpurse and hangers-on like John Beaver to the paragon of the man about town, Tony's friend Jock Grant-Menzies.

The novel's grounding in this society and even more its self-assured mastery of it advertise a noticeable development from *Black Mischief*'s briefer and more modest visits to Mayfair. In the earlier novel Waugh had, as it were, peeked over Basil Seal's shoulder for a day, rather than attempting a full-length study. *A Handful of Dust* shows that he had now settled comfortably into fashionable society—so comfortably, in fact, that his perspective has changed. The narrative voice maintains a general attitude of detachment from the novel's individual characters, but its social sympathies and proclivities are patent. No longer the curious but outside observer of high society, no longer even an admiring newcomer, Waugh now wrote as a veteran, condescending to look at the populous scene outside his club window as if at a rather alien and only distantly amusing spectacle.

This urbane outlook is most apparent whenever *A Handful of Dust* strays outside polite society. Social inferiors and social incompetents, like children, are treated with benign condescension or aversion. Simple servants like Ben the groom and Nanny the nurse, though admirable in their limited capacities, are patronized for their lack of sophistication. The tarts of the Old Hundredth, with their professional vulgarity, are treated affectionately, like pets. Less affectionate is the unconcealed contempt for Tony's unwelcome acquaintances at Brighton: Dan, Dan's friend, and Dan's girl "Baby" (no doubt a compliment to Teresa "Baby" Jungman). Dealing with children, whom the bachelor Waugh might prudently have avoided (in his fiction, that is), the humor sinks very low:

> "Now you are to go upstairs and say you are sorry to nanny and promise never to use that word about anyone again."
> "All right."
> "And because you have been so naughty to-day you are not to ride to-morrow."
> "To-morrow's Sunday."
> "Well, next day then."
> "But you said 'to-morrow.' It isn't fair to change now."
> "John, don't argue." (40)

Similarly precious conversations occur with Milly the tart's daughter, Winnie. The novel's two children reveal Waugh's comic genius floundering badly. Gone are the expansive and even promiscuous sympathies of *Decline and Fall,* the earlier enthusiasm for eccentric and unconventional character; the only peculiarity of many characters in *A Handful of Dust* is their lack of worldliness and style. The West End characters themselves may be, and indeed generally are, morally deplorable, but they can at least behave properly at a cocktail party. *A Handful of Dust* was not only written from a St. James perspective; it assumes urban worldliness as a rigid standard.

Implicit in *A Handful of Dust*'s focus on fashionable London and country house culture is Waugh's contracting imaginative scope. This might not have been a bad thing, had Waugh been another sort of writer—Jane Austen confined herself to an even narrower world—but Waugh's particular genius fed on diversity and eccentricity. There seems perilously little room for a Grimes or an Agatha Runcible in *A Handful of Dust;* all Waugh's zest for disorder and disorderly character, all his openness to diverse experience, had dwindled into a high regard for convention and decorum. The novel's moral indignation is confused by worldliness.

An instructive example of the reigning social standard is John Beaver, whose primary failing, the novel hints repeatedly, is that he is just not good club material. He is poor and pennypinching, for instance, hating to buy drinks at Brat's:

> ". . . well, I'm going down to lunch. You won't have another?"
> Beaver rose to go.

"Yes, I think I will."

"Oh, all right. Macdougal. Two more, please."

Macdougal said, "Shall I book them to you, sir?"

"Yes, if you will."

Later, at the bar, Jock said, "I made Beaver pay for a drink."

"He can't have liked that."

"He nearly died of it." (22)

Jock is one of the fellows: " 'Hullo, Jock old boy, what are you drinking?' or, more simply, 'Well, old boy?' " Jock is in; Beaver is out: "Six broad backs shut Beaver from the bar" (20). The sympathies of the broad-backed club members are the sympathies of the novel. When Beaver is later nominated for election to Brown's, to which Tony and Jock belong, it confirms Tony's discovery of universal moral chaos; when Beaver is blackballed, the good sense of Brown's members is re-established—there are at least vestiges of justice and decency left in the world, and Brown's is one of the last refuges. Even Mrs. Beaver taunts her son with his unclubbability, reminding him: "Your father was a member" of Brown's (279). Beaver senior was all right, at any rate, even if his son is a worm. Beginning with *A Handful of Dust,* the masculine exclusivity of the London gentlemen's club becomes an important value in Waugh's fiction.

The contrast between Jock's clubbability and Beaver's virtual exclusion from Brat's (and actual exclusion from Brown's) betrays perhaps a slight insecurity in Waugh's own position, or perhaps just self-satisfaction. The jokes at Beaver's expense insist almost too broadly on Waugh's respect for social status. One of the most damning indictments against Beaver, for example, is that he gladly accepts insulting last-minute luncheon invitations, since he is too unpopular to command real invitations. Contemplating such abject want of dignity seems to have afforded Waugh inordinate pleasure; in *Black Mischief* a character named Captain Cruttwell is similarly derided.

Jock Grant-Menzies, on the other hand, can afford to spurn last-minute summonses from desperate hostesses; "I decided when I got up that I'd have oysters here" at the club, he replies cavalierly (21). As the perfect type of the man about town, Jock reveals how strongly the St. James ideal enticed Waugh. A bachelor Member of Parliament, Jock gracefully spans the social spectrum, from clubland to the Old Hundredth; he glides through a succession of casual amours; he travels down to country houses for weekend visits and hunt meets. Money never seems to be a problem, and he enjoys the perquisites and status it confers with self-assurance and good taste. As an accomplished and debonair man of the world, a more elegant and socially acceptable version of Basil Seal, Jock seems in many respects to be what Waugh himself would like to have been. Tony Last, who with marriage and the duties of a squire has long since given up Jock's gay life, keeps up his club memberships and on his rare visits to London easily slips back through the front door of Brat's, but he is in retreat from London and all it represents, while Jock suggests the compelling allure that the man-of-the-world ethos held for Waugh.

If Jock's urbanity and worldliness represent Waugh's social aspirations, Tony Last suggests his continued fondness for the traditional domestic and feudal virtues, though now qualified by a severe judgment on their spiritual inadequacies. Tony is more than simply an elaboration of Paul Henty. In some respects he is even duller; Henty was, at least, well travelled, popular among hostesses, and appreciative of architecture and ballet. Tony can boast none of these advantages. He is old-fashioned, reclusive and, though not humorless, habitually sober and occasionally pompous. Above all, he is obsessively attached to Hetton, his inherited estate. Self-consciously emulating, even burlesquing, a Victorian squire, he is a dinosaur relict of an older, more dignified age, remote from the England of 1934. He lectures his son, for example, on *noblesse oblige:*

> . . . you were using a word which people of your age and class do not use. Poor people use certain expressions which gentlemen do not. You are a gentleman. When you grow up all this house and lots of other things besides will belong to you. You must learn to speak like someone who is going to have these things and to be considerate to people less fortunate than you, particularly women. (40)

Tony believes all this, and so does Waugh, wistfully; but they are both aware that modern England has abandoned such feudal, chivalric ideals. Tony is the last Victorian. Deliberately antiquated, insulating himself at Hetton from the horrors of contemporary life, especially as they are concentrated in places like London, Tony is a refugee from the twentieth century.

Hetton is his sanctuary, not just a place to hide but the very symbol of his withdrawal. Like its fictional antecedents—King's Thursday, Doubting Hall, the British Legation in Azania—Hetton stands apart from the tumult and complexity of the greater world. Like King's Thursday, especially, Hetton's comforts are austere, its domestic conveniences primitive; like Sir Samson Courteney's Legation stockaded against the rest of Azania, Hetton is moated. The County Guide Book calls Hetton "devoid of interest," and even Tony realizes that it is "not in the fashion"; the most that can be said is that it is "amusing"—in a quaint way. It is an architectural version of Tony himself; its battlemented Gothic elevations, moat, lack of modern amenities, and unfashionableness all have their parallels in his character. His bedroom is like an archaeological excavation, exposing shards and fossils from earlier stages of his life:

> He had taken nothing from the room since he had slept there, but every year added to its contents, so that now it formed a gallery representative of every phase of his adolescence—the framed picture of a dreadnought (a coloured supplement from *Chums*), all its guns spouting flame and smoke; a photographic group of his private school; a cabinet called 'the Museum,' filled with the fruits of a dozen desultory hobbies, eggs, butterflies, fossils, coins; his parents, in the leather diptych which had stood by his bed at school; Brenda, eight years ago when he had been trying to get engaged to her; Brenda with John, taken just after the christening; an aquatint of Hetton, as it had stood until his great-grandfather demolished it; some shelves of books, *Bevis, Woodwork at Home, Conjuring for All, The Young Visiters, The Law of Landlord and Tenant, Farewell to Arms.* (30)

Hetton's rooms, named after Arthurian characters—"Yseult, Elaine, Mordred and Merlin, Gawaine and Bedivere, Lancelot, Perceval, Tristram, Galahad, his own dressing room, Morgan le Fay, and Brenda's Guinivere" (28)—and decorated with friezes of Gothic text, represent the romantic medievalism of Tony's imagination.[12] Hetton is Tony, Tony is Hetton.

Tony's Victorian-Gothic freaks, as well as Hetton's, assert a quixotically heroic defiance of contemporary England. While Waugh's fondness for aristocratic style shines through the details of the West End scenes, his sentimental attachment to the old squirearchical values reveals itself in Tony at Hetton. Already, although he had not yet begun to act the role himself, Waugh relished the histrionically anachronistic character, later variants of which appear as the narrators' fathers in *Work Suspended* and *Brideshead Revisited.* Perhaps Waugh's preeminent creation of this type was himself, however, when after the Second World War he deliberately cultivated the role. Being out of touch with the times, or defiant of the times, was beginning, even as early as 1934, to seem an admirable idiosyncrasy.

Nevertheless, although splendidly reactionary, Tony has important failings. In particular, his religion is a bland acquiescence in the Established Church: a part of his feudal duties, the center of his Sunday morning routine, nothing more:

> Tony invariably wore a dark suit on Sundays and a stiff white collar. He went to church, where he sat in a large pitch pine pew, put in by his great

grandfather at the time of rebuilding the house, furnished with very high crimson hassocks and a fireplace, complete with iron grate and a little poker which his father used to rattle when any point in the sermon excited his disapproval. Since his father's day a fire had not been laid there; Tony had it in mind to revive the practice next winter. On Christmas Day and Harvest Thanksgiving Tony read the lessons from the back of the brass eagle.

When service was over he stood for a few minutes at the porch chatting affably with the vicar's sister and the people from the village. Then he returned home by a path across the fields. . . . That was the simple, mildly ceremonious order of his Sunday morning, which had evolved, more or less spontaneously, from the more severe practices of his parents; he adhered to it with great satisfaction. (50–51)

The old vicar's old sermons, written years earlier in India, are full of picturesque but inappropriate imagery; Tony and his fellow parishioners are resigned to their irrelevance, a token of the Established Church's polite inconsequence. Although Tony is a conscientious landlord and squire, a pious and decent gentleman of the old school, a wistful romantic, his virtues are, ultimately, inadequate.

In short, he lacks faith. "It was very painful," he remarks of his interview with the vicar after his son's death: "after all the last thing one wants to talk about at a time like this is religion" (182). Later, when Mr. Todd asks him, "Do you believe in God?" Tony replies weakly: "I suppose so. I've never really thought about it much" (328). At the moment of trial, Tony's faith is weighed—and found wanting. Waugh scarcely allows us to doubt Tony's principal deficiency. He is civilized, but that is all; spiritually he remains unredeemed. Vague piety and tepid conformity to the Established Church are not enough. "Enter not into judgment with Thy servant, O Lord," Tony sings at church on Sunday morning: a plea for Tony himself.

Yet despite the symbolic suggestions of Hetton and Tony—as emblems of older "humanist" values, of decency and *pietas*, though also of spiritual inadequacy—they are imaginatively informed by feelings more profound than Waugh's cultural ideology. Hetton is, above all else, home. Uncomfortable and almost ruinously expensive to maintain, Hetton has by modern standards of convenience little to recommend it. Aesthetically, too, it is deplorable—"the worst possible 1860," Waugh instructed an illustrator—with its sham medievalism and bulky unwieldiness.[13] But its worth is independent of all such incidental considerations. It is protective and stable, with the most ponderous Victorian solidity; it is full of rich associations: "all these things with which he had grown up were a source of constant delight and exultation to Tony; things of tender memory and proud possession" (28). Its exaggerated impracticality and ungainliness merely emphasize its real value; we love home not because it is beautiful, but simply because it is home: ". . . there was not a glazed brick or encaustic tile that was not dear to Tony's heart" (27). Hetton means, to Tony, continuity and family. "We've always lived here," he remarks characteristically, "and I hope John will be able to keep it on after me" (33). Like Christmas at Doubting Hall, Christmas at Hetton is traditional and ceremonious:

> This year, everything happened in its accustomed way; nothing seemed to menace the peace and stability of the house. The choir came up and sang carols in the pitch pine gallery, and later devoured hot punch and sweet biscuits. The vicar preached his usual Christmas sermon. (95)

But while family is welcome at Hetton, hardly anyone else is: "I don't keep up this house to be a hostel for a lot of bores to come and gossip in" (33). Privacy precedes hospitality. At Hetton Tony can shut out the world and lead his own life among those he loves and trusts; at home one is free to be oneself. Hetton owes something to actual country houses Waugh had visited, something to his admiration for the English country house as an institution, something to his interest in domestic architecture—but above all, Hetton springs from the Underhill of Waugh's youth, where his mother had pampered him and where Arthur Waugh had read Dickens aloud in the evenings, under the red-shaded lamp in the book room. Homeless, and with a strong prospect of being always homeless, Waugh created from this personal desideratum a mythic image of home. Tony Last's exile from his home echoes Waugh's own despairing lack of domestic stability or sanctuary. With Hetton, the rural retreats of the early novels reach their culmination.

London, on the other hand, dips to its nadir.

The changing face of London in the early novels is a good index to Waugh's withdrawal from contemporary life. Although the allure of London never died, his feelings about it became increasingly ambivalent during the 1930s, as his pleasure in its social richness was soured by contempt for its pernicious novelties and vulgarities. As a young man Waugh relished the neurotic energy and diversity of the metropolis; but as the years went on, his tastes narrowed to aristocratic London—and aristocratic London, Waugh felt with dread, was under siege. Relicts of an earlier elegance were preserved here and there—in club life, in remnants of eighteenth- and nineteenth-century architecture, in a few refined social circles—but London was for the most part a battleground of traditional England against the modern age, and the modern age was inexorably advancing.

The urbane figure of Jock represents something of the old aristocratic London, with the opportunities and pleasures available to an unattached and wealthy young man; but *A Handful of Dust*'s London is dominated by Mrs. Beaver. Perpetually busy with a fretful rodent voracity, she is gobbling a dish of yoghurt at the beginning, "the carton close under her chin" (13), and still gobbling at the end, busily trying to cash in on Tony's disappearance. Although there is something of Mr. Youkoumian in her entrepreneurial push and unscrupulousness, she is much less amiable. A hard businesswoman, she runs her interior decorating business with scroogelike rapacity, abusing her hired girls, rejoicing at news of a house fire that promises business.

Worse yet are her friends, a horrific clique of idle women including the social-climbing Polly Cockpurse and other characters named Veronica, Daisy, Sybil, and Souki. Their smartness is graced by neither elegance nor dignity. Bored, childless (apparently), purposeless, virtually homeless (excepting in each case the energumen Mrs. Beaver herself), they fill their days with gossip and a never-ending quest for novelty: new restaurants, new "bonesetters," new scandals, new fortunetellers, new lovers. Amused by the prospect of Brenda's "walkout" with John Beaver, these friends encourage her: ". . . with the exception of her sister's, opinion was greatly in favour of Brenda's adventure. The morning telephone buzzed with news of her. . . . The choice of Beaver raised the whole escapade into a realm of poetry for Polly and Daisy and Angela and all the gang of gossips" (91–92). Mrs. Beaver herself actively panders. *A Handful of Dust* reveals a remarkable loathing for these women: the usually romantic, sometimes troubadorish Waugh, whose closest friends and confidantes were almost always women, seems for the moment to verge on something close to misogyny.

Lonely and bored at Hetton, restless for society, Brenda Last sinks into Mrs. Beaver's inferno through her unaccountable infatuation with John Beaver. Her selection of this idle young man is bafflingly capricious; universally regarded as worthless, "second rate and a snob and, I should think, as cold as a fish" (as Brenda herself admits), unclubbable, unemployable—even Beaver seems perplexed by the glamorous Brenda's attentions (82). If his promotion seems enigmatic, however, Brenda's decline from Hetton into his mother's vicious London is, in the symbolic polarity of the novel, plain enough. Brenda's study of economics, the dismal science of getting and spending, implicitly rejects the nobler, more humane values of Hetton, while her flight from Hetton to one of Mrs. Beaver's London flats suggests her desertion of all finer ideals for the siren charms of rootless and amoral modern urban culture.

Mrs. Beaver's flats are an architectural realization of her spirit. By encouraging Brenda's adultery she not only helps out her incompetent son, but also advances her business interests, for one of the most profitable of her sidelines is converting townhouses into flats, campsites for the transient and adulterous, "fit for base love." Decorated in the latest and most execrable fashion, flashy chromium-plated walls in contrast to the elaborate and almost lost artistry of Hetton's molded plasterwork, the flats represent the meretricious displacing the elegant. Designed to facilitate the casual affair, Mrs. Beaver's flats gnaw away at the solid domestic foundation of Hetton. Mrs. Beaver is in the business of breaking up not simply houses, but also homes.

"They're going like hot cakes," she remarks of her flats; "I shall have to look about for another suitable house to split up" (84). The next suitable house turns out to be Hetton. The image of house-wrecking appears at the moment Brenda first kisses Beaver: ". . . an old house . . . was being demolished to make way for a block of flats" (77). Then Mrs. Beaver induces a willing Brenda to take a flat in one of the houses she has already broken up, where Brenda may teach John Beaver how to make love, an educational use of the real estate that Mrs. Beaver encourages. Finally Mrs. Beaver and her friends physically assault Hetton itself, travelling down at Brenda's invitation to assess how best to destroy the morning room, "an appalling room" (Mrs. Beaver), "a bit mouldy" (Polly), "horrible" (Daisy)—"I'd blow the whole thing sky–high" (Veronica) (127–28). Mrs. Beaver's ideas for the room—white chromium plating and natural sheepskin carpet—are predictable; and soon the workmen move in to strip it: ". . . mouldings of fleur-de-lis . . . littered the floor, fragments of tarnished gilding and dusty stencil-work" (146). The shattered decorations of the morning room presage the coming destruction of Tony's Gothic imaginative world, itself an elaborate gilt artifice out of place in the chromium-chic world of Mrs. Beaver. Crumbling plaster on the floor, a handful of dust literally, is all that remains of the morning room after Mrs. Beaver sets to work. Her adulterous clique has ravaged the innocence of Tony; the city of flats rises out of Hetton's ruins.

John Andrew's death precipitates the death of Hetton itself. Like Brenda's infatuation with Beaver, John Andrew's accident seems part of an increasingly irrational, disordered universe: "Everyone agreed that it was nobody's fault"; "No one to blame . . ."; " 'It wasn't anyone's fault,' they said" (166–67). When her son is killed, Brenda is as usual in London with Mrs. Beaver's gang, who are having their fortunes told by a footreader. When Jock breaks the news to her, "Thank God," she says in relief when she realizes that it is only her son who has been killed. The mother has been swallowed up by the adulteress; Tony's harmonious, reasonable world is turned upside down; the decent order of nature itself is subverted.

Tony, however, remains ignorant of Brenda's perfidy. So deeply ingrained are his chivalrous notions and his unreflecting faith in Brenda that, despite her erratic behavior, despite, even, her abrupt departure after John Andrew's funeral, he suspects nothing. The letter announcing her abandonment leaves him incredulous. "He had got into a habit of loving and trusting Brenda," the narrative voice comments ironically, but "love" and "trust" belong to the obsolete values of Hetton, not to Brenda's new circle. Even after her desertion, Tony naively continues to trust Brenda, until she reneges on their informal divorce settlement. This second betrayal—a betrayal of Hetton as much as of Tony—is so flagrant that even he can no longer mistake it. Tony's world collapses into dust, like the morning room.

From this point we follow Tony into the jungle. Leaving Hetton and London behind, except for brief glimpses, the narration descends into an underworld of bewilderment, disillusion, isolation, and fatal insight.

In a reminiscence written after Waugh's death, Harold Acton referred to *A Handful of Dust* as a "prose analogue" of *The Waste Land*, a comparison the novel's title and epigraph openly invite. Eliot had a revolutionary impact on some of Waugh's contemporaries; Cyril Connolly, for example, later wrote of "the veritable brainwashing, the total preoccupation, the drugged and haunted condition" Eliot had induced in him and others.[14] Not quite so dramatically shaken, Waugh nonetheless recognized that *The Waste Land*'s images of disintegration were apt for the experience he was trying to convey in *A Handful of Dust*. "I can connect / Nothing with nothing," Tony Last himself might well say when his world disintegrates, when the broken pieces of his life fall out in nightmare incoherence: *Alice in Wonderland* and *The Waste Land* fused together.

Though Tony's world begins to crack apart early in the novel, not until John Andrew's death does he take any notice. With his son's death, the apparent good order of Tony's life, its conformity to reasonableness and expectation, begins visibly to decay. The choral commentary on John Andrew's accident—"nobody's fault"—applies not just to this particular disaster, but to a universe in which, suddenly, events seem to occur merely by chance, in which accidents are no one's fault because no one is responsible for anything, because there is no system of order to be observed or violated. In Tony's coherent system, things happen by rule; in Mrs. Beaver's world, things happen willy-nilly.

Before John Andrew's accident, the mysteriously prophetic figure of Mrs. Rattery descends on Hetton like a bird of ill omen. A laconic, wandering, homeless woman, she has ostensibly come to keep Jock company; but she has actually come, it transpires, to foretell Tony's fortune at this critical hour. Staying with him after the accident, Mrs. Rattery, like *The Waste Land*'s Madame Sosostris with her Tarot deck, spreads out her cards for a four-deck patience game:

> Mrs. Rattery sat intent over her game, moving little groups of cards adroitly backward and forwards about the table like shuttles across a loom; under her fingers order grew out of chaos; she established sequence and precedence; the symbols before her became coherent, interrelated. (173–74)

Just as in Tony's world, order and meaning seem to prevail—but:

> Mrs. Rattery brooded over her chequer of cards and then drew them towards her into a heap, haphazard once more and without meaning; it had nearly come to a solution that time, but for a six of diamonds out of place, and a stubbornly congested patch at one corner, where nothing could be made to move. "It's a heart-breaking game," she said. (174–75)

The card game is an image of Tony's life: what had seemed orderly turns out to be haphazard, a game of chance in which there is no accounting for the deal: a card out of place and the ordered pattern breaks down. It is no one's fault. Next morning Mrs. Rattery flies off without saying goodbye, on to other patience games and other destinies; she is later reported in California. Tony is left behind with his losing hand, doomed to play out a game he cannot win.

Tony combines characteristics of several earlier Waugh heroes. Although (by Waugh's account) a "normal" person, he bears a family resemblance to the sequestered, benignly eccentric squires in earlier novels, most recently Sir Samson Courteney pottering about the British Legation in Azania, unconcerned with, scarcely aware of, the turbulence beyond the stockade. But with Tony this caricature merges with another character type, the sensitive, unlucky hero, especially *Vile Bodies*' Adam Symes, an unoffending young man buffeted and baffled by the modern age, longing for stability and privacy, a figure with origins in Waugh himself.

The grammar of Tony's imagination is based on Hetton, on images of Arthurian chivalry, on trust in Brenda. With John Andrew's death and Brenda's desertion, the syntax begins to scramble, and when Brenda's treason finally becomes manifest, all the customary rules prove nugatory. The pieces no longer fit together in any meaningful pattern: a jigsaw puzzle scattered on the floor. Spurred by the bizarre, portentously named Dr. Messinger, Tony leaves England, abandoning it to Mrs. Beaver's tribe, and sets off in search of "the City," a lost Incan civilization that in his brooding imagination soon grows into a model of chivalric order and beauty, a more glamorous and more graceful Hetton. But the new City is hidden deep in the jungle.

A Handful of Dust endows Tony's submergence in the jungle with a mythic significance it lacked for Paul Henty in "The Man Who Liked Dickens." No lost city draws Henty; he goes off to Brazil on a whim, to kill time. Tony, however, leaves England not simply for a change of scenery, but in quest of understanding. He does not know it. Imagining that he is looking for a Camelot, he is actually stumbling toward a more profound discovery. But he must first free himself from his customary assumptions and logical expectations. Civilization, apparently so well-ordered and rational, has proved so disordered and irrational that the meaning of his life must be sought in darker, stranger regions. Tony's expedition into the jungle is a descent into the undersea depths of the imagination, where the daylight mind cannot penetrate.

With Tony's introduction to Dr. Messinger and his involvement in Messinger's expedition, the novel's air of everyday plausibility, its concern with "normal" people, begins to slide into fantasy, and, as Tony sails further away from streets and pavements toward the trackless wilderness, his notions of the City grow increasingly fabulous:

> It was Gothic in character, all vanes and pinnacles, gargoyles, battlements, groining and tracery, pavilions and terraces, a transfigured Hetton, pennons and banners floating on the sweet breeze, everything luminous and translucent; a coral citadel crowning a green hill top sown with daisies, among groves and streams; a tapestry landscape filled with heraldic and fabulous animals and symmetrical, disproportionate blossom. (253)

As Tony penetrates deeper, irretrievably deep into the crepuscular forest, the narrative transitions between London and the jungle grow more abrupt and disjointed. By the time Dr. Messinger drowns, the novel has shaken itself free of normal people and conventional responses. "Dr Messinger's hat floated very slowly towards the Amazon and the water closed over his bald head" (308): the macabre humor suggests the changed atmosphere.

If A Handful of Dust acknowledges the influence of The Waste

Land, Dickens seems to loom behind the later chapters even more heavily, as conventional characters give way to eccentrics like Dr. Messinger and Mr. Todd. During his wanderings in 1933, Waugh had fortuitously discovered a cache of Dickens in a remote Jesuit mission in British Guiana and took *Martin Chuzzlewit* along with him when he plunged back into the bush. Perhaps this find, which (Waugh claimed) reintroduced him to the pleasure of reading, fused with the mad Mr. Christie, the inspiration for Mr. Todd, to create the grotesque quality of *A Handful of Dust*'s later chapters. If so, Dickens lent more than just gargoyle ornamentation to *A Handful of Dust;* he helped Waugh break free of the merely plausible and normal, to explore a wider range of imaginative possibilities.

Writing to Waugh about *A Handful of Dust,* Henry Yorke complained that after the credibility of the novel's English scenes, he had been deeply disappointed by the subsequent descent into fantasy:

> Most seriously though I dont think the Demerara trip is real at all, or rather I feel the end is so fantastic that it throws the rest out of proportion. Arent you mixing two things together? The first part of the book is convincing, a real picture of people one has met and may at any moment meet again. . . . But then to let Tony be detained by some madman introduces an entirely fresh note & we are with phantasy with a ph at once. . . . It seemed manufactured & not real.[15]

Apart from a sadly pedestrian notion of the "real," Yorke was of course right. Plodding through the jungle with the queer Dr. Messinger and the superstitious Indians, unknowingly approaching his destiny, the mad Mr. Todd, Tony Last leaves behind Waugh's "normal" people, Yorke's "real" world (the "real" for Tony had proved a meaningless enigma) and begins to probe the region of "phantasy," where truth lies concealed in strange images, inaccessible to the reasoning mind. In the fantastic jungle, mere logic does not apply. " 'From now onwards the map is valueless to us,' said Dr Messinger with relish," as he and Tony sink deeper into the jungle (278); the map suggests our need to reduce the world to manageable form by flattening and simplifying its irregular topography. Figuratively, the map has already proved useless to Tony, and he must now lose himself to find himself. "Time is different in Brazil," he eventually realizes (315); England and Brazil, the two parts of Tony's mind, work on different systems. The logic and chronology of the imagination are unconventional and unpredictable; it throws fragments of experience into new and surprising juxtaposition and combination. The clock and the syllogism are useless baggage in the jungle. Only by sailing away from England and jettisoning his cramped notions of the "real" can Tony piece together the disordered fragments of his life into meaning.

Contracting malaria, he alternates between wakefulness and fevered visions, in which images cross and recross in dreamlike confusion. Delirium dramatizes and heightens the incoherence of his experience:

> In Brazil she wore a ragged cotton gown of the same pattern as Rosa's. It was not unbecoming. Tony watched her for some time before he spoke. "Why are you dressed like that?"
>
> "Don't you like it? I got it from Polly."
>
> "It looks so dirty."
>
> "Well, Polly travels about a lot. You must get up now to go to the County Council meeting."
>
> "But it isn't Wednesday?"
>
> "No, but time is different in Brazil; surely you remember?"
>
> "I can't get as far as Pigstanton. I've got to stay here until Messinger comes back. I'm ill. He told me to be quiet. He's coming this evening."
>
> "But all the County Council are here. The Shameless Blonde brought them in her aeroplane."
>
> Sure enough they were all there. Reggie St. Cloud was chairman. He said, "I strongly object to Milly being on the committee. She is a woman of low repute."
>
> Tony protested. "She has a daughter. She has as much right here as Lady Cockpurse."
>
> "Order," said the Mayor. "I must ask you gentlemen to confine your remarks to the subject under discussion. We have to decide about the widening of the Bayton-Pigstanton road. There have been several complaints that it's impossible for the Green Line buses to turn the corner safely at Hetton Cross."
>
> "Green Line *rats*."
>
> "I said Green Line rats. Mechanical green line rats." (312–13)

These kaleidoscopic fragments alternate incongruously with images of the City until, as Tony stumbles up to Mr. Todd's ranch, the shattered images suddenly come together.

During his own South American wanderings, entertaining splendid visions of a place called Boa Vista, Waugh had been sharply disabused to find—instead of a shining city in the jungle—a bleak backwater. Perhaps this disappointment gave him the idea for Tony's dreadful discovery, deep in the jungle, when the broken pieces of his life finally converge in a moment of fevered illumination:

> I will tell you what I have learned in the forest, where time is different. There is no City. Mrs Beaver has covered it with chromium plating and

converted it into flats. Three guineas a week, each with a separate bathroom. Very suitable for base love. And Polly will be there. She and Mrs Beaver under the fallen battlements . . . (325)

The City and Mrs. Beaver, fused in a single deadly image, make the larger meaning of Tony's experience instantly plain. Yet despite the interest of this revelation, the more immediately relevant revelation is Mr. Todd, a doom of permanent exile.

Tony, in fact, does not even seem to remember his delirious vision of Mrs. Beaver when he recovers from his hallucinations; it evaporates like the bad dream it seemed to be. He looks forward to escaping Mr. Todd's insistent hospitality and daydreams about returning to England. But there is no escape from Mr. Todd; he is the nightmare that waking does not dispel, the destiny that no one can avoid. The slow eternity of a dantesque circle of Dickens becomes grimly clear with the success of Mr. Todd's ingenious plot to delude Tony's would-be rescuers. Critics have often noted the likely derivation of Mr. Todd's name from the German "tod," meaning death.

Back in England, life goes on. Hetton descends to some Last cousins and becomes a fox farm; despite Waugh's apparent disapproval, the change seems to inject some life into the old place. Brenda, with indiscreet alacrity, marries Tony's loyal friend Jock. Mrs. Beaver, too, is flourishing. Tony's absence from all this is only appropriate. Like earlier Waugh heroes, he is a private, domestic, wistfully nostalgic young man unable to attack the world with sufficient gusto and insensitivity. There had been a time when Waugh divided his sympathies between the hapless heroes like Tony and the anarchic world that invariably defeated them. But no longer. The once admirable energy of a Margot Beste-Chetwynde had come to seem merely savage in Mrs. Beaver. Perhaps Tony's endless cycle of Dickens reflects Waugh's own world-weariness: all the inexhaustible fertility of Dickens's fiction, as crowded as life itself, has become simply a long torment.[16]

But while savagery-versus-civilization was the announced theme, *A Handful of Dust*, like *Black Mischief*, probes more deeply than this tidy antithesis would suggest. Tony Last's epitaph, somewhat prematurely composed, reads simply:

ANTHONY LAST OF HETTON
EXPLORER

In *A Handful of Dust* Waugh explored his own disillusion and exile. The novel's most strongly felt themes are at once universal categories and intensely personal grievances—trust betrayed, innocence violated, illusions shattered, exile from home. Even more potently, *A Handful of Dust* depicts a mythic descent into the imaginative underworld, a journey into the nightmare regions that the daytime self half-recalls only in flickering shadows. The jungles of *Black Mischief* and *A Handful of Dust* seemed remote from the diversions of St. James and Madresfield—but they disturbed Waugh's repose and poisoned all his worldly pleasures and successes. Most critics agree in praising *A Handful of Dust* as one of Waugh's finest novels; many would say his finest. Never again did he put so much of his buried life into fiction.

7

Scoop: ". . . Inside the Park Everything Was Sweet and Still"

In July 1934, a few months after finishing *A Handful of Dust,* Waugh abruptly left England to hike across Spitzbergen. He had no particular interest in Spitzbergen and went on a whim, with only two days' notice. Two years earlier he had written:

> Those for whom the attraction of travel is primarily anthropological will always be puzzled at the zeal which again and again has driven men to the hideous privations and dangers of the Arctic Circle. Here there is no lost culture to be discovered; no clues to be picked up that hint at the origins of our own social structure or creeds.[1]

His experience in Spitzbergen confirmed this insight.

Back in England the following month, he turned up as usual on his parents' doorstep: "At 7 Evelyn arrived for dinner, with a moustache," Arthur Waugh recorded of his return. "Told us most exciting accounts of narrow escapes in the Arctic."[2] Despite these exciting accounts, the expedition failed to stimulate Waugh's appetite for the polar regions. "Just back from Spitzbergen which was hell—a fiasco very narrowly retrieved from disaster," he wrote to a friend.[3]

Although no book came out of the Spitzbergen adventure, it is in several respects a revealing episode. His departure from England on such short notice, so capriciously, for almost two months, testifies to his restlessness at the time, his lack of obligations, his lack of occupation. The abrupt decision to go also suggests his recurrent urge to break out of his routine and seek the exotic and extraordinary. He increasingly depended on foreign adventures to provide stimulus and material for his novels. His everyday experience, the life around him in England, interested him less as time went on; or at least it was not proving imaginatively fruitful. Having written *A Handful of Dust,* Waugh seems to have exhausted his existing stores of strongly felt experience—experience that needed fictional expression.

Soon, however, the vagaries of international politics fashioned a situation apparently made to order. In the summer of 1935, Haile Selassie's Abyssinia began to mobilize in anticipation of an Italian invasion and, Waugh later observed, "In the circumstances anyone who had actually spent a few weeks in Abyssinia itself, and had read the dozen or so books which constituted the entire English bibliography of the subject, might claim to be an expert."[4] His own claim to expertise persuaded the *Daily Mail* to send him to Addis Ababa as a special correspondent.

In 1930 Waugh had spent four weeks in Abyssinia, mostly in the capacity of tourist; in 1935 he spent almost four months there as a working journalist. It was a very different experience the second time. Partly the difference was due to the different occasions—a war as opposed to a coronation; partly it was due to Waugh himself. The thirst for novelty with which he approached the coronation five years earlier had vanished. In 1935 he was bored in Abyssinia, frustrated by his inability to find any news or see any fighting, at odds with the *Daily Mail,* exasperated by his press colleagues. Even more intolerable, the war dragged on much longer than Waugh, who had planned on a quick Italian victory, ever intended or desired to stay in Abyssinia.

Worse yet, part of the baggage he carried with him to Abyssinia was political partisanship: he was strongly pro-Italian. Since the Abyssinians were "by any possible standard an inferior race," Waugh imagined Italy—European and Catholic—to have something like a right, if not a duty, to introduce Christian civilization to the benighted country, forcibly if necessary.[5] Counter-Reformation zeal, stimulated by the writing of *Edmund Campion,* the biography he had recently finished, disposed him to regard Abyssinia as an ideal candidate for aggressive missionary activity. Ideologically committed, he was much less tolerant of Abyssinian quirks and anomalies, much less open to the comic aspect of his experience, than he had been in 1930.

One other event strongly influenced *Scoop.* His first marriage having been after long delay annulled by the Church, Waugh became engaged to Laura Herbert in the summer of 1936 and married her the following spring.

In the fall of 1936, just betrothed to Laura Herbert, Waugh needed money to get married, and *Waugh in Abyssinia,* the book he was writing about his experiences as a war correspondent, was unlikely to earn much. His Abyssinian venture had been undertaken to generate not only a war book, however, but also a novel; or at least this soon became his plan. "All this will make a funny novel so it isn't wasted," he had consoled himself during his tribulations in Addis Ababa.[6]

When *Waugh in Abyssinia* was finally out of the way in October, he quickly began writing this funny novel and within two weeks he had sped through a draft of the first two chapters. "It is light & excellent," he assured Peters.[7] As usual, he got off to a fast start and then slowed down; the third chapter was not finished until December. In the meantime he was pleasurably distracted by his attentions to Laura Herbert, his search for a house, a weekend in Belgium, social engagements, the crisis of Edward VIII's abdication—which he followed closely. "If it had not been for Simpson this would have been a very bitter week," he wrote as the climax approached.[8] The "as yet unnamed" novel progressed slowly. By April he had finished only five chapters, and here occurred another interruption, his marriage.

In May, on his honeymoon at the Herberts' villa in Portofino, he resumed work on the novel, "fairly well" the first week, "very badly" the next.[9] By July, back in England, he had grown unhappy about the whole thing. "The novel is to be entirely rewritten. It will be ready in time for publication before Christmas. It will be called SCOOP," he informed Peters's associate Roughead.[10] But in autumn he revised his plans again: "I have stopped work on the novel because I understood that there was no hope of serialization. The book couldn't come out before Christmas so there was no point in hurrying it."[11] Peters must have thought "hurrying" an odd concern, for by now Waugh had been working on this short novel for a year, several months longer already than he had spent on any of his earlier novels. Not fear of deleterious haste, but some combination of competing interests and difficulties with the manuscript evidently account for the novel's dilatory progress. He seems to have been struggling with his material, unsure of its direction, unsure how to set it right.[12]

In late November he revived it without much enthusiasm. Early in the new year it was still limping: "Work on *Scoop* going slowly, with infinite interruptions and distractions."[13] He eventually finished it in February 1938, after sixteen months of intermittent application.

In mood, *Scoop* is closer to *Decline and Fall* than to the more recent novels: light farce after the horrors of *A Handful of Dust* and *Black Mischief*. No macabre twists or bizarre tricks of fate disturb *Scoop*'s serene comic fantasy; from beginning to end it is the mellowest of Waugh's early novels, with an unprecedented absence of serious violence, insanity, or death. Perhaps *A Handful of Dust* helped to exorcise Waugh's demoniacal impulses; more likely *Scoop*'s sunny mood owes much to Laura Waugh. Its tone had been fixed by the auspicious occasion of their engagement. "This light-hearted tale was the fruit of a time of general anxiety and distress but, for its author, one of peculiar personal happiness," Waugh later wrote.[14] Set aside, for the time being, were his anxieties about the decline of European civilization.

The experience of William Boot, the retiring hero, echoes a familiar pattern of the early novels, that of the cloistered innocent thrust willy-nilly into a dangerously chaotic world. Here Waugh was working with a comfortable myth, one reflecting an ineradicable element of his sensibility and present in one way or another in all his early novels. Like the heroes of those other novels, William Boot has partly autobiographical origins.

But *Scoop* actually features two Boots, each of whom suggests a different aspect of Waugh. First on stage is John Courteney Boot—a successful young novelist, traveler, bachelor and man about town, well known to Lady Metroland's fashionable circle. The portrait is a self-parody, Waugh himself in his man-of-the-world aspect. Not only John Boot's general situation but specific details as well emphasize the resemblance. Boot's first book, for example, a biography of Rimbaud, recalls Waugh's debut with *Rossetti,* while Boot's latest book, *Waste of Time,* "a studiously modest description of some harrowing months among the Patagonian Indians," recalls *Ninety-Two Days,* Waugh's modest description of his tedious months in the hinterlands of British Guiana and Brazil; for that matter, *Waste of Time* might have served as a title for *Waugh in Abyssinia.* John Boot is looking to go abroad again, to escape from a pursuing woman; eventually he winds up in Antarctica, an unpromising location reminiscent of Waugh's fiasco in Spitzbergen. This Boot is also an intimate friend of Mrs. Stitch, a facsimile of Waugh's close friend Lady Diana Cooper.

The other Boot, William, knows nobody as stylish as Mrs. Stitch—indeed, he knows no one at all—and has no desire to go abroad; some day he would like to go up in an airplane, but aside from that he wants nothing more than to remain at Boot Magna, his family's country house somewhere near Taunton. Here he potters about and writes a nature column for the *Daily Beast,* a happy employment that allows him to stay home. In background and style, this Boot is by no means so autobiographical as the other Boot; but whereas John Boot represents the bachelor life Waugh had been leading for the previous eight or nine years, William Boot suggests Waugh's inclinations as he wrote *Scoop:* tired of his wandering years (and in particular of Abyssinia), looking for a house in the rural southwest in which to establish himself in relative seclusion. Modern England is headquartered in London, which William Boot hates even to visit—an attitude Waugh himself, once established in Gloucestershire, affected: "Alas, I don't come to London . . . I hate the place," he responded to an invitation in 1938.[15] Just as John Boot caricatures the urban, social Waugh, William Boot recalls Waugh in his newly adopted role of countryman and squire.

Scoop's plot echoes *Decline and Fall*'s: the hero exiled from a peaceful sanctuary and cast into the vortex, only to return finally to his sanctuary, more worldly-wise but no less retiring; and as hero, William Boot is a fictional cousin of *Decline and Fall*'s Paul Pennyfeather. In an excerpt from *Scoop* published in *Town and Country* in November 1937, Boot is made a clergyman, the Reverend William Boot, further suggesting the divinity student Pennyfeather. Both characters sprang from dim chapters in Waugh's life, his descent into schoolmastering and his introduction to competitive international journalism. In both cases he had fallen into an unfamiliar and awkward setting. Boot's bewilderment and incompetence burlesque Waugh's journalistic naiveté among the hardened correspondents in Addis Ababa—schoolgirl innocence in a bordello.

Boot distinguishes himself from the other correspondents not only by his incompetence, but also by falling in love, a tender emotion further associating him with both Paul Pennyfeather and with Waugh himself, whose home thoughts were a serious distraction from his Abyssinian interests. Boot's infatuation with Katchen, the unworldly cosmopolitan, is his first experience of love; unlike Waugh he has previously been "celibate and heart-whole," but perhaps the underwater imagery of Boot's feelings—". . . for the first time he was far from shore, submerged among deep waters, below wind and tide . . ." (173)—drew on Waugh's own emotions, for he had been landbound, as it were, for what must have seemed a long time. "Suffused and inflated and tipsy with love," William sounds much like Waugh writing to Laura Herbert in 1936. Yet Waugh's heroes never really emerge successful in love. The pattern of disappointment and loneliness, recurring in almost every novel up to *Unconditional Surrender,* was too deeply ingrained in Waugh's own patterns of feeling.

On the other hand, though unsuccessful in love, Boot (unlike Waugh) is wildly successful as a correspondent. Whereas Waugh missed the only scoop in Abyssinia, F. W. Rickett's Standard Oil coup, Boot stumbles onto a scoop in Ishmaelia when the other journalists rush out of town on a fool's errand. It was, in fact, Waugh himself who was out of town when, to his surprise and discomfiture, the Rickett story broke in Addis Ababa in 1935. The two journalists who scooped the Rickett story, Sir Percival Phillips of the *Daily Telegraph* and James Mills of the Associated Press, are caricatured in *Scoop* as two "pompous old cads" upstaged by the novice Boot.

Boot's improbable success in Ishmaelia is the happy fantasy at the center of *Scoop*'s light mood: innocence triumphant over worldliness and malevolence, a unique triumph in the early novels.

The English chapters of *Scoop* develop a comic theme quite unrelated to journalists, but more indicative of Waugh's real interests at the time. Just as William Boot's adventures as a special correspondent exaggerate Waugh's, so Boot's flight from the turbulence of Ishmaelia and London to the otiose routine of Boot Magna caricatures Waugh's eagerness to abandon his rootless urban life and settle in the country. *Scoop*, like *A Handful of Dust*, oscillates between country and city, but its benign mood dissolves the moral urgency of Hetton's conflict with Mrs. Beaver's London. *Scoop*'s London comprises some of the worst horrors of contemporary life, but the reproaches are now less indignant, almost resigned. Indeed, *Scoop*'s London is not without its appeal, embodied most notably in the radiant feminine charms of Mrs. Stitch, a tribute specifically to Lady Diana Cooper but also, more generally, to the aristocratic, urbane style that Waugh so deeply admired. But Mrs. Stitch is not typical of *Scoop*'s London; she represents an endangered species of elegance. More characteristic are Lord Copper, the press lord based on Lord Beaverbrook; the vulgar and neurotic headquarters of the *Daily Beast;* the insipid modern hotel in which William stays; the traffic jams that Mrs. Stitch, with magnificent élan, circumvents, or tries to, in her midget car; the "very bad and very expensive" restaurant in which Lord Copper holds his banquet. This is modern England, or at least a representative slice of it.

Houses are still being torn down in London; Mrs. Beaver and her kind are still at work, gnawing away: "East wind swept the street, carrying with it the exhaust gas of a hundred motors and coarse particles of Regency stucco from a once decent Nash façade that was being demolished across the way" (9). The housewrecking here, however, does not symbolize adultery and domestic disruption, but refers quite literally to the destruction of London's eighteenth- and nineteenth-century architecture, about which Waugh had recently written several admonitory, despairing articles. "Twenty years ago," he wrote in early 1937, for example, "we had the finest streets and squares in Europe. Where are they now? It is too painful to chronicle the destruction; ruthlessly, year by year, street by street, house after house of irreplaceable excellence has been destroyed."[16] The lament sprang from more than just sorrow for the ravaged houses. Mourning the London of his youth, Waugh saw the city's architectural decay as a visible emblem of the high civilized style crudely undermined by the twentieth century. Yet though the city he had loved was changing, Waugh was changing too. In *Decline and Fall*, a decade earlier, London had been green and vernal, Berkeley Square in April, sunshine and plovers' eggs at the Ritz. How blithe, too, had been the satire on architectural preservation in *Decline and Fall*, when the old King's Thursday was wantonly demolished. Now the crumbling houses crushed Waugh's spirits: "It is a subject for grief and resentment too bitter for temperate expression," he lamented, concluding with advice to foreign tourists coming for the coronation of George VI: "If our overseas visitors are wise they will turn their backs on London as soon as the last scrap of ermine has moved out of sight round the corner and set out to look for England a hundred miles away."[17] This, as it happened, was just where Waugh had purchased his own little piece of England, Piers Court in Gloucestershire.

Boot Magna also reposes at a far remove from the London of Copper House and concrete apartment flats. It parodies country house life at its most backward and isolated—"not pure fantasy," Waugh asserted twenty-five years later, but at least exaggerated and indeed rather like P. G. Wodehouse (whom Waugh certainly had in mind). But Boot Magna—provincial, anachronistic, eccentric—is also recognizably the latest of the early novels' rural sanctuaries. Shabby but comfortable, ritualistic and traditional, both communal and individualistic, Boot Magna has perfected the art of decent leisure; life there flows slowly, placidly, privately, among family, according to each one's own lights:

> In course of time each member of the Boot family had evolved an individual style of eating; before each plate was ranged a little store of seasonings and delicacies, all marked with their owner's initials—onion salt, Bombay duck, gherkins, garlic vinegar, Dijon mustard, pea-nut butter, icing sugar, varieties of biscuit from Bath and Tunbridge Wells, Parmesan cheese, and a dozen other jars and bottles and tins mingled incongruously with the heavy, Georgian silver; Uncle Theodore had a little spirit lamp and chafing dish with which he concocted a sauce. The dishes as sent in from the kitchen were rather the elementary materials of dinner, than the dinner itself. (287)

The benign eccentricities of the dinner table epitomize Boot Magna's character; Uncle Theodore's sauce is the sauce that flavors life.

Boot Magna is nevertheless not the sort of place in which one can imagine Waugh himself long flourishing; he would have greatly preferred elegant dining in London to the idiosyncratic cuisine of the Boots. Boot Magna's value has less to do with its practical advantages than with its spiritual opposition to London. The antithesis of city and country is embodied particularly in two contrasting figures, the countryman William Boot and the irredeemably urban Mr. Salter of the *Daily Beast,* both mild, domestic, private men, neither of whom relishes the fury of modern journalism in Lord Copper's employ:

> "Is there *nothing* you want?"
> "D'you know, I don't believe there is. Except to keep my job in *Lush Places* and go on living at home."
> It was a familiar cry; during his fifteen years of service with the Megalopolitan Company Mr Salter had heard it upon the lips of countless distressed colleagues; upon his own. . . . His heart bled for William but he was true to the austere traditions of his service. (41–42)

Despite similar natures, however, Boot and Salter inhabit radically different spheres, and during the course of the novel they exchange, like the country mouse and the city mouse, frightful visits to each other's home ground. First Boot is summoned to London to interview Salter:

> It was always a solemn thing for a Boot to go to London; solemn as a funeral for William on this afternoon. Once or twice on the way to the station, once or twice as the train stopped on the route to Paddington, William was tempted to give up the expedition in despair. Why should he commit himself to this abominable city merely to be railed at and, for all he knew of Lord Copper's temperament, physically assaulted? . . .
>
> . . . It was always the way; the moment he left the confines of Boot Magna he found himself in a foreign and hostile world. There was a train back at ten o'clock that night. Wild horses would not keep him from it. (27–28)

Boot's visit to London turns out even worse than he expected, propelling him directly and unwillingly to Africa. Balancing his metropolitan adventure, however, is Salter's intimidating excursion to Boot Magna at the end of the novel. Salter is a product of the modern suburban experience:

> He had been born in West Kensington and educated at a large London day-school. When not engaged in one or other capacity in the vast Megalopolitan organization he led a life of blameless domesticity in Welwyn Garden City. . . . Normal life, as he saw it, consisted in regular journeys by electric train, monthly cheques, communal amusements and a cosy horizon of slates and chimneys. (31–32)

His train ride to Somerset parallels Boot's train ride to London:

> ... at Taunton, he had left the express, and changed into a train such as
> he did not know existed outside the imagination of his Balkan correspon-
> dents; a single tram-like, one-class coach, which had pottered about in
> desultory fashion through a system of narrow, under-populated val-
> leys. ... there had been very old, unhygienic men and women, such as
> you never saw in the Underground, who ought long ago to have been put
> away in some public institution; there had been women carrying a multi-
> tude of atrocious little baskets and parcels which they piled on the seats;
> one of them had put a hamper containing a live turkey under Mr Salter's
> feet. It had been a horrible journey. (273)

And from this point Salter's visit to the country grows worse.

Although it would be difficult to demonstrate the debt, perhaps Salter's journey into the West Country owed something to Waugh's experiences as a newcomer to rural Gloucestershire. What seems more certain, however, is that during his months of househunting and then during his early months at Piers Court—that is, as he slowly wrote and rewrote *Scoop*—he was frequently reminded of the gulf between the rural England where he sought refuge and the metropolis he was fleeing. In theory and to some extent in fact London repre-sented almost everything he deplored in contemporary English culture, but it had been his home base ever since childhood and remained his natural habitat. His 1937 article in *Nash's*, for example, advising foreign visitors to eschew London, nonetheless included urbane advice about London restaurants, too:

> Sovrani's move to Knightsbridge is also a move in the right direction.
> There is no reason why all our eating should be done in one square half-
> mile. I believe there will be a good chance of prosperity for someone who
> will open a first-rate restaurant in the Victoria region between Chelsea and
> Westminster.[18]

"First-rate" restaurants were nothing he needed to worry about in Stinchcombe, near Dursley, Gloucestershire, but he knew a great deal more about fashionable dining than he did about Laura's cows. Out-side of visits to country houses and an intermittent yen for the quiet life, there was little of the countryman in Waugh. He could easily satirize the odious modern London encountered by Boot; but Salter's harrowing sortie into rural Somerset was closer to Waugh's own experience. He was not altogether at home among hedgerows and yokels.

The sharp oppositions between Boot Magna and London—not the

adventures in Ishmaelia or the satire on journalists—reveal the tendencies of Waugh's imaginative energies as he wrote *Scoop*. The novel catches him at a moment of transition, abandoning his man-about-town life, deserting the city—the once beautiful, now corrupt mistress—and contentedly settling down in the country. *Scoop* is the product not simply of a retreat from London but of marriage, of establishing a home and family, of adopting a wholly new way of life. Like *A Handful of Dust*'s Hetton, Boot Magna is an image of home, but home as a place to be celebrated and enjoyed rather than lost and mourned.

Ostensibly, however, *Scoop* is not about country and city, but *A Novel about Journalists,* according to the subtitle in early editions. In this respect, it caricatures Waugh's experience as a war correspondent in 1935. William Boot's outfitting in London, his journey to Africa, the train to Jacksonburg, the hotel, the Pension Dressler, the Excelsior Movie-Sound News company, the cabling jargon and haphazard system of message distribution, the *ad hoc* press association and its unruly polyglot meetings, Corker's souvenirs, the journalists' expedition to Laku, the stuck lorry—the originals of all these elements and others appear in *Waugh in Abyssinia,* sometimes nearly word for word. But though the correspondents in Abyssinia excited his contempt and occasionally his wrath, *Scoop*'s satire on the journalists is generally good-humored. Time and distance, perhaps, had softened much of the animus pervading *Waugh in Abyssinia.*

Scoop also includes a vein of political satire. Although Ishmaelia is in Africa, its ideological divisions are plainly indebted to the Spanish Civil War. But *Scoop*'s political satire is neutralized and trivialized, with fascists and communists both routed by a merely venal, non-ideological regime. Characters named Mr. Baldwin and Dr. Benito seem to insinuate political allegory into the novel, but the idea is hardly pursued consistently enough to demonstrate that Waugh had any real political argument in mind. The political references were primarily a topical joke. Fascism and communism dominated international politics (as Waugh wrote, the civil war in Spain was agitating political enthusiasts of all creeds) and vexed the nation's domestic tranquillity, but Waugh's chief interests were now domestic in a narrower sense.

Although a product of happy times for Waugh personally, however, *Scoop* was far from a spontaneous effusion of good feeling; it had cost him more than usual pains to write. He usually revised carefully—revision was the only part of writing that he professed to enjoy—but the manuscript of *Scoop* reveals more working over than that of any earlier novel. His diaries and correspondence confirm his difficulties. In his diaries, for example, he noted at a relatively early point that the novel had "good material but shaky structure."[19] Five months later he decided that it had to be rewritten, and several months later yet, still stuck, he put it aside. Only on the third try, evidently, did he finally manage to hammer it into shape.

Yet despite *Scoop*'s protracted gestation, few would propose it as one of Waugh's more distinguished offspring, and critical commentary on *Scoop* is slight and tepid. Robert Murray Davis, for example, a strong admirer of Waugh, claims only that *Scoop* is "good farce," "lighthearted farce in which Waugh made unexpected technical advances" (though most readers "probably noticed nothing new in *Scoop*"), conceding that Waugh's "aesthetic and thematic resolutions in *Scoop* were unstable."[20] Jeffrey Heath, more than an admirer, admits that *Scoop* is "an unprecedentedly serene book," evidently lacking in much, though not all, of the moral severity he detects in the earlier novels; Waugh's "imagination does not seem to have been fully engaged with his subject."[21]

One critic who does greatly admire *Scoop*, D. Paul Farr, praises the novel's civilized style, based, he believes, on the conversational style of pre-1914 Oxford, informal but classically educated and allusive, a style that exposes by contrast the vulgarity of *Scoop*'s journalists and their language. By way of demonstration, Farr cites, among other things, *Scoop*'s "informal (but rarely colloquial), specific and humorous" diction; its use of colloquialism, cliché, and uncommon words for special purposes, like undercutting; its "judicious use of figurative language"; its preponderance of single-clause sentences; its judicious use of periodic sentences and anticlimax; its *double-entendres* and puns; its use of *deus ex machina;* its use of speech for characterization.[22] An impressive catalog of rhetorical resources—but here are two similar passages to consider:

> She was a large shabby woman of unbounded energy. When William confronted her she was scolding a group of native peasants from the dining-room steps. The meaning of her words was hidden from William; from the peasants also, for she spoke Ishmaelite, and bad Ishmaelite at that, while they knew only a tribal patois; but the tone was unmistakable. The peasants did not mind. This was a daily occurrence. Always at dawn they appeared outside Frau Dressler's dining-room and exposed their wares—red peppers, green vegetables, eggs, poultry, and fresh local cheese. Every hour or so Frau Dressler asked them their prices and told them to be off. Always at half-past eleven, when it was time for her to

begin cooking the mid-day dinner, she made her purchases at the price which all parties had long ago decided would be the just one.

She was a housewife of formidable efficiency. Daily from dawn until noon a miniature market was held on the steps of the dining-room. Half a dozen native hawkers squatted patiently, displaying meat, eggs and vegetables. Every half-hour she or Mr. Heft would emerge, disparage the goods, ask the price, and, in simulated rage, tell the salesmen to be off. Eventually, when it was time to start cooking luncheon, she made her purchases.

The second passage appears to be an admirable condensation of the first: Waugh the craftsman carefully honing down the edge of his prose to razor sharpness. But in fact the second version is the earlier, from *Waugh in Abyssinia*. Lifting the paragraph for *Scoop*, Waugh doubled its length but scarcely doubled its interest—indeed, despite the padding the later version adds almost nothing of value to the paragraph, while sacrificing the conciseness and understatement of Waugh's most effective comic writing. The two paragraphs epitomize the writing of *Scoop:* a great deal of working and reworking of the material—but the inspiration lacking.

Scoop's setting also suggests a lack of enthusiasm for the material. Although indebted in many ways to Abyssinia, *Scoop*'s Ishmaelia little resembles *Black Mischief*'s Azania, which had bubbled with semicivilized and savage energy. Ishmaelia, to the contrary, is not only sedate but bland. Instead of the enthusiastic (eventually mad) Seth, the placid Jackson clan governs Ishmaelia with a pedestrian polity of nepotism, corruption, and tropical inertia. The American-dominated republic of Liberia (which Waugh had never visited) seems to have been partly if not mostly the model. Nothing like the turbulent confluence of cultures in Azania animates Ishmaelia. At the British Legation, in place of the dotty Sir Samson and the "swift, gay" Prudence, a dreary diplomat named Bannister follows local affairs all too closely and accurately. And while Azania lurches into anarchy, Ishmaelia's revolution dwindles into a minor, quickly pacified disturbance, only briefly rippling Jacksonburg's tranquillity.

Such contrasts appear to owe less to the needs of the plot than to the differences between Waugh's excursions to Abyssinia in 1930 and in 1935. On his first visit he had found Addis Ababa alive with confusion and conflict. Five years later, though "little changed in character and appearance," it inspired only dull loathing. The change was largely in Waugh himself. In 1930 he had been unattached, hungry for experience, in love with anarchy; and coronation week provided a rich diet of stimulus. When he arrived in 1935, Addis

Ababa was just as anarchic, but the novelty was gone, nor was he so receptive or so impressionable. He was, in truth, a little jaded, and he had (as he admitted) left half of himself in England. The half of him in Abyssinia was bored and disgruntled, and his ambiguous admiration for the Abyssinians had hardened into contempt. His frustrating experience in Addis Ababa proved almost equally frustrating when he tried to exploit it fictionally. Ordinarily Waugh's fiction thrived on difficult experiences, but Abyssinia presented a new sort of difficulty: indifference. He was simply not very interested in his material.

With *Scoop*, in fact, he was for the first time writing a novel about an experience that had not really possessed his imagination. Plot and theme offer evidence to the same effect. The satire on journalists sprang from a merely temporary annoyance. Waugh later explained:

> This novel is a light satire on modern journalism, not a schoolboy's adventure story of plot, counterplot, capture and escape. Such incidents as provoke this misconception are extraneous to the main theme which is to expose the pretensions of foreign correspondents, popularized in countless novels, plays, autobiographies and films, to be heroes, statesmen and diplomats.[23]

The debunking of foreign correspondents is amusing and effective, perhaps a worthy public service, but Waugh's interest in foreign correspondents was brief and superficial; beyond his few irksome months in Abyssinia, they simply did not matter to him. The novel's plot, with its "extraneous" adventure incidents, also suggests perfunctory involvement in his own story. Well-made, carefully constructed, stocked with mystery characters and machinations, it is more elaborate than any of his earlier plots, several of which had been entirely improvisational; but the attention he devoted to the plot and structure of *Scoop* seems less a result of extraordinary ambition than a necessary substitute for the novel's lack of strong autobiographical impetus. Rather than drawing strength from personal experience, Waugh merely fashioned the Ishmaelian revolution as a makeshift scaffolding for the satiric theme.

It may seem churlish to emphasize *Scoop*'s shallow imaginative roots. It is perhaps the happiest of Waugh's novels; though it is more specifically satiric than most, the satire is generally stingless. Indeed, the novel's mellowness and gentleness are in striking contrast to the violence and death—often gruesome—of the earlier novels. Even the most caddish of *Scoop*'s journalists escapes unscathed, while the wicked Dr. Benito and his associates simply disappear. Except for a weak-minded bumpkin casually reported to be "gravely" injured when a truck overturns, the most serious injury is inflicted by a goat butting one of Dr. Benito's gestapo. Even here, the goat is actuated less by malice than by springtime high spirits, and the victim's pride is more seriously wounded than his person.

Scoop is remarkable, too, for its charitable distribution of justice. Waugh's earlier novels had underscored the gross and capricious inequities of fortune: sympathetic figures invariably abused, cads seldom chastised. William Boot is the first of Waugh's heroes to emerge perceptibly better off than he began; for, though he ends where he started, he has become considerably richer along the way. And very much unlike *A Handful of Dust,* which had ended with a nightmare fantasy of lonely captivity, *Scoop* ends with a sanguine fantasy of universal prosperity, "a calm and vinous optimism" (306). Even Lord Copper, in his way, shares in this cheerful conclusion, with a future "full to surfeit of things which no sane man seriously coveted" (306). *Scoop's* last pages welcome the future. Waugh had emerged, rejuvenated and hopeful, from his dark passage between marriages. He had given up on the larger world, but he thought that marriage and rural privacy would restore order to his universe.

The favorite refrain of Boot's Uncle Theodore is "Change and decay in all around I see," a parody, perhaps intentional, of Waugh's own outlook. *Scoop* is a honeymoon novel, a vacation from troubles and ambitions. Personal optimism bulked larger, for the time, than the encircling chaos—"falling towers" in every direction.

But *Scoop's* relative serenity accompanies its relative lack of intensity. It did not spring from real troubles in Waugh's life, from the kind of disturbance that stimulated his most memorable fictions. He was too contented. The 1935–36 Abyssinian journeys were mere digressions from the main concerns of his life. He had strong opinions about the Abyssinian matter, but little solid interest; his correspondence and *Waugh in Abyssinia* testify abundantly to his apathy. So he seized on an almost adventitious element of the experience, one that lent itself handily to satire—the journalists. His earlier novels had sprung from much deeper imaginative sources.

"What is it, Mr. Harsanyi?" asks a character in Willa Cather's *Song of the Lark,* marveling at Harsanyi's pupil, the singer Thea Kronborg. "You know all about her. What's her secret?"

"Her secret?" answers Harsanyi. "It is every artist's secret . . . passion. That is all. It is an open secret, and perfectly safe. Like heroism, it is inimitable in cheap materials." *Scoop* lacks passion, the pressure of deeply felt experience.

Just a few weeks after *Scoop* was published, Waugh read a manuscript sent along by an aspiring novelist and returned it with some advice:

> My real criticism is that the book owes its origin to an impulse to write *a* book, not this particular book. Your imagination was not so obsessed by your subject that it had to find literary expression. And that is the only way—at least while you are learning the trade—that a good book can result.[24]

Surely Waugh was thinking here of *Scoop* itself, a good book, the labor of a professional craftsman, but not the product of an obsessed imagination. Next time, he would try something different.

8

The War and *Brideshead Revisited:* "I Do Not Want Any More Experiences"

Happily married, pottering about the garden of Piers Court, to all appearances a contented squire, Waugh had by 1938 settled into country life. Not since his childhood at Underhill had he known such a stable and ordered home life. It may have been a little too stable and ordered. With *Scoop* finished, he had no major writing project in hand, and when rainy weather thwarted his landscaping projects he had few other diversions. Nor did the role of country gentleman promise to generate much fictional material of the sort he had found in London and abroad. Soon growing restless at Piers Court, he began to look for opportunities to travel, and in July he sailed for Mexico, hired by "a very rich chap" to write a book about the confiscation of foreign-owned oil properties by the Mexican government.

It was an unusual, even bizarre subject for Waugh, but that alone does not account for the dismal results of the trip. More damaging, as he himself seems to have realized, was the swamp of ideological controversy he waded into. Mexico, he wrote with despair in *Robbery under Law: The Mexican Object-Lesson*, "is waste land, part of a dead or, at any rate, a dying planet. Politics, everywhere destructive, have here dried up the place, frozen it, cracked it and powdered it to dust" (3). His own involvement in the ideological controversies swirling about Mexico had similar results for himself. Absorbed in political questions, he was unable to interest himself in the actual Mexico around him: a place he had never been, a large and diverse country, a totally different culture from his own. There should have been something there, besides politics, to engage his attention, but he failed to find it. He does not even seem to have been looking very hard. Instead, *Robbery under Law* is polemical in content, rancorous in tone—by much the dreariest of his travel books.

The experience and the book together spoke ominously of Waugh's state of mind on the eve of the Second World War. A few months before his arrival, Graham Greene too had travelled to Mexico. Although loathing it fully as much as Waugh, he produced from his visit first a fine travel book, *The Lawless Roads,* and then one of his finest novels, *The Power and the Glory.* Waugh, on the other hand, managed to go to Mexico, spend more than a month looking about, and yet see almost nothing really to interest him. In earlier years he had been stimulated by much less, but Mexico elicited only vexation and disgust. Such a morose response—such deadness of perception and imaginative torpor—augured badly for his fiction.

As the Second World War approached, Waugh began writing a novel, recording in his diary in late July 1939: "I have rewritten the first chapter of the novel about six times and at last got it into tolerable shape."[1] He wrote in the mornings, sitting in the library opposite a portrait of George III, and gardened in the afternoon. Despite this agreeable routine, the novel was still "going very slowly" three weeks later.[2] In September, several weeks after war had been declared, he wrote to A. D. Peters's associate William Roughead: "Re novel. About 15,000 words were done & jolly well done before the war. Its fate depends on mine. If no one wants my patriotic services at once I think I may retire to the Faro islands & finish it."[3] He did in fact retire to Chagford for several weeks, but, eventually obtaining a commission with the Royal Marines, he reported for duty in the first week of December, leaving his unfinished manuscript with Peters. "Here is the first ¼ of the novel. Whether it is ever finished depends on the leisure I get in the Marines."[4] But the Marines kept him busy, and as the weeks passed the novel grew cold. Before long he gave up on it.

"So far as it went," he wrote of *Work Suspended,* "this was my best writing."[5] It was different, at any rate. With *Work Suspended* he threw out the old formula and started all over again. Perhaps this was why he had to rewrite the first chapter six times: he was beginning not his sixth novel, but his first—of a new kind.

Although sharp, the break with his earlier fiction was not without warning. Various of his ideas and opinions had been creeping into his novels, but comic fantasy did not really lend his thoughts the dignified context he felt they deserved. This was a problem of decorum. Artistic ambition also urged him to change. Believing with some justification that he had mastered comic fiction, he felt he needed to progress to more challenging forms; and he seems to have imagined, especially, that a more elaborately stylized prose, more conventional characters and standards of plausibility, and a first-person narrator would produce the effect he sought. The anarchic, farcical imp of the early fiction was to be kept suppressed: this was to be literature, not mere entertainment.

Such a development had been incubating at least five years earlier, when he congratulated himself on *A Handful of Dust*'s "normal people," English comic characters having become too easy. Two years after that, visiting Jerusalem, he had thought about taking up historical fiction:

> I was of an age then—thirty-two—when, after I had struck lucky with three or four light novels, it did not seem entirely absurd, at any rate to myself, to look about for a suitable "life's work"; (one learns later that life itself is work enough). So elated was I about the beauties about me that I there and then began vaguely planning a series of books—semi-historic, semi-poetic fiction, I did not quite know what—about the long, intricate, intimate relations between England and the Holy Places.[6]

Although he later wrote a semihistorical book, *Helena,* on this theme, the concept never fully materialized; but his dismissal of the "three or four light novels" with which he had "struck lucky" suggests that in ambitious moments, as early as 1935, he thought his early novels trifles, his "life's work" not yet begun. Like Graham Greene, he seems to have begun dividing his fiction into two categories: "entertainments" and "novels." *A Handful of Dust* might almost have qualified as a novel, in this system, but none of the other early farces was more than an entertainment. Waugh intended to erect more imposing literary monuments, and *Work Suspended* would be the first of them. Readers expecting another *Scoop* would find themselves very much surprised.

As far as it goes, *Work Suspended* concerns a character named John Plant, talking mostly about himself. By profession, Plant is a writer of detective novels. His story begins in Fez, where he is writing one of these; but learning of his father's death in England and coincidentally embarrassed by an incident involving a prostitute and the police, he returns to London to sell his father's house and find one for himself in the country. In London he meets the man who killed his father, Atwater, and the new wife, Lucy, of an old friend, Roger. Although Lucy is pregnant, Plant becomes infatuated with her. *Work Suspended* breaks off inconclusively shortly after she gives birth to a son.

No blueprint of the rest survives, but, however one wishes to fill in the later chapters, it is evident from the opening paragraphs that Waugh was striking out in a new direction. In several almost explicitly autobiographical passages he seems to discuss his motives. Plant is a thirty-three-year-old bachelor (Waugh's age at the time of his second marriage) and "a serious writer" of detective novels, of which he has written seven:

> I had a naturally ingenious and constructive mind and the taste for writing. I was youthfully zealous of good fame. There seemed few ways, of which a writer need not be ashamed, by which he could make a decent living. To produce something, saleable in large quantities to the public, which had absolutely nothing of myself in it; to sell something for which the kind of people I liked and respected would have a use; that was what I sought, and detective stories fulfilled the purpose. They were an art which admitted of classical canons of technique and taste. Their writing was painful—though much less painful than any other form would have been—because I have the unhappy combination of being both lazy and fastidious. (5)

Like Waugh, Plant does his serious writing outside London, "away from telephones and parties and things" (5–6). Although parsimonious and somewhat ascetic—unlike Waugh—Plant the writer is otherwise quite like Waugh as he saw himself in 1939: a serious craftsman who had mastered a respectable but narrow kind of popular fiction. Having decided that he has done all he can with detective novels, Plant is feeling restless about his writing. Like Waugh with *Scoop*, he is bogged down with his current novel, *Murder at Mountrichard Castle*, explaining to his publisher: "I have been writing for over eight years . . . and am nearing a climacteric." He feels himself "in danger of turning into a stock best-seller." He also feels "in danger of becoming purely a technical expert. . . . of becoming mechanical, turning out year after year the kind of book I know I can write well. I feel I have got as good as I ever can be at this particular sort of writing. I need new worlds to conquer" (42–43). Though intended half-facetiously, this last remark glances at Waugh's ambitions in *Work Suspended*. Plant tells his publisher that he wants to make "just some new technical experiments. I don't suppose the average reader will notice them at all" (44). But if Plant intends his next novel to differ from his earlier novels as sharply as *Work Suspended* differs from *Scoop*, this too is ironical, or at least disingenuous.

One learns no more about Plant's experiments in fiction, but the nature of Waugh's innovations is plain. The narration of *Work Suspended*, for example, is leisurely, discursive, confessional, sporadically ornamental. The narrative voice of the earlier novels had, ordinarily, been ironically unobtrusive; in *Work Suspended* it is conspicuous: loquacious, sometimes effusive, enamored of amplitude and tropes:

> For the civilised man there are none of those swift transitions of joy and pain which possess the savage; words form slowly like pus about his hurts; there are no clean wounds for him; first a numbness, then a long festering, then a scar ever ready to reopen. Not until they have assumed the livery of the defence can his emotions pass through the lines; sometimes they come massed in a wooden horse, sometimes as single spies, but there is always a Fifth Column among the garrison ready to receive them. Sabotage behind the lines, a blind raised and lowered at a lighted window, a wire cut, a bolt loosened, a file disordered—that is how the civilised man is undone. (41)

Although more elaborate and confused than most of the fragment's metaphorical flourishes, this progress from pus-filled sores to Trojan horses, Fifth Columns, and disordered files, all in the space of two sentences—this remarkable and disheartening sequence of images illustrates very well the stylistic ambition of *Work Suspended*. Discussing his books, Plant justifies and applauds literary embellishment:

> I despised a purely functional novel as I despised contemporary architecture; the girders and struts of the plot require adornment and concealment; I relish the masked buttresses, false domes, superfluous columns, all the subterfuges of literary architecture and the plaster and gilt of its decoration. (2)

The taste for baroque, the architectural analogy, the contempt for functionalist styles—all suggest that here, as often, Plant speaks for Waugh, issuing a manifesto in justification of *Work Suspended* itself.

Martin Stannard, remarking that *Work Suspended* exhibits a "more conventional and committed prose style than that of the five early novels," states (accurately, I believe) that "even when allowance is made for the narrating persona, Waugh appears to be laying his literary soul open in an entirely new fashion."[7] For Stannard, the fragment is "an innovation, a fictional approach which allowed controlled sentimentality and sensuous description." He sees *Work Suspended*'s new style as the product of artistic ambition and greater emotional complexity. My own guess is that the elaborate, self-revelatory style is more a product of declining imaginative energies. In *Work Suspended*, I believe, Waugh misunderstood his own gifts. Concreteness, conciseness, understatement, exact diction, vernacular vigor—these were his strengths. Luxurious prose enfeebled him, or perhaps the reverse: his prose may have swelled to compensate for a flagging of imaginative power. Among other things, *Work Suspended* represents a failure in self-criticism.

If the rhetorical texture suggests a radical change in technique—or at least an "experiment"—the innovation (for Waugh) of first-person narration confirms that something odd is afoot. The early novels had usually adhered to the artifice of an impersonal, aloof narrator, seldom commenting directly on the action. John Plant, on the other hand, not only is involved in the action but also liberally interjects his opinions, prejudices, and sentiments. His discursiveness and his confessional impulse, or habit, are striking departures from Waugh's earlier fiction. For the first time, the narration focuses not on action—characters encountering and conflicting with other characters—but on the narrator himself; the teller overwhelms the tale.

Although similar to Waugh in several specifics, especially to the bachelor Waugh of a few years earlier, Plant is no more (and perhaps less) autobiographical in detail than several earlier Waugh heroes. The temptation of first-person narration for Waugh, however, was to make the narrator a puppet voice, and this was a temptation he could not resist, or did not try to, in *Work Suspended*. Plant's ideas and opinions are almost invariably Waugh's. Satirizing the architectural decline of London, for example, or the vogue of Marxism among English writers, Plant *is* Waugh. But Plant borrows more than just his politics and aesthetics; he also borrows a complete set of attitudes. Unlike, say, the diffident, naive Paul Pennyfeather or the wistfully Victorian Tony Last, Plant is the worldly and prosperous author Waugh had become in the 1930s: the clubman and man of the world, very conscious of his superior status, narrow in his tastes, patronizing, knowing, somewhat cynical. He is very free with information about himself; only a year or two earlier Waugh had frowned at the "elaborately over-self-explanatory personality of Mr. Auden," but Auden could hardly surpass John Plant in garrulous self-revelation.[8] Plant has opinions about everything and is glad to share them. To live is to change, and Waugh's heroes ought not to have remained static, but the metamorphosis of Adam Symes, the wistful and unknown young novelist, into the worldly and prosperous novelist John Plant does not suggest a happy development.

Plant's character is well illustrated by his attitude toward Arthur Atwater, the down-at-heels hosiery salesman who in a fit of ill temper has driven over Plant's father. Moody—alternately jaunty and morose—vulgar in deportment and language, raffish, Atwater descends from Captain Grimes and anticipates the Hooper of *Brideshead Revisited*. Like them, he is not a gentleman. He does not, for example, belong to a good club; his club, the Wimpole, is not just unfashionable but disreputable. Neither Plant nor a cab driver asked to go there has ever heard of it, and Plant seems to feel himself on rather a daring lark when he allows himself to be taken to the Wimpole—like Tony Last and Jock sampling low life at the Old Hundredth. It is, Plant thinks, "a new and glorious idea" for a slumming expedition. The Wimpole is vulgar:

> The room into which he led me was entirely empty. It was at once bar, lounge and dining-room, but mostly bar, for which a kind of film-set had been erected, built far into the room, with oak rafters, a thatched roof, a wrought iron lantern and an inn-sign painted in mock heraldry with quartered bottles and tankards. (142)

This was certainly not the decor of the St. James' Club. The members of the Wimpole are, like Atwater, shiftless and unsavory; many prefer, like Atwater, to go by a pseudonym:

> "By the way, I may as well explain, I'm known as Norton at the club."
> "Why?"
> "Lots of the chaps there use a different name. I expect it's the same at your club."
> "I shouldn't be surprised," I said. (141)

Often the members are unable to come up with their subscription: "Most of the chaps one time or another have been shown the door. I expect it's the same at your club. No disgrace attached" (137–38). The joke turns here, rather ponderously, on the social superiority of Plant's club. Plant's smirks at the Wimpole discredit Atwater and the Wimpole less, however, than they expose Plant's own very conventional standards. People who speak like Atwater and belong to "free and easy" clubs like the Wimpole are not quite the sort of people he generally chooses to associate with. Atwater's value to Plant is that he allows Plant to feel gratifyingly superior. "You're paying me for my entertainment value. You think I'm a kind of monkey," Atwater accuses Plant as they watch the apes at the zoo, and Plant concedes the accuracy of this charge (140). While Atwater distresses Plant's finer sensibilities, he also flatters Plant's self-esteem.

Plant's bland complacency betrays the narrowing of Waugh's sympathies over the preceding decade. A few years earlier Atwater would have been more than a zoo curiosity; he might have been portrayed with the sympathy accorded Grimes and Agatha Runcible and Youkoumian. If Grimes were to emerge from the mists of Egdon Heath to join a London club, it would more likely be the Wimpole than the St. James'. Grimes and Atwater are kindred scapegraces: neither can hold a job; both are dishonest—indeed, criminally inclined; both are "good scouts" and good drinking companions. There had been a time when Waugh was glad to go drinking with Grimes, but that time had passed. All of Atwater's Grimesian potential is squashed by Plant's oppressive respectability. Ten years earlier, Waugh's imagination had ranged across the spectrum, delighting especially in the raffish, but Atwater was a weed outside the little garden Waugh was now content to cultivate.

To criticize a book on the evidence of only two chapters may be unjust; the end might have redeemed the beginning. The fragment contains suggestions of riddle and allegory, but the complete scheme and eventual purposes remain a matter for conjecture. What exists is largely a character study of John Plant, incomplete, but adequate to yield an insight into Waugh in 1939. Weary of the world's diversity and disorder, he hoped to substitute in their place, for fictional purposes, a combination of ornate prose, "technical experiments" in narration, a voluble first-person narrator, and perhaps other devices not fully apparent in the novel's fragmentary state. But all this was poor compensation for the vitality and imaginative expansiveness that were missing.

The truncation of this novel-to-be may have been just as well, not only because it terminated Plant but also because the Second World War, reviving Waugh's listless interest in life, gave him much better material. When the war was imminent, he considered his prospects:

> My inclinations are all to join the army as a private. Laura is better placed than most wives, and if I could let the house for the duration very well placed financially. I have to consider thirty years of novel-writing ahead of me. Nothing would be more likely than work in a government office to finish me as a writer; nothing more likely to stimulate me than a complete change of habit.[9]

By 1939 he had spent his fictional capital and badly needed an infusion. Although he eventually tired of the war and the army, in the meantime they generously replenished his reserves. It is hard to see what he could have written about for the next twenty-five years had the war not interposed to rescue him from himself.

Although during the summer of 1939 he had tried to disregard the war's approach, once he found military employment he entered into the spirit of it fully: rejuvenated; happily freed from domestic routine, workaday concerns, and the necessity of having to write; cheered by the camaraderie and old-fashioned customs of the Marines, by the promise of adventure, and even by the physical exertion of training, so very different from his sedentary life at Piers Court. His patriotism and chivalry were stirred by the almost palpable evil of

Hitler's Germany and Stalin's Soviet Union in shameless collabora-
tion. As the war began, Waugh felt much like Guy Crouchback in
Men at Arms: "The enemy at last was plain in view, huge and hateful,
all disguise cast off. It was the Modern Age in arms. Whatever the
outcome there was a place for him in that battle" (5). When in the
spring of 1940 the German army swept through Holland and
Belgium, conquered France, and left England isolated and
beleaguered, the war took on an added heroic dimension: England
stood alone in defense of European civilization, holding the pass
against the barbarians. The Battle of Britain ensued; German invasion
seemed imminent; it was Britain's "finest hour."

At the end of 1940 he transferred from the Marines to the Special
Services Brigade, popularly known as the Commandos, an elite force
"originally intended to supply raiding parties, primarily against the
occupied coast of France."[10] They "had a gaiety and independence
which I thought would prove valuable in action," he later wrote.[11]
Finding himself among friends, enjoying the loose discipline and
special privileges of the Commandos, and content with the prospect
of hazardous operations, Waugh was happy: "The whole thing was a
delightful holiday from the Royal Marines."[12] In February 1941 he
sailed with his Commando battalion for the Mediterranean; in April
took part in an unsuccessful night raid on Bardia, on the coast of
German-occupied Libya; and at the end of May landed in Crete with
his Commando unit to reinforce British troops retreating before a
German assault. Narrowly escaping capture, he returned safely to
Egypt after a dangerous and exhausting week that was, as it turned
out, his most strenuous combat experience in the war. During a
circuitous voyage back to England by way of South Africa, the West
Indies, and Iceland, enjoying "comfort and leisure and negligible
duties, a large cabin with a table and a pile of army stationery," and
with the prospect of returning home—during this seven-week cruise
he wrote *Put Out More Flags.*[13]

One of the most quickly written of his novels and "the only book I
have written purely for pleasure," *Put Out More Flags* distills the first
two years of the war into comedy.[14] Though light, picaresque, and
unambitious, it is in its modest way successful. *Put Out More Flags*
reverts to an earlier spirit and to an earlier hero. In 1930 the ferment
of Haile Selassie's Abyssinia had given birth to Basil Seal; now the
spectacle of England mobilizing for war prompted his renaissance.
Put Out More Flags follows Basil's exploits through the dislocations
and confusion of the early months of the war, up to the summer of
1940. As in Azania, he prospers with brazen self-assertion, and when
Basil is on stage *Put Out More Flags* is farcical and satiric, Waugh
plainly enjoying his hero's wayward, indeed criminal, career. The

Second World War had resuscitated the comic imp that had seemed so very moribund in *Work Suspended*. Much to Waugh's delight, there was trouble everywhere, and everything was a-muddle.

Basil Seal dominates but does not monopolize. Displaying a revived interest in character, *Put Out More Flags* offers sympathetic studies of several other quite disparate figures: Angela Lyne, Basil's superbly elegant and unhappy mistress; Alastair Trumpington, last seen in *Black Mischief* as a decayed Bright Young Person; Ambrose Silk, an aesthete of Waugh's generation at Oxford, now washed up on a barren strand of young left-wing dilettantes. Waugh was encountering the world with reawakened alertness and sympathy; the first two years of the war had been an imaginative tonic.

Put Out More Flags is, finally, a sketch not only of England bumbling into war, but of England deciding to win the war. In the national danger, the lost generation of the 1920s finds a chance to redeem itself. Alastair Trumpington, for example, enlists in the ranks, then volunteers for the Commandos, and at some point in the war (beyond the end of the novel) is killed, his widow Sonia later explaining:

> "You see he'd never done anything for the country and though we were always broke we had lots of money really and lots of fun. I believe he thought that perhaps if we hadn't had so much fun perhaps there wouldn't have been any war. Though how he could blame himself for Hitler I never quite saw. . . . At least I do now in a way," she added. "He went into the ranks as a kind of penance or whatever it's called that religious people are always supposed to do." (125)

Peter Pastmaster, another alumnus of *Decline and Fall* and another of the idle rich, marries to beget an heir and also enlists in the Commandos. Even Basil Seal, after several months of disruptive private adventuring "when there wasn't any real war," is ready to do his bit after Dunkirk; he too joins the Commandos, explaining: "There's only one serious occupation for a chap now, that's killing Germans. I have an idea I shall rather enjoy it" (255). This general turn to duty in the hour of crisis, even among the least public-spirited, reflects something of Waugh's own spirit in 1940. The perennially deluded old fool Sir Joseph Mainwaring unexpectedly stumbles onto the meaning of England's peril: "The war has entered into a new and more glorious phase" (246). In dedicating the novel to Randolph Churchill, Waugh noted that it dealt with "the survivors of the world we both knew ten years ago," the Bright Young People, during "that odd, dead period before the Churchillian renaissance." And the novel's final lines echo the theme of national rebirth, again in the words of Sir Joseph:

"There's a new spirit abroad," he said. "I see it on every side."
And, poor booby, he was bang right. (256)

Characteristically, Waugh's favorite period of the war was a time of immense trouble for England.

It has, however, been argued by one critic, Claire Hopley, that the novel's exuberance actually masks an antiwar theme: ". . . much of the exhilaration that *Put Out More Flags* generates is destructive, fostered in the reader because the story the book has to tell is that war lays waste to good and hopeful possibilities."[15] Hopley detects this theme primarily in what one character, Angela Lyne, does not say: ". . . as Basil says, 'She doesn't like the war.' This is an understatement of her feelings and, because they are not otherwise verbalized, the reader experiences them as complete organic antipathy." That war is destructive can hardly be denied, but it seems hazardous to infer from Angela's silence on the subject that Waugh himself thought "that war is unspeakable." In 1939, a few days before the war began, he had written in his diary of a papal plea for peace: "The Pope's appeal was in terms so general and trite that it passes unnoticed here, where no one doubts that peace is preferable to war."[16] In the abstract, Waugh recognized the advantages of peace, but *Put Out More Flags* does not seem seriously concerned with such pacific sentiments. His personal experiences of the war had been imaginatively reviving. Indeed, although Hopley argues that Waugh deplored the war because, among other things, it destroyed aesthetic creativity, *Put Out More Flags* itself is evidence that the dislocations and even the destructiveness of the war had greatly helped to reawaken his own creative powers.

Two epigraphs preface the novel, both lifted—perhaps a result of eclectic reading at sea—from Chinese sages. Together they suggest *Put Out More Flags'* fusion of Waugh's old comic and new martial spirits. The first quotation, supplying the title, alludes to the war's farcical aspect: "A man getting drunk at a farewell party should strike a musical tone, in order to strengthen his spirit . . . and a drunk military man should order gallons and put out more flags in order to increase his military splendour." But the second quotation asserts that this bacchic spirit must now give way to heroic endeavor: "A little injustice in the heart can be drowned by wine; but a great injustice in the world can be drowned only by the sword." Even Basil Seal, heretofore a rebel, feels inclined for the first time to enlist in the national cause. And so too Waugh. The spring of 1940 wakened his sleeping patriotism; *this* war was a challenge, a serious and rather exciting one. There was trouble everywhere; the times were dangerous and invigorating. Sated with two years of rural quiet, Waugh rejoiced in the hurly-burly. He was greatly enjoying the war, and *Put Out More Flags* shows it.

Even as he wrote *Put Out More Flags*, however, his martial gusto was waning. Waugh's war essentially repeated the pattern of his early novels; *Put Out More Flags* is the *Decline and Fall* of his military career, while *Brideshead Revisited*, written in 1944, shows Waugh as weary with the war as *Work Suspended* had shown him weary with peace five years earlier. The war recharged his imaginative energies—but not for long.

The charms of the army inevitably staled. For someone of Waugh's restless temperament and self-indulgent habits, the routine, regulations, discipline, and stops-and-starts of military life could only grow irksome with long acquaintance. When his Commando unit disbanded after the fall of Crete and he was reposted to the Marines, the reunion was markedly less delightful than the honeymoon two years earlier. He was not to see combat again, nor even to get overseas again until the last year of the war, and even then, though nearly killed in a plane crash, not in a strictly military capacity. The nature of modern warfare—mechanistic, high-explosive, and bureaucratic—must have helped to dampen his ardor. Discussing *Men at Arms*, the first volume of his later war trilogy, Waugh explained that it "was a kind of uncelebration, a history of Guy Crouchback's disillusion with the army. Guy has old fashioned ideas of honour and illusions of chivalry; we see these being used up and destroyed by his encounters with the realities of army life."[17] What perverted the crusade absolutely was the Soviet Union's entry into the war in June 1941, just after the disgrace (as Waugh considered it) of Crete. Instead of the lone champion of civilization, courageously resisting the evils of the modern age, Britain became ingloriously allied with one of the chief of those evils, the darling of the left-wing ideologues Waugh despised—Stalin's murderous police state. In Waugh's eyes, this unholy alliance vitiated the very purpose of the war.

On top of these discouragements, Waugh's personal military unfitness landed him in difficulties. In 1942 he rejoined the Commandos and spent the next year "soldiering among friends" once more; but as an officer he suffered the grave disability of alienating both inferiors and superiors. In March 1943 his brigade commander, a candid friend, informed him that he was "so unpopular as to be unemployable," prompting Waugh to observe: "My future very uncertain."[18] It was actually more certain than he knew, for he had already been written out of the Commandos' plans. When his unit embarked for the Mediterranean three months later, Waugh was left behind, and the following month he was forced to resign from the Commandos "for the Brigade's good," having been informed that "I had done nothing but discredit to the Brigade since I had joined it."[19] This humiliating ejection, just as his former comrades were about to see action, effectively removed him from the war for the next year. The tide of the war had now shifted, too, and Waugh, who had soldiered loyally in adversity, now languished unwanted in prosperity. He felt greatly misused, though he had mostly himself to blame.

Even before his disgrace, however, his diaries show him sliding into a devitalizing boredom. By March 1943 not only his waking hours but even his dreams had grown tedious:

> A night disturbed by a sort of nightmare that is becoming more frequent with me and I am inclined to believe is peculiar to myself. Dreams of unendurable boredom—of reading page after page of dullness, of being told endless, pointless jokes, of sitting through cinema films devoid of interest.[20]

It was as if he had been visited by Tony Last's fate in the Brazilian jungle. In August, after being dropped from the Commandos, he consoled himself with reveries about Art:

> I have got so bored with everything military that I can no longer remember the simplest details. I dislike the Army. I want to get to work again. I do not want any more experiences in life. I have quite enough bottled and carefully laid in the cellar, some still ripening, most ready for drinking, a little beginning to lose its body. I wrote to Frank very early in the war to say that its chief use would be to cure artists of the illusion that they were men of action. It has worked its cure with me. I have succeeded, too, in dissociating myself very largely with the rest of the world. I am not impatient of its manifest follies and don't want to influence opinions or events, or expose humbug or anything of that kind. I don't want to be of service to anyone or anything. I simply want to do my work as an artist.[21]

A few weeks later he wrote to Laura that he was "fighting the Giant Boredom as best I can."[22] He was back where he had been in the summer of 1939, although now his oppressive ennui was aggravated by meaningless military assignments and he could no longer console himself by pitchforking the compost heap. He had been soldiering for four years, with little visible success; he felt himself a virtual prisoner of the army until, sometime in the indefinite future, the war ended.

Disillusioned, embittered by failure, savaged by boredom, he decided to write a novel. Early in 1944, citing his general inaptitude for military service, he requested a three-month leave of absence, noting in his diary: "After hanging on in London alone (Laura down with mumps) leading a more and more limited life in the vicious spiral of boredom and lassitude, I decided to escape . . ."[23] Thus, like Achilles, he dropped out of the war, though the Allied cause did not suffer perceptibly from his absence.

Feeling "full of literary power," he retreated to the civilian quiet of Chagford to begin writing *Brideshead Revisited*. Although periodically recalled to duty for brief spells, most of which he spent at the bar of White's Club, he made steady progress on the novel, the excellence of which he never doubted. "It is *very* good," he informed Peters soon after beginning, and later he congratulated himself in his diary: "English writers, at forty, either set about prophesying or acquiring a style. Thank God I think I am beginning to acquire a style."[24] Such overripe self-satisfaction was an ominous clue to what he was about. On D-day he "wrote a fine passage of Lord Marchmain's death agonies," and two days later he finished the epilogue.[25] Soon after, the mysterious quirks of war carried him to Yugoslavia where, a presentation edition of *Brideshead Revisited* having been printed and sent off to his friends, he eagerly awaited news of its reception. "Do please keep your ear to the ground & report what they say," he directed Nancy Mitford. "For the first time since 1928, I am eager about a book."[26]

Not all his friends admired the novel so unreservedly as Waugh did—Nancy Mitford herself had reservations—but he remained convinced that it was a masterpiece. "It seems to be a success and I think it should be," he wrote to his now-widowed mother. "I believe it will go on being read for many years."[27] It marked, he thought, the beginning of his career as a serious novelist: "I think perhaps it is the first of my novels rather than the last," he confided in his diary, and to Laura he referred to "this book which I regard as my first important one."[28] But whether his first important novel was also a good one remains a vexed critical question.

Brideshead Revisited has been the most written about and most critically controversial of Waugh's novels. Reactions to it range between extremes of admiration and abhorrence. Ultimately, one's opinion of the novel will reflect what aspects (if any) of Waugh's fiction one values. As is probably clear from the preceding chapters, I value Waugh's early novels for their glad embrace of the world's vitality, diversity, and disorder; their sympathy with the unconventional and eccentric; their liberating comic gusto; their imaginative conversion of personal troubles, impulses, and tensions into contemporary fables with ironic texture and recurrent mythic patterns.

By these standards, *Brideshead Revisited,* despite its ambition and splendor, is seriously wanting.

Born of resentment and desperate boredom, the novel begins with a prologue reproducing more or less exactly Waugh's own bleak mood in 1944. "I am not I," he asserted in a brief, mannered "Author's Note," but the "I" of the story, Charles Ryder, often resembles Waugh all too closely in both circumstance and temperament. A painter by occupation, Ryder is about Waugh's age and like Waugh a captain in the army. After a honeymoon with the army in the early years of the war, Ryder has come to loathe it and to feel himself mightily ill-used. He has lost all interest in his own duties and in the war generally. He hates, in fact, not just the army, represented by his dull-witted commanding officer, but modern England itself, represented by the proletarian subaltern Hooper. Feeling himself surrounded and beset by incompetence, pettiness, nastiness, and vulgarity, Ryder describes his melancholy state with such convincing pathos that he very much seems not merely a chip off the old block Waugh, but the old block itself.

Sunk in despondency, Ryder is stirred to reminiscence by the mention of Brideshead, poignant memories of which momentarily divert him from the hated army and the accursed war. "My theme is memory, that winged host that soared about me one grey morning of war-time," he later explains. For Ryder, the past offers an escape from the present; for Waugh *Brideshead* itself was an escape, not only into the past but also into golden, timeless fantasies. Whatever else *Brideshead* might be—a triumph of style, a moral allegory, an enduring literary classic—it served most immediately as a simple imaginative vacation from his midwar, midwinter gloom, "a beaker full of the warm South"—lush tropical prose, honey-sweet nostalgia, romantic passion, tragic pathos, and a delicious quaff of the high civilized style of the Catholic, aristocratic Marchmains and their splendid, secluded baroque palace.

The early chapters are awash in nostalgia. Ryder's reminiscences immediately transport him back to a lost Arcadia—Oxford in the early 1920s, the Oxford of Waugh's and Ryder's youth. With the mention of Brideshead, Ryder instantly recalls "a cloudless day in June, when the ditches were white with fools' parsley and meadowsweet and the air heavy with all the scents of summer; it was a day of peculiar splendour, such as our climate affords once or twice in the year, when leaf and flower and bird and sun-lit stone and shadow seem all to proclaim the glory of God" (20). Oxford is, figuratively, the June of Ryder's life. Under the liberating influence of the beautiful, charming, and doomed young aristocrat Sebastian Flyte, he breaks out of the cocoon of a wintry childhood and emerges a butterfly, sipping nectar. For a few splendid months, life is supremely good. *Brideshead Revisited* excels in its re-creation of Oxford, that enchanted place of discovery and great expectations in Waugh's own life. The early chapters spill over with wondrous novelties: the great house Brideshead itself; the baroque; Venice—"I was drowning in honey, stingless" (90); wine—"Ought we to be drunk *every* night?" (75); and love. These chapters are also the richest in characters: Anthony Blanche, the stuttering exquisite; Ryder's father, the graciously malicious recluse; Mr. Samgrass, the society don; Lord Brideshead, the lay Jesuit; Sebastian, the aristocratic Peter Pan. Waugh himself was living once again, in his fiction, and the fiction itself came alive.

But by 1944, the early summer of Ryder's life has long since vanished. Oxford itself has vanished, in fact, "submerged now and obliterated, irrecoverable as Lyonnesse, so quickly have the waters come flooding in" (20)—the floodwaters of the modern age, that is; but in mourning Oxford, Ryder mourns his own youth as well. Filled with regret for time past, deeply elegiac, the early chapters are suffused with a Wordsworthian intimation that growing up inexorably alienates one from the lifegiving source. Sebastian, unable or unwilling to abandon childhood, retains his irresponsibility and his teddy bear; Ryder becomes an adult and finds the experience deadening. "Here at the age of thirty-nine," he remarks in the prologue, "I began to be old" (9), a remark well describing Waugh's 1944 condition, except that he had just turned forty. *Brideshead Revisited* betrays Waugh sinking into a premature old age from which, despite occasional stirrings, he never perfectly recovered. As the novel progresses from Oxford to the Second World War, Charles Ryder changes from an undergraduate into his own hibernal father.

Nostalgia for youth dominates the early chapters, but the novel is also heavy with wartime nostalgia for sumptuary pleasures. Waugh's hunger for luxury is poignantly expressed in frequent, sometimes rhapsodic accounts of delicacies—plovers' eggs, sweet Turkish cigarettes, lobster newburg, fresh strawberries, *caneton à la presse,* cognac, and, above all, wine:

> I rejoiced in the Burgundy. How can I describe it? The Pathetic Fallacy resounds in all our praise of wine. For centuries every language has been strained to define its beauty, and has produced only wild conceits or the stock epithets of the trade. This Burgundy seemed to me, then, serene and triumphant, a reminder that the world was an older and better place than Rex knew, that mankind in its long passion had learned another wisdom than his. (155)

Wine is the symbol and sacrament of the world's good things, of which Rex Mottram is ignorant and of which Ryder is unfairly deprived by the war. Even Waugh later had reservations about *Brideshead*'s epicurean lust, writing to Graham Greene, for example, in 1950: "Talking of re-reading, I re-read *Brideshead* and was appalled. I can find many excuses—that it was the product Consule Bracken of spam, Nissen huts, black-out—but it wont do for peacetime."[29] And later he told an interviewer:

> It is very much a child of its time. Had it not been written when it was, at a very bad time in the war when there was nothing to eat, it would have been a different book. The fact that it is rich in evocative description—in gluttonous writing—is a direct result of the privations and austerity of the times.[30]

The diaries give a slightly less harrowing impression of Waugh's privations; certainly as he wrote *Brideshead* he was seldom without wine, once having some of his private stock of claret fetched from Piers Court; noting later, during Lent, that he "drank a great deal of good wine which is getting scarcer daily but still procurable by those who take the trouble"; treating his old Oxford friends John Sutro and Harold Acton to "a fine dinner—gulls' eggs, consommé, partridge, haddock on toast, Perrier Jouet '28, nearly a bottle a head, liqueur brandy, Partaga cigars—an unusual feast for these times"; another time drinking "champagne at £5 a bottle" at White's.[31] Indeed, when in London during the winter and spring of 1944, as he often was, he seems seldom to have been quite sober.

But wistfulness for youth and thirst for wine are only prologue. If the first half of *Brideshead* shows Waugh fleeing from a threadbare present into a richer past, the second part introduces the even more seductive fancy of erotic passion. *Et in Arcadia Ego* traces Ryder's youthful love for Sebastian Flyte from its beginning to its decay, as Sebastian, dipsomaniac and oppressed by his mother, drifts off to Morocco. "Friend of my youth, you are dead!" Ryder might well have echoed John Betjeman's lament, and as Sebastian dies to Ryder, Ryder dies too, in spirit. A decade of "dry empty years" follows, until Ryder meets Sebastian again—resurrected in the form of his sister Julia. Immediately falling in love with her, Ryder resumes his love for Sebastian; but this is a more adult version of that earlier love. His love for Sebastian had been naughty but schoolboyish; his love for Julia is erotic and, indeed, adulterous. Sebastian had only a teddy bear, but Julia is a woman with a husband (and Ryder has a wife, for that matter). Passion and sin are adult complications of which the undergraduate Ryder had been essentially innocent.

Waugh had seldom treated love very seriously in his fiction, but now he resolved to treat it very seriously indeed. "To write of someone loved, of oneself loving, above all of oneself being loved—how can these things be done with propriety? How can they be done at all?" John Plant had asked rhetorically in *Work Suspended* (81). Ryder writes of such things in passages such as this:

> "A hundred days wasted out of two years and a bit . . . not a day when you were not in my heart; not a day's coldness or mistrust or disappointment."
> "Never that."
> We fell silent; only the birds spoke in a multitude of small, clear voices in the lime-trees; only the waters spoke among their carved stones. (244)

Tender feeling by the fountain drains into a swamp of banality. Scenes like this one, or that of Ryder and Julia making love in the storm—Ryder "made free of her narrow loins" while "the waves still broke and thundered on the prow" (228–29)—reveal a startlingly unguarded sentimentality. The absence of irony, of detachment, of any critical self-awareness in the romance business of the novel testifies to Waugh's complete, debilitating absorption in his own self-mesmerizing inventions.

What did he find so compelling in the affair of Julia and Charles? Was it inspired by his own courtship and marriage, allowing him to relive the happy peacetime years with Laura? Perhaps, but the circumstantial resemblances are few, and Julia, in particular—married, sophisticated, glamorous, "experienced," guilt-ridden—seems very unlike the shy and virginal young Laura Herbert. Indeed, Julia suggests rather a succubus born of wartime celibacy, and the bathos of Ryder's and Julia's romance, somewhat like the vivid epicurean passages, may be largely a produce of womanless Nissen huts.

But even more revealing of Waugh's mood than the strictly amorous passages is Julia's and Charles's mood of beleaguered isolation. They meet on board ship, "orphans in the storm," and each finds in the other a perfect antidote to their respective disappointments: Julia's childless and loveless marriage to the crass politician Rex Mottram, Ryder's equally loveless marriage and his awareness of artistic failure. Except for the occasionally bothersome matter of religion, Ryder and Julia are perfect soulmates, both refugees from a hostile and ugly world. "Oh, my darling, why is it that love makes me hate the world? It's supposed to have quite the opposite effect. I feel as though all mankind, and God, too, were in a conspiracy against us," says Ryder (speaking somewhat out of character for a strident agnostic). Julia agrees, "They are, they are"; and Ryder continues: "But we've got our happiness in spite of them; here and now, we've taken possession of it. They can't hurt us, can they?" (242). Cloistered at Brideshead, Ryder and Julia can ignore "them," just as Waugh did in writing *Brideshead Revisited,* abstracting himself in a lush fantasy of immured and self-sufficient love.

Of all *Brideshead Revisited*'s consoling fancies, however, the most lavish and most alluring is the high aristocratic setting. The great house Brideshead and the noble Marchmain family lend the novel the distinctively opulent and glamorous flavor accounting for much of its embarrassing popular success (especially in the egalitarian United States). Nothing betrays *Brideshead*'s fairy-tale wishfulness so plainly as its daydreams of aristocratic life. "I reserve the right to deal with the kind of people I know best," Waugh asserted rather grandly in 1946, referring to *Brideshead Revisited;* but families like the March-mains were not really the people he knew best—they represented the style he most admired.[32] Not everyone was certain that such people even existed. Lady Pansy Lamb, for instance, an aristocrat who ought to have known, told Waugh that

> . . . all the richness of your invention, the magical embroideries you fling around your characters cannot make me nostalgic about the world I knew in the 1920s. And yet it was the same world as you describe, or at any rate impinged on it. I was a debutante in 1922, & though neither smart nor rich went to three dances in historic houses, Norfolk House, Dorchester House, Grosvenor House & may have seen Julia Flyte. Yet, even in retrospect it all seems very dull. . . . Nobody was brilliant, beautiful, rich & owner of a wonderful home though some were one or the other. . . . You see English Society of the 20s as something baroque and magnificent on its last legs. . . . I fled from it because it seemed prosperous, bourgeois and practical and I believe it still is.[33]

Katherine Asquith, another aristocrat, thought (in Waugh's words) "that the characters did not exist either in real life or faery."[34]

Faery is just where they did exist, however—a private faery of Waugh's own happy imagining. He endowed the Marchmains with everything he thought most fascinating and admirable: nobility, antiquity, wealth, charm, elegance, and Roman Catholicism. They live in a beautiful baroque palace in an enchanted valley. They accept the perquisites of their station and wealth with inimitable *sprezzatura;* they practice their Catholicism and speak its language by second nature. For Waugh, born an outsider to both aristocracy and Catholicism, this confident mastery of aristocratic, Catholic style, this "unbought grace of life" he admired and emulated (but could never attain), stood at the very highest pitch of desirability. Participating vicariously in the affairs of the Marchmains—gliding along the marble and gilt corridors of Brideshead, kneeling beside them in the Art Nouveau chapel—he could at least take such comfort as daydreams can provide.

For Waugh, the writing of *Brideshead* was an imaginative furlough. For Ryder, Brideshead has a quick and even more dramatically anaesthetic effect:

> . . . on the instant, it was as though someone had switched off the wireless, and a voice that had been bawling in my ears, incessantly, fatuously, for days beyond number, had been suddenly cut short; an immense silence followed, empty at first, but gradually, as my outraged sense regained authority, full of a multitude of sweet and natural and long-forgotten sounds: for he had spoken a name that was so familiar to me, a conjuror's name of such ancient power, that, at its mere sound, the phantoms of those haunted late years began to take flight. (17–18)

Although not so mystical, Waugh's experience was analogous. Writing *Brideshead Revisited* in the quiet and familiar comfort of the Easton Court Hotel, far from the army, far from the Hoopers and the hateful wireless sets, he dropped out of the present and fled into a rich private landscape that was immensely more interesting and gratifying than gray wartime England. All Waugh's fiction dealt in fantasy; what sets *Brideshead* apart is its rapt, humorless, self-indulgent absorption in Waugh's fantasies, hobbyhorses and prejudices, to such an extreme that he could hardly disentangle and detach himself from his own inventions. *Brideshead Revisited* takes itself much too seriously.

For argument's sake, at least, Waugh might have conceded *Brideshead's* various defects of style and substance without prejudice to its most important element, as he thought: its religious theme. Although to his annoyance many readers missed it, this theme was for him the point of the novel. Going to Hollywood in 1947 to discuss with MGM the possibility of making a film of it, he was distressed to discover that the scriptwriter assigned to the project "sees Brideshead purely as a love story." MGM did not really understand the novel: "None of them see the theological implication," he complained, and, rather than dilute the implication and turn *Brideshead* into an English *Gone With the Wind*, he went home and took his novel with him, foregoing, as A. D. Peters delicately phrased it, "the one chance in his life of making a killing."[35]

He had been struck by the religious theme in the autumn of 1943, when Hubert Duggan, a friend from Oxford days and a lapsed Catholic who now lay dying in London, unexpectedly made the sign

of the cross when anointed by a priest, signifying (as Waugh con-
strued it) his assent to the sacrament. In view of Duggan's errant life,
Waugh was deeply impressed by this contrite gesture. "We spent the
day watching for a spark of gratitude for the love of God and saw the
spark."[36] Duggan's acquiescence in the last rites prompted the idea
that the Faith could reclaim a soul, however wandering and aban-
doned, from the very edge of doom: "Betwixt the stirrup and the
ground / Mercy I asked, mercy I found." The point was not that
Catholics ordinarily behaved better than others; from the saintliness
of Cordelia to the virtual apostasy of Julia, the Marchmains exhibit a
wide variety of spiritual aptitudes. But once initiated in the Faith,
they can never, despite themselves, wholly relinquish it. The Hound
of Heaven is relentless. Cordelia foresees His jealous reclamation of
the wandering Marchmains: ". . . the family haven't been very con-
stant, have they? There's him gone"—her father—"and Sebastian
gone and Julia gone. But God won't let them go for long, you know"
(194). *Brideshead* hints at a Calvinistic notion of unconditional elec-
tion: chosen for salvation, the Marchmains cannot escape their des-
tiny.

The final chapter illustrates Cordelia's thesis, as a quick train of
conversions propels the novel to its conclusion. Julia's return to the
Faith, initiating the sequence, has been anticipated several chapters
earlier by her rhapsody on the theme of guilt: "*Living in sin*, with sin,
by sin, for sin, every hour, every day, year in, year out. Waking up
with sin in the morning, seeing the curtains drawn on sin," and so on
(251). Not until her father's imminent death determines her to go for
the priest, however, does she decide to renounce her adulterous love.
"I saw to-day there was one thing unforgivable—like things in the
schoolroom, so bad they are unpunishable, that only Mummy could
deal with—the bad thing I was on the point of doing, that I'm not
quite bad enough to do; to set up a rival good to God's," she explains,
somewhat incoherently, to the annoyed Ryder (298).

Her repentance is the critical event, spurring the novel's other
erring souls to reform. In theological terms, she has responded to
God's grace. In human terms, the credit belongs to her Catholic
girlhood: "You see, I can't get all that sort of thing out of my mind,
quite—Death, Judgment, Heaven, Hell, Nanny Hawkins, and the
Catechism. It becomes a part of oneself, if they give it one early
enough" (227). This is why she fetches the priest for her father and
abjures Charles Ryder; at the moment of crisis her sleeping faith
awakes. *Brideshead* reveals not only faith in divine grace, but also
confidence in the influence of a Catholic upbringing, which has given
Julia reserves of faith and acuteness of conscience unavailable to Lord

Marchmain, let alone to Ryder. Waugh, looking in from the outside, envied such "cradle Catholics" their almost instinctive Catholic reflexes.

Ryder, during his pagan phase, likens Julia's religious promptings to a Pre-Raphaelite painting—Holman-Hunt's *The Awakened Conscience,* which portrays a young woman suddenly struck by remorse as her piano-playing paramour unwittingly sings a tune evoking memories of her innocent past. As Hunt describes the scene, "I arranged the two figures to present the woman recalling the memory of her childish home, and breaking away from her gilded cage with a startled awakening while her shallow companion still sings on, ignorantly intensifying her repentant purpose."[37] His own purpose, Hunt explained, was to represent "in actual life the manner in which the appeal of the spirit of heavenly love calls a soul to abandon a lower life," or, again, to represent "the appeal of the Spirit of Righteousness to the sinner."[38] As a young man Waugh had been deeply moved by this painting, in *Rossetti* calling it "singularly beautiful"; in the "Essay on the Pre-Raphaelite Brotherhood" praising it with less restraint as, "perhaps, the noblest painting by any Englishman."[39]

Waugh's admiration for the painting may have faded, but it suggests how deeply appealing to him was the notion of childhood's grip on the conscience. Julia's awakened conscience seems, by her own admission, essentially a nostalgic impulse, as her references to the schoolroom and Nanny Hawkins and "Mummy," for example, suggest. Waugh thought of *Brideshead* as a Catholic work, but there is nothing specifically Catholic about guilt and remorse. Descended from the popular Victorian type of the fallen woman struck by contrition, Julia seems essentially nondenominational. Her contrition is a dramatic convention used not only by Holman-Hunt but also, for example, by Dickens, who had no theological interest whatever. Hunt, in fact, meditating upon "the willing conversion and instantaneous resolve for a higher life" (eventually illustrated by *The Awakened Conscience*), had been "deeply touched by the pathos of the search by old Peggotty after little Emily, when she had become an outcast" in *David Copperfield.*[40] A strongly Victorian, Pre-Raphaelite strain lurks beneath the Catholic gilding of *Brideshead Revisited;* this was, after all, the same Waugh who had stood rapt before the rich romantic mysticism of Rossetti's *Beata Beatrix.*

Lord Marchmain's reconciliation succeeds Julia's. Ryder attributes Marchmain's dying gesture of contrition to divine intercession, and readers scarcely know enough about Marchmain to speculate on any human motives involved. Readers do know Ryder fairly well by this time, however. Through most of the novel he has been a sceptic, occasionally an outspoken one; but as Lord Marchmain sinks toward death and a priest administers the last rites, Ryder prays for a sign, "if only of courtesy, if only for the sake of the woman I loved" (296). When Marchmain crosses himself, Ryder comments, "Then I knew that the sign I had asked for was not a little thing, not a passing nod of recognition, and a phrase came back to me from my childhood of the veil of the temple being rent from top to bottom" (296–97). He too is reminded of childhood lessons, and this apparently providential sign moves him to embrace the Church.

The actual working out of his conversion is accomplished off stage. Nevertheless, a reader is entitled to ask: what exactly persuades Ryder to embrace the Church? His intimate acquaintance with the Marchmains has certainly been a central influence, but the Marchmains seem a better recommendation for aristocratic wealth than for Catholicism. Both Julia's and Lord Marchmain's spiritual homecomings are dramatic, but they would be a convincing demonstration of the truth of Catholic dogma only to an observer already predisposed to acknowledge it. Perhaps, despite his sceptical bluster, Ryder is in fact predisposed, but there are few clues to indicate this. One critic sympathetic to *Brideshead* argues, reasonably, that Waugh's difficult task was "to present a novel in the realistic tradition which would make plain or strongly urge the reality of God's becoming the crucial fact of life for some characters who appear indifferent to such a possibility, or who scoff at or resist any such notion."[41] God becomes the "crucial fact" for Ryder at Marchmain's deathbed: "When Marchmain then makes the sign of the cross Ryder knows very well that his prayer has been answered, disastrously for his secular dreams of Julia and Brideshead Castle." But this slides over a critical problem of motivation: how does Ryder "know very well that his prayer has been answered"? Another plausible possibility is that Marchmain's sign only coincidentally followed Ryder's prayer; and, given a choice between coincidence and providence, would not a firm-minded sceptic opt for coincidence? However satisfying Ryder's conversion may be homiletically, humanly it seems arbitrary.

It is unfortunate, too, that Ryder's new faith coexists with such pagan gloom and self-absorption. In the prologue and epilogue, set some four or five years after Lord Marchmain's death, Ryder remains intolerant and peevish, resentful of the various daily affronts to his ease and dignity, complacently assured of his own superior sensibility, full of self-pity: "I never built anything, and I forfeited the right to watch my son grow up. I'm homeless, childless, middle-aged, loveless, Hooper" (303). All this is very true, yet he is still glad to be himself rather than Hooper. The question of Ryder's character is not, in theory, directly pertinent to the validity of the novel's theological theme; but practically speaking, he is hardly a strong recommendation for the faith he has embraced.

Apart from its religious theme, which may or may not be persuasive, *Brideshead Revisited* has autobiographical implications that can scarcely be avoided.

Ryder is at first a lonely and too well behaved undergraduate, like Waugh during his first terms at Oxford some twenty years earlier. Ryder's circumstances are somewhat grander than Waugh's were—Ryder is, for example, from a cadet branch of a landed family and matriculates at a better college than Waugh's Hertford—but he nevertheless languishes amid dull companions, allowing Oxford's precious opportunities to slip away. With the advent of Sebastian, however, a much wider prospect opens. Sebastian introduces Ryder to an ambrosial Oxford, "an enclosed and enchanted garden"; but when Sebastian one day carries him off to his ancestral home, Brideshead, Ryder encounters something more wonderful than even Oxford—an Elysian palace and style of life unimaginably beyond anything in his narrow background. Brideshead, as he first sees it, glimmers with romantic possibilities; he awakens into a dream:

> We drove on and in the early afternoon came to our destination: wrought iron gates and twin, classical lodges on a village green, an avenue, more gates, open park-land, a turn in the drive; and suddenly a new and secret landscape opened before us. We were at the head of a valley and below us, half a mile distant, prone in the sunlight, grey and gold amid a screen of boskage, shone the dome and columns of an old house. (32)

"What a place to live in!" Ryder exclaims, entranced by the vision; all at once his own modest background seems cramped and stifling, while his love for Sebastian expands to encompass the magnificent establishment of which Sebastian is a product. As events show, Ryder's affection is transferred easily among different residents of Brideshead, but his love of Brideshead itself never diminishes. Free run of the palace with Sebastian is a prelapsarian experience: "I . . . believed myself very near heaven, during those languid days at Brideshead," Ryder recalls of his first summer there (71).

Brideshead is more than just a big house; it embodies a way of life and a spirit, "the high civilized style." It is pure faery, "an enchanted palace," and here occurs the first of Ryder's religious experiences, his conversion to the baroque. His love of the baroque embraces much more than just an architectural style:

Here under that high and insolent dome, under those tricky ceilings; here, as I passed through those arches and broken pediments to the pillared shade beyond and sat, hour by hour, before the fountain, probing its shadows, tracing its lingering echoes, rejoicing in all its clustered feats of daring and invention, I felt a whole new system of nerves alive within me, as though the water that spurted and bubbled among its stones was indeed a life-giving spring. (73)

"If it was mine I'd never live anywhere else," Ryder remarks of Brideshead, echoing Waugh's sentiments exactly.

Although Brideshead's magnetic allure never fails, it does change in character, however. There are actually two Bridesheads in the novel: the magical palace of Ryder's youth and the comfortable hideaway of his middle age. After Oxford, Sebastian and Brideshead slip out of Ryder's life. As Waugh himself had unsuccessfully proposed to his father years earlier, Ryder (with *his* father's encouragement) goes to Paris to become a painter and, unlike Waugh at Heatherley's, proves to have a passable aptitude, especially for painting old houses. He makes a career, in fact, of two of Waugh's favorite avocations, architecture and painting, but the narration hurries through Ryder's life and career between 1926 and 1936, years of public success but inner decline. "For nearly ten years I was thus borne along a road outwardly full of change and incident, but never during that time, except sometimes in my painting—and that at longer and longer intervals—did I come alive as I had been during the time of my friendship with Sebastian" (198). Artistically he feels a failure.

Uninspired in England, like Waugh he travels abroad—in Ryder's case to the jungles and ruins of Central America and Mexico. Echoing the worry of John Plant in *Work Suspended,* he realizes that technical mastery is an imperfect substitute for the creative impulse. It was an anxiety to which, in Waugh's case, *Scoop* lent a measure of credibility; and, rather like Waugh's 1935 journey to Abyssinia, Ryder's trip to the jungle has ambiguous results. The public and the critics are fooled by his jungle paintings, but the more astute Anthony Blanche immediately detects a fraud: "t-t-terrible t-t-tripe" (236). In detail, of course, this hardly resembles Waugh's experience, but familiar notes echo: growing artistic skill coupled with loss of "the intensity and singleness and the belief that it was not all done by hand—in a word, the inspiration" (199); the search abroad for renewed inspiration; outward prosperity and inner restlessness.

Ryder's artistic frustration is discouraging, of course, but what poisons his life is an unhappy marriage. He despises his wife, who has been unfaithful; the marriage survives, but only formally, a leaden weight on his spirit. When she meets him in New York after his two-year jungle sojourn, he sinks into profound despondency at the prospect of returning to England with her. His old life oppresses him, but he is unable to make a new one. Just at this nadir, however, he fortuitously meets Julia, and, promptly abandoning his wife, he is presently re-established at Brideshead. But Julia's Brideshead, though aesthetically as splendid as ever, lacks the enchanting vernal quality of Sebastian's Brideshead of fifteen years earlier. When Ryder was an undergraduate, Brideshead crouched magically in its valley, as if all the world's loveliness and mystery were wrapped up and hidden within. Now, revisited, that green expectancy has grown sere. The adult Ryder, wearied by life, cannot return to that youthful world, so full of romantic possibility and opportunity, "so various, so beautiful, so new"; that world which beckoned so seductively, once. Instead, Brideshead the second time around has become an island fortress, to which Ryder flees like a refugee from the world beyond the valley, where Rex and Celia and ignorant armies of Hoopers are massed in ugly and menacing array. At Brideshead, Ryder can cloister himself in love and luxury and baroque beauty. When the notion that Julia might inherit the house enters his head, he savors the possibility of enjoying such comfortable sequestration in perpetuity:

> It opened a prospect; the prospect one gained at the turn of the avenue, as I had first seen it with Sebastian, of the secluded valley, the lakes falling away one below the other, the old house in the foreground, the rest of the world abandoned and forgotten; a world of its own of peace and love and beauty; a soldier's dream in a foreign bivouac; such a prospect perhaps as a high pinnacle of the temple afforded after the hungry days in the desert and the jackal-haunted nights. Need I reproach myself if sometimes I was rapt in the vision? (282)

"I do not want any more experiences in life," Waugh had written the year before, and Ryder displays exactly the same attitude. Brideshead is Waugh's daydream of the best possible place to hide from a world of disagreeable people and discouraging novelties.

The earlier novels had often evinced a similar impulse of retreat; but not until *Brideshead* did this impulse, now grown somewhat self-righteous to boot, dominate a novel. Ryder's progress from Sebastian to Julia duplicates Waugh's progress from Oxford's liberating influence, reflected in *Decline and Fall,* to his withdrawal from the army and the Second World War; and *Brideshead Revisited* is a product of the declining vitality that it traces. Waugh had turned inward, from the incorrigibly weedy life around him into a closed hothouse of gaudy but delicate flowers. His sympathies had contracted disastrously; his preoccupation with style betrayed imaginative enervation. *Brideshead Revisited* suffers not from lack of inventiveness, but from lack of gusto for the world—crowded, foolish, chaotic, brutal, insensitive, vulgar, ugly, anything and everything, but alive. Waugh's imagination, thrown back on itself, languished for lack of sustenance. Nothing is impossible, but it is difficult to be both anchoritically indifferent to the world and, at the same time, a novelist.

Waugh concluded his single volume of autobiography with a chapter titled "In Which Our Hero's Fortunes Fall Very Low," referring to his 1925 exile in North Wales. The phrase would have applied even better to 1944. In worldly terms he was a successful man, and *Brideshead Revisited* would soon make him much more successful; but imaginatively he was in a deep slough.

Epilogue

Waugh's transition from man about town to crusty old squire had begun in 1937 with his second marriage and his self-exile in Gloucestershire, but the Second World War was the experience that confirmed and perfected the metamorphosis. He returned to civilian status in 1945 about twenty years older than he had been in 1939, resolved to have nothing or at least very little to do with the world beyond Piers Court. His hair was still thick and brown, but his spirit had turned gray, and, except for bibulous visits to London and occasional rejuvenating adventures in the greater world, his last twenty years were sedate, secluded, increasingly torpid. "Early" Waugh gave way to "late" Waugh.

His later fiction falls into two principal categories. The first comprises occasional works: several short novels, or long stories, inspired by specific, extraordinary experiences—*Scott-King's Modern Europe* (1947) by a literary congress in Spain; *The Loved One* (1948) by a trip to Los Angeles; *The Ordeal of Gilbert Pinfold* (1957) by a spell of madness. In origin these resembled the earlier novels: Waugh stimulated to fiction by encounters with the world, and by trouble; indeed, *The Ordeal of Gilbert Pinfold* records one of the most bizarre and troubling incidents in Waugh's life. These short books, especially *The Loved One* and *Pinfold*, rank among Waugh's best fiction.

But such occasional stories were preliminaries to, or digressions from, the major work of his last two decades, the war trilogy comprising *Men at Arms* (1952), *Officers and Gentlemen* (1955), and *Unconditional Surrender* (1961), combined in the single-volume *Sword of Honour* the year before Waugh's death. An estimate of Waugh's later career must rest heavily on the trilogy. Exploiting his experience of the Second World War for material, *Sword of Honour* expresses his most serious thinking about life, as the apparently meaningless and discouraging confusion of the novel's world, the accidents and cross-purposes and disappointments, all fall into a pattern of divine purpose. It is an immensely more catholic and magnanimous work of fiction than *Brideshead Revisited;* Waugh had escaped the imaginative hothouse and gotten outdoors again.

The trilogy preserves Waugh at his ripest and most mellow; or, in the metaphor Waugh himself might have preferred, *Sword of Honour* is a vintage wine patiently aged, brought to full maturity and prime for the table. It is not a sparkling wine, like the early novels; it is not a wine for bacchanalian celebration, but one for sipping with judicious appreciation. To ask whether it fulfills the promise of the early novels poses an unanswerable question. It rounds off Waugh's career, speaking for Waugh the patriarch as the early novels had spoken for Waugh the young man.

Like *Brideshead Revisited,* the trilogy has a "theological implication," but Waugh's faith seems to have reached a higher stage. *Sword of Honour* revolves about another old Catholic family—these were now, like the rural retreats of the earlier novels, the moral centers of his fiction—but there is none of the theatrical Pre-Raphaelite religion of *Brideshead.* The theme of the trilogy, reserved until the last volume, was an idea expressed in Waugh's essay "St Helena Empress": "What we can learn from Helena is something about the workings of God; that He wants a different thing from each of us, laborious or easy, conspicuous or quite private, but something which only we can do and for which we were each created."[1] In *Men at Arms* Guy Crouchback, the protagonist, returns to England in 1939 from a long self-imposed exile in Italy to throw himself into the war, thinking that he is enlisting in a grand crusade against the Modern Age. He ends, in *Unconditional Surrender,* by realizing that his ordained mission is more modest, though no less important—to give a home to one unwanted child:

> "What is one child more or less in all the misery?"
> "I can't do anything about all those others. This is just one case where I can help. And only I, really. . . ." (193)

All of which illustrates the precept of Guy's saintly father, the novel's moral paradigm: "Quantitative judgments don't apply. If only one soul was saved, that is full compensation for any amount of 'loss of face'" (194). This was a great progress from Waugh's bellicose, imperialistic Catholicism of the 1930s; it was, in fact, almost a specific disavowal of such great ambitions. The world's follies and miseries were too vast to contemplate, let alone amend. One could hope to accomplish only one's own limited, perhaps "quite private," task, to tend one's own garden well. God asked no more of his weak and erring children.

Waugh arrived at this theological assertion in response to disillusion—with the Second World War specifically, with life itself more generally. In a sentiment attributed to Scott-King in *Scott-King's*

Modern Europe, the Second World War somewhere along the way "cast its heroic and chivalrous disguise and became a sweaty tug-of-war between teams of indistinguishable louts" (5). In *Officers and Gentlemen* Guy Crouchback recognizes, after the fall of Crete and the pusillanimous flight of his aristocratic friend Ivor Claire, that what he had thought a noble war was just as morally gray as the world which had produced it:

> It was just such a sunny, breezy Mediterranean day two years before when he read of the Russo-German alliance, when a decade of shame seemed to be ending in light and reason, when the Enemy was plain in view, huge and hateful, all disguise cast off; the modern age in arms.
>
> Now that hallucination was dissolved, like the whales and turtles on the voyage from Crete, and he was back after less than two years' pilgrimage in a Holy Land of illusion in the old ambiguous world, where priests were spies and gallant friends proved traitors and his country was led blundering into dishonour. (321–22)

Commitment to causes and countries is ultimately vain; even commitment to ideals and heroes, for the beautiful young Ivor Claire has been Guy Crouchback's model of the aristocratic ideal. For Guy, Claire's cowardice is sadly disillusioning; for Waugh himself, long enamored of that same ideal, it was perhaps the ultimate renunciation of his own worldly vanities.

After the debacle on Crete, Guy withdraws from the army and the war. Waugh himself later explained *Sword of Honour*'s complementary themes of withdrawal and personal mission in a note to a reviewer:

> May I commend two points to your attention 1) The character of all the Crouchback family of withdrawal from the world, at its lowest in mad Ivo, at its highest in the father. This explains much of Guy's failure to re-enter the world in the army 2) The idea that God creates no man without a special purpose. Guy's was to rescue Trimmer's son from a disastrous upbringing.[2]

At the end of *Unconditional Surrender* Guy retires to private life, on the home farm of the old family estate. Even more representative of the trilogy's spirit of withdrawal is Guy's nephew, Tony Box-Bender; after five years as a German prisoner of war, he retires to a monastery.

Sword of Honour contains many fine comic episodes; it is fully capable of laughing at life, but in the end it recoils from it. In its benign tolerance it differs from *Brideshead Revisited;* but in its weariness with life it differs also from the earlier novels. The trilogy's lack of zest perfectly expresses Waugh's spirit in the last fifteen years of his life. His ennui was, indeed, the greatest threat to his fiction during those years. Like Gilbert Pinfold, he was often afflicted with devitalizing boredom:

> The tiny kindling of charity which came to him through his religion, sufficed only to temper his disgust and change it to boredom. There was a phrase in the '30s: "It is later than you think," which was designed to cause uneasiness. It was never later than Mr. Pinfold thought. At intervals during the day and night he would look at his watch and learn always with disappointment how little of his life was past, how much there was still ahead of him. He wished no one ill, but he looked at the world *sub specie aeternitatis* and he found it flat as a map. (7–8)

Waugh's diaries, though only intermittent after 1945, frequently evince the same state:

> I am a very much older man than this time last year, physically infirm and lethargic. Mentally I have reached a stage of non-attachment which if combined with a high state of prayer—as it is not—would be edifying.

> Success has brought idleness as its dead fruit.

> Clocks barely moving. Has half an hour past? no five minutes.

> My life is really too empty for a diarist. The morning post, the newspaper, the crossword, gin.

> Resolved: to regard humankind with benevolence and detachment, like an elderly host whose young and indulged wife has asked a lot of people to the house whose names he does not know.

> *Abjuring the realm.* To make an *interior* act of renunciation and to become a stranger in the world; to watch one's fellow-countrymen, as one used to watch foreigners, curious of their habits, patient of their absurdities, indifferent to their animosities—that is the secret of happiness in this century of the common man.

> The church, in our last agony, anoints the organs of sense, sealing the ears against the assaults of sound. But nature, in God's Providence, does this long before. One has heard all the world has to say, and wants no more of it.[3]

Tired of his own life and of the world around him, he found it more and more difficult to work himself up to fiction. It took him a decade to write the war trilogy, and by the time he finished the last volume he was dealing with material that was more than fifteen years old. Except for a few isolated incidents and trips, his experience across those intervening years had been imaginatively a void.

The result was inanition. He was aware that sloth, the sin of joylessness and despair, had a grip on him. Gilbert Pinfold, in his late forties, "spent most of the day in an armchair. He ate less, drank more, and grew corpulent" (10). Later, in an essay on sloth, Waugh wrote in plain self-reference: "Sloth is not primarily the temptation of the young. Medical science has oppressed us with a new huge burden of longevity. It is in that last undesired decade, when passion is cold, appetites feeble, curiosity dulled, and experience has begotten cynicism, that *accidia* lies in wait as the final temptation to destruction."[4] The following year he noted in his diary: "All fates are 'worse than death'."[5] This was not the right frame of mind for writing fiction—at least not the sort of fiction for which Waugh was most gifted. His genius was the ability to re-create life. Even the most spiritually healthy attributes of his condition—philosophical detachment, resignation, readiness for death—were inhospitable to his talents. In simplest terms, the imaginative problem of Waugh's later years was that he sickened of the very stuff which nourished his fiction. There was no fictional form to express his aversion to life—at least no form that he knew of. Fiction required characters and action, and Waugh no longer had the heart for either.

He would not have been so good a novelist had his temperament not been so complex and troubled; but those temperamental complexities and troubles eventually defeated him. The early novels remain the springtime and high summer of his genius, before the ambiguous autumn.

Notes

For quotations from Waugh's novels I have used the first English edition (London: Chapman and Hall) in each case, except where otherwise noted and except for *Decline and Fall,* for which I have used the 1962 revised edition (London: Chapman and Hall) because of its restoration of the manuscript text (for the textual history of *Decline and Fall,* see P. A. Doyle, *"Decline and Fall:* Two Versions," *Evelyn Waugh Newsletter* 1 (Autumn 1967): 4–5, and Robert Murray Davis, *Evelyn Waugh, Writer* (Norman, Oklahoma: Pilgrim Books, 1981), pp. 38–50).

For all other books by Waugh I cite or quote from the first English edition, except where noted otherwise.

Abbreviations and short titles in the notes refer to the following sources:

HRC: The Evelyn Waugh collection at the Humanities Research Center at the University of Texas at Austin.

Catalogue: Robert Murray Davis, *A Catalogue of the Evelyn Waugh Collection at the Humanities Research Center, the University of Texas at Austin* (Troy, New York: Whitston Publishing Company, 1981). For all unpublished material at HRC, I have given the *Catalogue* numbering.

Diaries: Michael Davie, ed., *The Diaries of Evelyn Waugh* (London: Weidenfeld and Nicolson, 1976). I have used the dates supplied in this edition, which are sometimes editorial. In one or two cases my reading differs from Davie's.

Letters: Mark Amory, ed., *The Letters of Evelyn Waugh* (London: Weidenfeld and Nicolson, 1980). In a few cases my reading differs from Amory's.

Essays: Donat Gallagher, ed., *The Essays, Articles and Reviews of Evelyn Waugh* (Boston: Little, Brown, 1984).

Arthur Waugh diaries: the manuscript diaries of Arthur Waugh, in the Alec Waugh archive in the Department of Special Collections of the Mugar Memorial Library of Boston University.

Preface

1. Margaret Morriss and D. J. Dooley, "Introduction," in *Evelyn Waugh: A Reference Guide* (Boston: G. K. Hall, 1984), pp. ix–xvi.

2. "A Pilot All at Sea," *Tablet* 186 (10 November 1945): 225–26 (*Essays,* pp. 281–82).

Chapter 1. Introduction: "I Hope There Will Be Trouble"

1. "Evelyn Waugh—The Man," ed. Christopher Sykes, in *Good Talk,* ed. Derwent May (London: Gollancz, 1968), p. 15.

2. James F. Carens, *The Satiric Art of Evelyn Waugh* (Seattle: University of Washington Press, 1966).

3. Ian Littlewood, *The Writings of Evelyn Waugh* (Totowa, N.J.: Barnes & Noble, 1983), p. 53.

4. Jeffrey Heath, *The Picturesque Prison: Evelyn Waugh and His Writing* (Kingston and Montreal: McGill-Queen's University Press, 1982).

5. Martin Stannard, *Evelyn Waugh: The Early Years 1903–1939* (New York: W. W. Norton, 1987).

6. Littlewood, *Writings of Waugh*, p. 1.

7. *A Little Learning*, p. 197.

8. *Diaries*, 25 January 1925.

9. Anne Fleming, "Yours Affec: Evelyn," in *Evelyn Waugh and His World*, ed. David Pryce-Jones (Boston: Little, Brown, 1973), p. 238.

10. Christopher Hollis, "Introductory Memoir," in John St John, *To the War with Waugh* (London: Leo Cooper, 1973), p. v.

11. Alec Waugh, *The Early Years of Alec Waugh* (New York: Farrar, Straus, 1963), p. 22.

12. "Evelyn Waugh—The Man," pp. 18–19.

13. *Diaries*, 18 September 1939.

14. Aldous Huxley, *Antic Hay* (New York: George H. Doran, 1923), p. 185.

15. Robert Murray Davis, *Evelyn Waugh, Writer* (Norman, Oklahoma: Pilgrim Books, 1981).

16. "Fan-Fare," *Life Magazine*, 8 April 1946, p. 60 (*Essays*, pp. 300–304).

Chapter 2. Oxford and the Years of Ferment: "I Did Not Set Out to Be a Writer"

1. *A Little Learning*, p. 181; MS of *A Little Learning*, HRC (*Catalogue* item C85).

2. A. L. Rowse, *A Cornishman at Oxford* (London: Jonathan Cape, 1965), p. 67.

3. Maurice Bowra, *Memories 1898–1939* (London: Weidenfeld and Nicolson, 1966), pp. 154–55.

4. Christopher Hollis, *Oxford in the Twenties* (London: William Heinemann, 1976), p. 97.

5. Quoted in *Letters*, p. 20n.

6. Alec Waugh, "My Brother Evelyn," in *My Brother Evelyn and Other Portraits* (New York: Farrar, Straus and Giroux, 1967), p. 172.

7. Quoted in "The Oxford University Railway Club," *The Cherwell*, 8 December 1923, pp. 142–43.

8. To Dudley Carew, undated (June/July 1924), HRC (*Catalogue* item E53).

9. *Diaries*, 21 June 1924.

10. Ibid., 6 and 7 September 1927.

11. To Harold Acton, undated (December 1924) (*Letters*, p. 20).

12. Quoted in Christopher Sykes, *Evelyn Waugh: A Biography* (1975; revised edition Harmondsworth, Middlesex: Penguin Books, 1977), p. 95.

13. To Harold Acton, undated (February 1925) (*Letters*, p. 22).

14. *A Little Learning*, p. 223.

15. To Harold Acton, undated (February/March 1925) (*Letters*, p. 23).

16. *Diaries*, 28 May 1925.

17. Ibid., 26 August 1925.

18. *Georgian Stories, 1926*, [ed. Alec Waugh] (London: Chapman and Hall, 1926), pp. 253–91; reprinted in *Evelyn Waugh, Apprentice*, ed. Robert Murray Davis (Norman, Oklahoma: Pilgrim Books, 1985), pp. 155–85.

19. *Diaries*, 5 May 1925.

20. Ibid., 30 October 1926.

21. "P. R. B.: An Essay on the Pre-Raphaelite Brotherhood, 1847–1854" (London: privately printed by Alastair Graham, 1926).

22. *Diaries*, 14 November 1925.

Chapter 3. *Decline and Fall:* "Grimes, You Wretch!"

1. *Diaries*, 3 September 1927.

2. Dudley Carew, *A Fragment of Friendship* (London: Everest Books, 1974), pp. 81–82.

3. Anthony Powell, *Messengers of Day*, vol. 2 of *The Memoirs of Anthony Powell* (New York: Holt, Rinehart and Winston, 1978), p. 22.

4. To Harold Acton, undated (early 1928) (*Letters*, p. 25).

5. To Anthony Powell, 7 April 1928 (*Letters*, p. 27).

6. Preface to *Decline and Fall*, revised ed. (London: Chapman and Hall, 1962), p. 11.

7. To Harold Acton, undated (September/October 1928) (*Letters*, p. 28).

8. The comic rhetoric of this passage is discussed in detail in Walter Nash, *The Language of Humour* (London: Longman, 1985), pp. 22–25.

9. Jeffrey Heath, *Picturesque Prison*, warns against being seduced into liking Waugh's bad characters: "The discrepancy between the levels of action and parable creates an ambivalent tone of condemnation and compassion; as a result of this deceptive tone Waugh is able to ambush readers who mistakenly sympathize with characters whom he in fact deplores" (122). I think that this comment confuses fiction with life. Characters like Lady Circumference—based on the mother of Waugh's friend Alastair Graham—might be boring and awful as houseguests or neighbors and might even be morally deplorable; but they may be fascinating and even sympathetic characters in fiction, where they are aesthetic objects to which we respond with different standards. Replying, years after *Decline and Fall*, to an interviewer who mentioned fictional characters like Pistol and Moll Flanders, Waugh remarked: "Ah, the criminal classes. . . . They have always had a certain fascination." To assert that the dramatic interest of Falstaff (to take another example) is that he demonstrates Shakespeare's disapprobation of robbery, cowardice, lying, lechery, and drunkenness not only would be banal, but would altogether mistake Shakespeare's, and our, attitude to Falstaff.

10. Good discussions of Waugh's comic style may be found in William J. Cook, Jr., *Masks, Modes, and Morals: The Art of Evelyn Waugh* (Rutherford, N.J.: Fairleigh Dickinson University Press, 1971); and in Littlewood, *Writings of Waugh*, pp. 36–65.

11. *Diaries*, 2 October 1927.

12. Ibid., 14 May 1925.

13. Ibid., 3 July 1925.

14. Claud Cockburn, "Evelyn Waugh's Lost Rabbit," *The Atlantic*, December 1973, p. 54.

15. *Diaries*, 8 February 1927.

16. Nikolaus Pevsner, *Pioneers of the Modern Movement: From William Morris to Walter Gropius* (New York: Frederick A. Stokes, 1937), pp. 205–6.

17. *Diaries*, 6 October 1927.

18. Ibid., 11 September 1925.

19. Jerome Meckier, "Circle, Symbol and Parody in Evelyn Waugh's *Decline and Fall*," *Contemporary Literature* 20 (1979): 51–75.

Chapter 4. *Vile Bodies:* "A Sharp Disturbance"

1. To Arthur Waugh, undated (March 1929) (*Letters*, p. 32); to A. D. Peters, 29 March 1929, HRC (*Catalogue* item E100).

2. To Henry Yorke, undated (June 1929) (*Letters*, pp. 35–36).

3. Preface to *Vile Bodies*, new ed. (London: Chapman and Hall, 1965), p. 7.

4. Alec Waugh, "My Brother Evelyn," p. 190.

5. To Henry Yorke, undated (June/July 1929) (*Letters*, p. 36).

6. There are conflicting accounts of precisely what happened during this period; see Stannard, *Early Years*, p. 183.

7. To Catherine and Arthur Waugh, undated (early August 1929) (*Letters*, p. 38).

8. To Harold Acton, undated (August 1929) (*Letters*, p. 39).

9. To Lady Mary Lygon, undated (September 1936) (*Letters*, pp. 111–12).

10. Preface to *Vile Bodies*, new ed., p. 7.

11. Ibid.

12. Julian Jebb, ed., "Evelyn Waugh: An Interview," number 30 in "The Art of Fiction" series, *Paris Review* 8 (Summer–Fall 1963): 78.

13. "Ronald Firbank," *Life and Letters* 2 (March 1929): 191–96 (*Essays*, pp. 56–59).

14. Preface to *Vile Bodies*, new ed., p. 7.

15. To Ronald Knox, 14 May 1945 (*Letters*, p. 206).

16. MS of *A Little Hope*, HRC (*Catalogue* item C90).

17. Alec Waugh, "My Brother Evelyn," p. 189.

18. *Evelyn Waugh Newsletter* 1 (Spring 1967): 1.

19. To Henry Yorke, 20 July 1929 (*Letters*, p. 36).

20. Preface to *Vile Bodies*, new ed., p. 7.

21. Martin Stannard, *Early Years*, puts the transition at the beginning of chapter 7 (*Early Years*, p. 206). I cannot detect a change of mood in chapter 7. External evidence is slim.

22. To Harold Acton, undated (August 1929) (*Letters*, p. 39).

23. *Times* (London), 18 August 1929.

24. Alvin B. Kernan, "The Wall and the Jungle: The Early Novels of Evelyn Waugh," *Yale Review* 53 (1963): 199–220.

25. Stephen Jay Greenblatt, *Three Modern Satirists: Waugh, Orwell, Huxley* (New Haven: Yale University Press, 1965), pp. 13–14.

26. Heath, *Picturesque Prison*, pp. 81, 82.

27. *Diaries*, 2 June 1947.

28. To Henry Yorke, undated (September 1929) (*Letters*, p. 39).

29. Martin Stannard (*Early Years*, p. 199) comments on this passage, "Shades of

the prison house," and denounces the apparent peacefulness of Christmas at Doubting Hall: "But in Waugh's hands this apparent evocation of the solid and continuous becomes pastiche. Festive Dickensian camaraderie had no place in his sceptical vision. . . . Nina and Adam's happiness is mocked as radically sentimental. . . . Their simplicity and innocence are reviewed as decadence and ignorance. . . . There is a vague sense of *malaise*, of sickness, but each has only a partial, egocentric, vision of the collective tragedy, the relentless decline into barbarism." This seems to me the sledgehammer of moral indignation battering at a light and fond caricature of an Edwardian country-house Christmas. I think Waugh's attitude was not ferociously censorious, but amused and wistful. The lamblike innocence of the scene is plainly an image meant to be set against the battlefield wasteland that immediately follows. The ironic contrast would be lost if the Christmas scene were equally vicious.

   30. To Henry Yorke, undated (September 1929) (*Letters*, p. 39).

Chapter 5. *Black Mischief:* "Sunless, Forbidden Places"

   1. To A. D. Peters, undated (late January 1930), HRC (*Catalogue* item E125).
   2. *Diaries*, 2 July 1930.
   3. Ibid., 8 July 1930.
   4. Ibid., 18 August 1930.
   5. Quoted in Sykes, *Biography*, p. 156.
   6. To Penelope Betjeman, 10 February 1948 (*Letters*, p. 267).
   7. To Edith Sitwell, 9 August 1955 (*Letters*, p. 451).
   8. "Converted to Rome: Why It Has Happened to Me," *Daily Express*, 20 October 1930, p. 10 (*Essays*, pp. 103–5).
   9. Arthur Waugh diaries, 27 September 1930.
   10. *Remote People*, pp. 44, 53.
   11. Ibid., p. 29.
   12. To Catherine and Arthur Waugh, 16 November 1930 (*Letters*, p. 51).
   13. Quoted in Donat Gallagher, "New Discoveries in Waugh Bibliography III," *Evelyn Waugh Newsletter* 17 (Spring 1983): 8.
   14. Arthur Waugh diaries, 9 March 1931.
   15. *Remote People*, p. 63.
   16. To Catherine and Arthur Waugh, 16 November 1930 (*Letters*, pp. 51–52).
   17. *Remote People*, p. 63.
   18. Ibid., p. 82.
   19. "To an Unknown Old Man," unpublished typescript of a BBC talk delivered 28 November 1932, HRC (*Catalogue* item C9).
   20. *Black Mischief*, p. 22. The text actually reads "The whole might of Evolution rides behind him"; *him* is a misprint for *me*, corrected in later editions.
   21. "To an Unknown Old Man."
   22. *A Little Learning*, p. 205.
   23. To Henry Yorke, undated (November 1930) (*Letters*, p. 51).
   24. "An Open Letter to His Eminence the Cardinal Archbishop of Westminster," May 1933 (*Letters*, p. 77).
   25. *Remote People*, p. 164.
   26. Heath, *Picturesque Prison*, p. 103.
   27. *Diaries*, 3 November 1930.
   28. "Converted to Rome," p. 10.

29. *Remote People*, p. 163.
30. "Converted to Rome," p. 10.

Chapter 6. *A Handful of Dust:* "From Now Onwards the Map Is Valueless . . ."

1. Arthur Waugh diaries, 1 May 1933.
2. To Henry Yorke, undated (early May 1933) (*Letters*, p. 71).
3. To Katherine Asquith, undated (January 1934) (*Letters*, p. 83).
4. Ibid.
5. To Henry Yorke, undated (September 1934) (*Letters*, p. 88).
6. Jerome Meckier, "Why the Man Who Liked Dickens Reads Dickens Instead of Conrad: Waugh's *A Handful of Dust*," *Novel: A Forum on Fiction* 13 (1980): 171–87.
7. Ann Pasternak Slater, "Waugh's *A Handful of Dust:* Right Things in Wrong Places," *Essays in Criticism* 32 (1982): 48–68.
8. "The Man Who Liked Dickens," *Nash's Pall Mall Magazine* (November 1933): 18–21, 80, 82–83.
9. "Fan-Fare," *Life*, 8 April 1946, p. 58.
10. To Henry Yorke, undated (September 1934) (*Letters*, p. 88).
11. To Lady Mary Lygon, undated (October 1933) (*Letters*, p. 81).
12. For a detailed exegesis of *A Handful of Dust*'s literary allusions, see Nicholas Joost, "*A Handful of Dust:* Evelyn Waugh and the Novel of Manners," *Papers on Language and Literature* 12 (1976): 177–96.
13. To Tom Driberg, undated (ca. 1 September 1934) (*Letters*, p. 88).
14. Cyril Connolly, "T. S. Eliot: 1," in *The Evening Colonnade* (New York: Harcourt Brace Jovanovich, 1975), p. 207.
15. Quoted in Sykes, *Biography*, pp. 201–2.
16. Waugh's choice of Dickens as Tony Last's reading matter has provoked much critical discussion. Jerome Meckier, for example, holds that Dickens was selected because he was not only symbolically but also personally responsible for the decline of Western civilization: "At other times an imitator of Dickens, Waugh puts the works of Boz in Mr. Todd's hut for a very satirical reason: he considers the Inimitable largely responsible for the breakdown of social restraints" ("Why the Man Who Liked Dickens Reads Dickens Instead of Conrad," p. 171). I cannot subscribe to this notion, since it seems to place a disproportionate burden of historical guilt on a mere novelist and to read a great deal more into the text of Waugh's novel than is actually there. In "The Man Who Liked Dickens," of course, Paul Henty is also sentenced to lifetime Dickens, and certainly this story has little to do with the decline of Western civilization.

Dickens in the jungle was initially suggested to Waugh by the Jesuit fathers' mission library in British Guiana. The middle-class Victorian English novelist among the illiterate Indians of remote South America must have seemed pleasantly incongruous. Waugh's own relationship with Dickens may have made the irony even more attractive. Waugh's father had introduced him to Dickens, and the influence of Dickens on Waugh was longstanding and pervasive. Waugh's attitude toward Dickens seems to me to have been ambivalent in a filial way, both admiring and occasionally rebellious. The use of Dickens in *A Handful of Dust* may have been partially to taunt his paternal authority. There may also be in the use of Dickens simply a joke about too much of a good thing.

Chapter 7. *Scoop:* ". . . Inside the Park Everything Was Sweet and Still"

1. "The Cold North," *Spectator* 148 (18 June 1932): 869.
2. Arthur Waugh diaries, 28 August 1934.
3. To Tom Driberg, undated (ca. 1 September 1934) (*Letters*, p. 88).
4. *Waugh in Abyssinia*, p. 49.
5. Ibid., p. 35.
6. To Laura Herbert, October 1935 (*Letters*, p. 100).
7. To A. D. Peters, undated (ca. 25 October 1936), HRC (*Catalogue* item E298).
8. *Diaries*, 8 December 1936.
9. Ibid., 16 and 17 May 1937.
10. To W. N. Roughead, undated (ca. 7 July 1937), HRC (*Catalogue* item E321).
11. To A. D. Peters, undated (ca. 1 October 1937), HRC (*Catalogue* item E328).
12. *Scoop's* protracted and complex composition is discussed in Davis, *EW, Writer*, pp. 87–105.
13. *Diaries*, 10 January 1938.
14. Preface to *Scoop*, new ed. (London: Chapman and Hall, 1954), p. 9.
15. To Mory McLaren, undated (ca. 19 May 1938), an unpublished letter in the BBC Written Archives Centre, Caversham Park, Reading.
16. "In Preparation . . . Hostesses and Housebreakers Get Ready for the Coronation," *Nash's Pall Mall Magazine*, April 1937, p. 10.
17. Ibid., pp. 10, 11.
18. Ibid., p. 10.
19. *Diaries*, 4 February 1937.
20. Davis, *EW, Writer*, pp. 90, 105.
21. Heath, *Picturesque Prison*, pp. 124–25.
22. D. Paul Farr, "The Novelist's Coup: Style as Satiric Norm in *Scoop*," *Connecticut Review*, 8, no. 2 (1975): 42–54.
23. "Memorandum for Messrs. Endfield and Fisz," 12 April 1957, HRC (*Catalogue* item C50).
24. To Alexander Comfort, 29 June (1938) (*Letters*, p. 118).

Chapter 8. The War and *Brideshead Revisited:* "I Do Not Want Any More Experiences"

1. *Diaries*, 27 July 1939.
2. Ibid., 17 August 1939.
3. To W. N. Roughead, undated (late September 1939) (*Letters*, p. 127).
4. To A. D. Peters, undated (ca. 7 December 1939), HRC (*Catalogue* item E375).
5. Dedicatory note, *Work Suspended*.
6. Preface, *The Holy Places*.
7. Martin Stannard, "*Work Suspended:* Waugh's Climacteric," *Essays in Criticism* 28 (1978): 302–20; a revised version of this article, including the quoted passages, appears in Stannard, *Early Years*, pp. 490–91.
8. "Bloomsbury's Farthest North," *Night and Day*, 12 August 1937, p. 25.
9. *Diaries*, 27 August 1939.
10. Ibid., "Memorandum on LAYFORCE," p. 489.
11. Ibid., p. 491.

12. Ibid.
13. Preface, *Put Out More Flags*, new ed. (London: Chapman and Hall, 1967), p. 7.
14. Ibid.
15. Claire Hopley, "The Significance of Exhilaration and Silence in *Put Out More Flags*," *Modern Fiction Studies* 30 (1984): 83–97.
16. *Diaries*, 25 August 1939.
17. Jebb, "Evelyn Waugh: An Interview," p. 82.
18. *Diaries*, 23 March 1943.
19. Ibid., to Brigadier R. E. Laycock, 19 July 1943, p. 544.
20. Ibid., 21 March 1943.
21. Ibid., 29 August 1943.
22. To Laura Waugh, undated (28 September 1943) (*Letters*, pp. 171–72).
23. *Diaries*, 31 January 1944.
24. To A. D. Peters, 8 February 1944, HRC (*Letters*, p. 177); *Diaries*, 21 March 1944.
25. *Diaries*, 6 June 1944.
26. To Nancy Mitford, 7 January 1945 (*Letters*, p. 196).
27. To Catherine Waugh, 5 February 1945 (*Letters*, p. 200).
28. *Diaries*, 21 May 1944; to Laura Waugh, 7 January 1945 (*Letters*, p. 195).
29. To Graham Greene, 27 March (1950) (*Letters*, p. 322).
30. Jebb, "Evelyn Waugh: An Interview," p. 83.
31. *Diaries*, 8 February, 3 April, 4 and 11 May 1944.
32. "Fan-Fare," *Life*, 8 April 1946, p. 60.
33. Quoted in *Letters*, p. 199; in Sykes, *Biography*, p. 342.
34. To Ronald Knox, 14 May 1945 (*Letters*, p. 206).
35. *Diaries*, 7 February 1947; "Evelyn Waugh—The Man," p. 29.
36. *Diaries*, 13 October 1943.
37. W. Holman-Hunt, *Pre-Raphaelitism and the Pre-Raphaelite Brotherhood*, 2d ed., two vols. (London: Chapman and Hall, 1913), 2:347.
38. Ibid., pp. 346, 403.
39. *Rossetti*, p. 62; "An Essay on the Pre Raphaelite Brotherhood."
40. Holman-Hunt, 2:346.
41. Joseph Hynes, "Two Affairs Revisited," *Twentieth Century Literature* 33, no. 2 (1987): 234–53.

Epilogue

1. *The Holy Places*, p. 13.
2. To W. J. Igoe, 4 August (1961) (*Letters*, p. 571).
3. *Diaries*, 28 October 1947, 16 August 1948, 2 January 1954, 12 July 1955, 17 November 1944, 9 May 1962, 9 May 1962.
4. "Evelyn Waugh on Sloth," *Sunday Times* (London), 7 January 1962, magazine section, p. 21 (*Essays*, pp. 572–76).
5. *Diaries*, 3 September 1963.

Select Bibliography

A *Bibliography of Evelyn Waugh* (1986) lists more than four thousand items by or about Waugh. For studying Waugh's life and writing up to 1945, the following books are particularly pertinent or useful (or at least provocative). For works by Waugh, except those collected and published posthumously, I give only the original date of publication; most have gone through multiple printings and editions, and most remain in print.

Works by Evelyn Waugh

FICTION

Decline and Fall. 1928. Rev. ed., 1962.

Vile Bodies. 1930.

Black Mischief. 1932.

A Handful of Dust. 1934.

Mr. Loveday's Little Outing and Other Sad Stories. 1936.

Scoop. 1938.

Put Out More Flags. 1942.

Work Suspended: Two Chapters of an Unfinished Novel. 1942.

Brideshead Revisited. 1945.

Scott-King's Modern Europe. 1947.

The Loved One. 1948.

Helena. 1950.

Men At Arms. 1952.

Officers and Gentlemen. 1955.

The Ordeal of Gilbert Pinfold. 1957.

Unconditional Surrender (U.S. title: *The End of the Battle*). 1961.

Sword of Honour (combining *Men at Arms, Officers and Gentlemen,* and *Unconditional Surrender*). 1965.

Evelyn Waugh, Apprentice: The Early Writings, 1910–1927. Edited by Robert Murray Davis. Norman, Oklahoma: Pilgrim Books, 1985.

NONFICTION

P. R. B. An Essay on the Pre-Raphaelite Brotherhood, 1847–1854. 1926.

Rossetti: His Life and Works. 1928.

Labels: A Mediterranean Journal (U.S. title: *A Bachelor Abroad*). 1930.

Remote People (U.S. title: *They Were Still Dancing*). 1931.

Ninety-Two Days. 1934.

Edmund Campion. 1935.

Waugh in Abyssinia. 1936.

Robbery under Law: The Mexican Object-Lesson (U.S. title: *Mexico: An Object Lesson*). 1939.

The Holy Places. 1952.

A Little Learning: The First Volume of an Autobiography. 1964.

The Diaries of Evelyn Waugh. Edited by Michael Davie. London: Weidenfeld and Nicolson, 1976; Boston: Little, Brown, 1976.

The Letters of Evelyn Waugh. Edited by Mark Amory. London: Weidenfeld and Nicolson, 1980; New Haven and New York: Ticknor & Fields, 1980.

The Essays, Articles and Reviews of Evelyn Waugh. Edited by Donat Gallagher. London: Methuen, 1983; Boston: Little, Brown, 1984.

Memoirs

Acton, Harold. *Memoirs of an Aesthete.* London: Methuen, 1948.

Bowra, C. M. *Memories 1898–1939.* London: Weidenfeld and Nicolson, 1966; Cambridge: Harvard University Press, 1967.

Carew, Dudley. *A Fragment of Friendship.* London: Everest Books, 1974.

Cooper, Diana. *The Light of Common Day.* London: Rupert Hart-Davis, 1959; Boston: Houghton, Mifflin, 1959.

Hollis, Christopher. *Along the Road to Frome.* London: George G. Harrap and Co., 1958.

———. *Oxford in the Twenties.* London: Heinemann, 1976.

Mosley, Diana Mitford. *A Life of Contrasts.* London: Hamish Hamilton, 1977.

Powell, Anthony. *Infants of the Spring.* Vol. 1 of *The Memoirs of Anthony Powell.* London: Heinemann, 1976; New York: Holt, Rinehart and Winston, 1977.

———. *Messengers of Day.* Vol. 2 of *The Memoirs of Anthony Powell.* London: Heinemann, 1978; New York: Holt, Rinehart and Winston, 1978.

Pryce-Jones, David, ed. *Evelyn Waugh and His World.* London: Weidenfeld and Nicolson, 1973; Boston: Little, Brown, 1973.

Sykes, Christopher, ed. "Evelyn Waugh—The Man." In *Good Talk,* edited by Derwent May. London: Gollancz, 1968.

Waugh, Alec. *The Early Years of Alec Waugh.* London: Cassell, 1962; New York: Farrar, Straus, 1963.

———. *My Brother Evelyn and Other Profiles.* London: Cassell, 1967; New York: Farrar, Straus and Giroux, 1967 (as *My Brother Evelyn and Other Portraits*).

———. *A Year to Remember: A Reminiscence of 1931.* London: W. H. Allen, 1975.

Waugh, Arthur. *One Man's Road.* London: Chapman and Hall, 1931.

Biographies and Critical Works

Carens, James F. *The Satiric Art of Evelyn Waugh.* Seattle and London: University of Washington Press, 1966.

Davis, Robert Murray. *Evelyn Waugh, Writer.* Norman, Oklahoma: Pilgrim Books, 1981.

Heath, Jeffrey. *The Picturesque Prison: Evelyn Waugh and His Writing.* Kingston and Montreal: McGill-Queen's University Press, 1982; London: Weidenfeld and Nicolson, 1982.

Littlewood, Ian. *The Writings of Evelyn Waugh.* Oxford: Blackwell, 1983; Totowa, New Jersey: Barnes & Noble, 1983.

Stannard, Martin. *Evelyn Waugh: The Early Years 1903–1939.* London: J. M. Dent, 1986; New York: W. W. Norton, 1987.

———, ed. *Evelyn Waugh: The Critical Heritage.* London and Boston: Routledge & Kegan Paul, 1984.

Stopp, Frederick J. *Evelyn Waugh: Portrait of an Artist.* London: Chapman and Hall, 1958; Boston: Little, Brown, 1958.

Sykes, Christopher. *Evelyn Waugh: A Biography.* London: Collins, 1975; Boston: Little, Brown, 1975.

Bibliographies

Davis, Robert Murray. *A Catalogue of the Evelyn Waugh Collection at the Humanities Research Center, the University of Texas at Austin.* Troy, New York: Whitston Publishing Company, 1981.

Davis, Robert Murray; Paul A. Doyle, Donat Gallagher, Charles E. Linck, and Winnifred M. Bogaards, eds. *A Bibliography of Evelyn Waugh.* Troy, New York: Whitston Publishing Company, 1986.

Morriss, Margaret, and D. J. Dooley. *Evelyn Waugh: A Reference Guide.* Boston: G. K. Hall, 1984.

Index

Abyssinia, 24, 68, 120, 123; and *Black Mischief*, 78–80, 82, 88–89; and *Scoop*, 130–31

Acton, Sir Harold, 30–31, 37, 38, 59, 67, 112; at Oxford, 19, 28–29, 79

Antic Hay (Huxley), 21–22

Asquith, Katharine, 98–99, 152

Awakened Conscience, The (Holman-Hunt), 155

"Balance, The," 31–33, 62, 64, 72, 102

Beata Beatrix (Rossetti), 35, 155

Beaverbrook, Lord, 124

Betjeman, Sir John, 14, 38

Betjeman, Penelope, 77

Black Mischief, 18, 23, 24, 71, 78–97, 103, 105, 113, 117, 118, 121, 130, 143; artistic ambitions of, 78–79; Azanian vigor in, 80–81; Basil Seal and caddishness in, 85–88, 90–91, 95–96; cultural theme in, 81–84; complex motives of, 94–95; Emperor Seth and progress in, 82–84; jungle and savage violation in, 92–94; Legation and innocence in, 89–91; origins of in Abyssinia, 79–80; and Prudence, 90–91; sex in, 87–88

Bowra, Sir Maurice, 28

Brideshead Revisited, 14, 27–28, 29, 33, 35, 43, 107, 139, 145–60, 161; autobiographical echoes in, 148, 157–59; background and composition of, 145–47; Brideshead as revelation and sanctuary in, 157–60; criticism of, 15–16, 23–24, 156; as product of withdrawal, 159–60; religious theme of, 153–57; as wartime anodyne, 148–53

Carens, James, 15–16, 18

Carew, Dudley, 37

Cather, Willa, 132

Connolly, Cyril, 9, 112

Conrad, Joseph, 94

Cooper, Lady Diana, 122, 124

Crease, Francis, 29

D'Arcy, Rev. Martin, S. J., 76–77

Davis, Robert Murray, 23, 129

Decline and Fall, 13–14, 15, 25, 27, 37–57, 60, 62, 64, 69, 74, 79, 80, 84, 87, 91, 121, 123, 125, 139, 140–41, 143; comic style of, 38–42; criticism of, 15–18, 56; extemporaneous composition of, 43–45; influence of William Morris and Kelmscott in, 50–52; liberating influence of Grimes in, 45–49, 54; Margot Beste-Chetwynde as successor to Grimes in, 52, 54; Paul Pennyfeather's ambiguous end in, 54–57; Paul Pennyfeather and Oxford in, 42–43, 46–47, 54–55

Dickens, Charles, 28–29, 155; and *A Handful of Dust*, 101, 115, 117, 171 n.16

Duggan, Hubert, 153–54

Edmund Campion, 120

Eliot, T. S., 21, 112

Eminent Victorians (Strachey), 34

"Essay on the Pre-Raphaelite Brotherhood, 1847–1854, An," 33–34, 155

Farr, D. Paul, 129

Firbank, Ronald, 62, 71

Fleming, Anne, 19

Gardner, Hon. Evelyn, 58–59, 60, 65, 102

Graham, Alastair, 34, 38, 44, 45, 78, 168 n.9

Graham, Mrs. (mother of Alastair), 44, 168 n.9

Green, Henry. *See* Yorke, Henry

Greenblatt, Stephen Jay, 70

177